Praise for
Becoming a Life Change Artist

"Beautifully and skillfully written, this book manages to warm your heart and inspire the creative genius in us all. Deciding to make changes in your life is never easy, but this book will give you the courage and the creative tools to do so."
—EVA SELHUB, M.D., clinical instructor of medicine at Harvard Medical School and author of *The Love Response: Your Prescription to Turn Off Fear, Anger, and Anxiety to Achieve Vibrant Health and Transform Your Life*

"Fred Mandell and Kathleen Jordan bring a fresh idea to the literature of reinvention—using the skills of successful artists as a model for how to respond to the sparks that tell us it is time for some kind of life shift. Anyone with a creative urge will be grateful for this book. *Becoming a Life Change Artist* is a godsend not just for would-be artists but also for anyone on the path to a more fully realized or authentic life."
—MARCI ALBOHER, author of *One Person/Multiple Careers* and former Shifting Careers columnist/blogger for *The New York Times*

"*Becoming a Life Change Artist* is a must-read book. The artists' anecdotes are brilliantly insightful and completely relevant to everyday lives. Mandell and Jordan show us how to develop our personal creativity and demonstrate how it can help us navigate the often messy journey of change. It's a rare and innovative book that is both inspirational and practical . . . and a terrific read. The book is a winner!"
—HELEN DENNIS, author, lecturer, entrepreneur, columnist, and coauthor of *Project Renewment: The First Retirement Model for Career Women*

"Fred Mandell and Kathleen Jordan's book is a message reminding us that creativity is ageless. An important contribution and an inspiration to us all."
—HARRY R. MOODY, director of Academic Affairs for AARP

"Fred Mandell and Kathleen Jordan do a masterful job painting a picture of midlife transitions, all too often do-it-yourself projects fraught with as many roadblocks as opportunities. This book helps ease the burden of going solo. It's your map to a successful encore."
—MARC FREEDMAN, founder and CEO of Civic Ventures

"This is not just a book about life change—it's about both leadership of yourself and how to lead an organization. The creative skills Mandell and Jordan talk about will help you become a better leader."
—SPENSER SEGAL, CEO of ActiFi, Inc.

"*Becoming a Life Change Artist* is a page-turner—at once inspiring and practical, fun and serious. The stories Fred and Kathleen tell and the creative techniques they share will change the way you look at yourself and the world around you."
—DOUG LENNICK, coauthor of *Moral Intelligence: Enhancing Business Performance and Leadership Success* and CEO, The Lennick Aberman Group

BECOMING

A

LIFE CHANGE

ARTIST

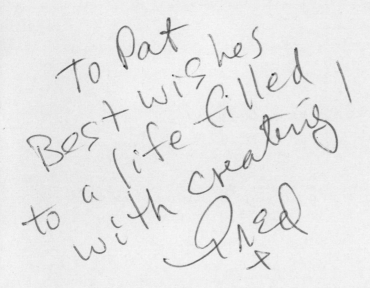

To Pat
Best wishes
to a life filled
with creating!
Fred
x

AVERY

a member of Penguin Group (USA) Inc.

New Yrok

BECOMING

A

LIFE CHANGE

ARTIST

7 Creative Skills to Reinvent Yourself

at Any Stage of Life

FRED MANDELL, PH.D.,
& KATHLEEN JORDAN, PH.D.

Published by the Penguin Group
Penguin Group (USA) Inc., 375 Hudson Street, New York, New York 10014, USA •
Penguin Group (Canada), 90 Eglinton Avenue East, Suite 700, Toronto,
Ontario M4P 2Y3, Canada (a division of Pearson Penguin Canada Inc.) •
Penguin Books Ltd, 80 Strand, London WC2R 0RL, England • Penguin Ireland,
25 St Stephen's Green, Dublin 2, Ireland (a division of Penguin Books Ltd) •
Penguin Group (Australia), 250 Camberwell Road, Camberwell, Victoria 3124,
Australia (a division of Pearson Australia Group Pty Ltd) • Penguin Books India Pvt Ltd,
11 Community Centre, Panchsheel Park, New Delhi–110 017, India •
Penguin Group (NZ), 67 Apollo Drive, Rosedale, North Shore 0632, New Zealand
(a division of Pearson New Zealand Ltd) • Penguin Books (South Africa) (Pty) Ltd,
24 Sturdee Avenue, Rosebank, Johannesburg 2196, South Africa

Penguin Books Ltd, Registered Offices:
80 Strand, London WC2R 0RL, England

Most Avery books are available at special quantity discounts for bulk purchase for sales
promotions, premiums, fund-raising, and educational needs. Special books or book excerpts
also can be created to fit specific needs. For details, write Penguin Group (USA) Inc.
Special Markets, 375 Hudson Street, New York, NY 10014.

Library of Congress Cataloging-in-Publication Data

Mandell, Fred.
Becoming a life change artist : 7 creative skills to reinvent yourself at any stage of life /
Fred Mandell and Kathleen Jordan.
p.   cm.
ISBN 978-1-58333-404-1
1. Self-realization.   2. Change (Psychology).   3. Career changes.
I. Jordan, Kathleen.   II. Title.
BF637.S4M3374   2010   2010015252
158.1—dc22

Printed in the United States of America
1   3   5   7   9   10   8   6   4   2

BOOK DESIGN BY AMANDA DEWEY

While the authors have made every effort to provide accurate telephone numbers and
Internet addresses at the time of publication, neither the publisher nor the authors assume
any responsibility for errors, or for changes that occur after publication. Further, the
publisher does not have any control over and does not assume any responsibility for author
or third-party websites or their content.

Fred dedicates *Becoming a Life Change Artist*
to Karen, his life partner and co-creator, still full of surprises,
and to Jacob, Hinda, Becky, Julie, and Baylor, each a blessing every day.

Kathleen dedicates *Becoming a Life Change Artist*
to her mother, Agnes Kelly Smith, life change artist extraordinaire.

ACKNOWLEDGMENTS

The seed for this book was unexpectedly sown from a postcard I received over a dozen years ago from Warren Bennis. Bennis had gotten his hands on a keynote presentation on leadership I had delivered and sent me the postcard from England with these words: "Turn it into a book!" In the end, though, I could not write that book because by then I was in transition from business executive to my artwork. Bennis's sweeping intelligence, generosity, and interest were key nutrients for the seed that became this book and confirm my long-standing belief that we too often do not even realize the seeds we sow.

I would also like to thank each member of the Lennick Aberman Group—Doug Lennick, Ben Smith, Rick Aberman, Judy Skoglund, Jim Choat, Chuck Wachendorfer, Kay May—for first encouraging me to explore the connection between the arts, leadership, and innovation. The Group provided a supportive home for the early testing and development of the ideas that came to form the core of *Becoming*. Thanks also to Kate Cannon for helping to make the connection between emotional and creative intelligence, and for personally embodying both. I am especially indebted to two business leaders—Peter Lefferts, who took the risk of recruiting me to the Minneapolis heartland, and Susan Plimpton, who was the first to welcome me there. Their intellectual curiosity and personal encouragement kept the fires burning during the incubation stage of *Becoming*. George Klavens, M.D., student of Erik Erikson, has been a gentle mentor and coach to many a creative and an insightful and penetrating mischief-maker to me. The twinkle in his eye and wisdom from his lips have led me both deeper and in new directions.

The Telling Group—Meg Newhouse, Sharon Sokoloff, Roberta Taylor, Paula Solomon, Barbara Abramowitz, Donna Singer, Cyndi Jones, Kit Harrington Hayes, Doug Dickson, Joan Ditzion, Scott Schillin—has played a unique role in the writing of *Becoming*. The actual writing of the book took place during the year this group met regularly to discuss each member's transition experience and to chronicle their journey in words and images on a remarkable canvas. The richness of the discussions, the openness and true sense of community, the fearless willingness to take risks acted as a source of inspiration and insight.

I want to thank Carol Greenfield, a catalyst of the first order, who first hoodwinked me back into organizational life just as I was beginning to hole myself up in the studio.

Harry Moody at various points, by virtue of his enthusiasm, verve for viewing personal change through the arts, and his quirkiness of thought, has acted as a refreshing blend of ideas and activism. I want to give special thanks to Richard Leider for being a pathfinder in exploring the territories of internal and external continents. I first learned of Richard's work in Minneapolis and he has been most generous with his ideas and offers of support. Helen Dennis is a unique sense-maker who has the ability to take emerging realities on the ground and place them in a broader context before most of us have any idea of what's going on. Her initial excitement regarding the ideas in *Becoming* gave me a sense that those ideas now in book form held real possibilities for making a difference in the world. And I want to acknowledge the profound impact that Nancy Fernandez Mills's friendship has had on me as well as on the ideas and textures in the book. Nancy is a remarkably talented storyteller and seeker whose integrity and self-insight set the standard for all life change artists. I especially want to thank Donna Krone, gifted coach and friend, who one day asked me the singularly most powerful truth-seeking question. Without that question, *Becoming* may never have been written.

Roger Junk, spirited and joy-loving sculptor and teacher in the Heartland, first exposed me to the multifaceted crafts of sculpture and to the exhilaration of seeing the finished product brought to life by my own hands. I also want to express my appreciation to Tim Harney, gifted artist, guardian of artistic integrity, insightful critic, and gesticulating teacher, for challenging me to go deeper and truer in my engagement with the creative process.

I need to acknowledge the lasting impact of all those over the years who helped inform, influence, and inspire curiosity about ideas great and small, one of whom referred me to Goethe, who, to paraphrase, said, *If you would find the universal, pursue the particular in every direction.* Such a thought is humbling and, I believe, defines the essence of living the life of both an artist and a life change artist, because the pursuit never ends.

I want to express the deepest appreciation for the folks I interviewed for *Becoming.* Many of these interviews were conducted over the phone due to distance, but if they could have been by my side they would have seen the wonder and admiration as well as the tears I experienced as a result of their courage, self-reflection, and openness. I hope the way we have represented their stories conveys an essential truth of their lives.

Thanks to Esmond Harmsworth of Zachary Shuster Harmsworth Literary Agency for his initial encouragement, and to Joanne Wyckoff, our agent at ZSH Literary, who has acted as fierce champion, emotional buoy, and savvy guide. The keen eye, discriminating instincts, and plain good old-fashioned rigor of our editor, Lucia Watson, has played a magical role in turning an interesting manuscript into a real book. In fact, we would like to thank the entire Penguin Avery team for their enthusiasm, creativity, and support from the very start. And we want to offer a special thanks to Bill Shinker, publishing visionary, who has been there each step of the way and who made the simple but gloriously energizing statement: "We would love to publish your book."

If collaboration were a kingdom, then my coauthor, Kathy Jordan, would be its enlightened ruler. She has remarkable character and talents, both technical and creative, which have made our work together on the book the most memorable working experience of my life.

Members of my extended family, all in their own way, have left their imprint on me and *Becoming*. I have been blessed to be part of a family of uniquely incredible characters who each contributed in often unsuspecting ways to the writing of this book. So I want to thank Judy, Danny, Jed, Mimsi, Susie, Mary, Richard, Julie, Abby, Matt, and Nina. And of course, Ben, gentle teacher.

At one point when I was contemplating a major life change, I gathered my family around and let them know that such a change would have an economic impact on the family and that I would not be able to provide the same level of financial support. One of my daughters, then a teenager, quickly responded: "But Dad, you provide for us in so many other ways." For this gift of permission I am eternally grateful. I was once asked to briefly describe my family. The two words that flashed into my mind were "love" and "volume." We are a loving and often cacophonous clan. I wouldn't have it any other way. To say *Becoming* would never have become without them is an understatement of the first magnitude.

—*Fred Mandell*

I am indebted to the hundred intrepid life change artists who generously shared their life change experiences with us. Whether or not your story appears on these pages, you have profoundly shaped our understanding of the creative process of life change. You are the heart of this book.

I join my coauthor in thanking those who helped turn our dream of doing this book into reality: our literary agents, Esmond Harmsworth and Joanne Wyckoff, of Zachary Shuster Harmsworth. Esmond saw the hidden potential in our initial book proposal. Joanne held our feet to the fire to produce a polished proposal, and is God's gift to any author lucky enough to have her as an agent. Lucia Watson, our editor at Avery, made our book tighter and stronger, and Miriam Rich kept me calm with her reassuring manner during hectic times.

Thanks to publishing executive Carol Franco and her husband, the author Kent Linebeck, who first encouraged me to write professionally and provided invaluable advice. Writing this book would have seemed too overwhelming had it not been for Fred Kiel and Doug Lennick, who trusted me to help write their 2005 book, *Moral Intelligence: Enhancing Business Performance and Leadership Success. Becoming a Life Change Artist* would never have come into being if Doug Lennick had not introduced me to our colleague and my now coauthor, Fred Mandell. That encounter marked the beginning of a creative collaboration that has been the highlight of my professional life.

I have been fortunate to have been mentored in editorial skills by my friend and colleague Jane Heifetz, executive editor at Harvard Business Publishing, and to have learned so much about the craft of writing from my friend and colleague Laurie Keller Johnson, a masterly writer.

No one endures the rigors of book writing without the love and inspiration of countless friends and family. I want to especially thank the following: my dearest friend, Andrea Shanley, whose wisdom and nurturing spirit always sustain me, and her husband, Bob, investment manager turned poverty fighter, one of my favorite life change artists; Nancy Fernandez Mills, Emmy-winning journalist, creator and producer of the PBS series *Boomers! Redefining Life After 50!* and entrepreneur, yoga teacher, and nutritional counselor, for her distinctive insights about living creatively after fifty; Julia Hughes Jones and Donna Krone, for being extraordinary life change role models; and "The Porcini Pals," Sara Cummins, Carol Franco, Rosalie Kerr, Perry McIntosh, Caroline Michel, Toni Smit, and Judy Uhl, for their joyous energy and unending support.

My deep appreciation goes to my family: to my amazing aunt

Dorothy, who demonstrates how to live an active and vibrant life at any age; to my talented accountant and sister Dottie Smith, who always told me I had a book in me; to "The Sergeant," my sister Barbara Smith, whose inner strength and sense of humor always lift me up; to my beautiful niece, Allison Smith, and to my brother, Bill Smith, who always knows the perfect time to send a few bottles of great red wine to lubricate the writing process. Most of all, I thank my daughter, Erin Smith Livermore, for her unconditional love and common sense. Erin and her remarkable husband, Doug Livermore, have graced me with the ultimate inspiration for this book, my granddaughter, Mackenzie Kathleen.

—Kathleen Jordan

Contents

Part Three

LIVING CREATIVELY

Foreword:
Rekindling Your Fire

For the past three decades, I have led annual walking safaris in Tanzania with small groups of people I call "inventurers"—individuals who adventure inward through outdoor immersion experiences.

On a recent Africa trek, I found myself, late one evening, sitting around a campfire with a collection of elders from a tribe of hunter gatherers known as the Hadza. Still living as our ancient ancestors did, the Hadza reside in a primeval-looking baobab forest. As the flames of the evening's fire morphed into smoldering coals, one Hadza elder asked me, "Who are the elders of your tribe?"

I found myself stumped. I also found myself intrigued. My tribe? What is that? My elders? What does it mean to be an elder? The very concept of "elder" seemed foreign. And yet it was clear to me that the man's question begged for an answer.

Enter *Becoming a Life Change Artist*. This book answers the question. It invites us to rekindle our fire and to become "enthusiastic explorers"—elders who choose to live in the third age of our lives in ways characterized by aliveness. Joseph Campbell once suggested that we are not searching for the meaning of life. We are searching for the experience of being "alive."

Becoming a Life Change Artist teaches us the art of being fully alive. It introduces us to individuals who see the third age as an empty canvas, a blank page, or a hunk of clay to be shaped on purpose. These are people who inspire us by stoking their fires—rekindling the smoldering coals of passion and purpose.

We each have an artist in our soul. Perhaps our "artist within" shows up in a visual art like painting, sculpture, or photography. Or maybe in another form, such as leading, parenting, teaching, or being a caring friend. The artist within knows no limits.

Sitting around the fire in Africa, I ask people, "What matters to you most in life?" Frequently, they look up in surprise. Many say it's been a long time since they thought about that question. Seems strange, doesn't it? How unusual that we can go years on this planet without pausing to wonder if we are focusing on what matters most.

Fred Mandell and Kathleen Jordan help us focus on what matters most in our lives. I have many development books on my shelf, but the fresh framework of their book makes the content so much more alive. It's one of those rare books that changes the way you think about, well, everything! And as we age, we must take the time to think about, well, everything! We must not let our creative coals smolder or, worse yet, our fire go out. We must stoke the fires of passion and purpose. We must rekindle the creative skills that can transform our lives. As we practice our life change artistry, things change dramatically.

I still ponder the question, "Who are the elders of your tribe?" And I have come to define "tribe" as people on a "shared path." Readers of this book are perhaps on a shared path. They are "enthusiastic explorers" who dare to ask of life everything good and beautiful.

The fired-up people you meet in this book burn with the beacon that guides them—their way of navigating the process of life change.

Their incandescence is powerfully illuminating. As they forge ahead, led by the rekindled fires of creativity, they light the way into the third-age future.

—*Richard J. Leider*
Founder and Chairman, The Inventure Group

Introduction

A business executive becomes an award-winning high school teacher at the age of fifty-seven.

A waitress and mother of four returns to college at age forty-one and is now working on her doctorate.

A neurosurgeon is forced to leave his profession because of a heart condition and finds a new passion.

A single mother on welfare becomes a physician.

A Hollywood entertainer becomes a rabbi at the age of fifty-eight.

An entrepreneur sells his first business start-up for multimillions of dollars at age twenty-one.

A twenty-year career engineer decides she wants to be a stay-at-home mom.

A New York City cop earns a Ph.D. in psychology while working the night shift and then becomes a successful artist.

What do these people have in common? Obviously, they have all gone through major changes that have hopefully made their lives more fulfilling. Apart from that, it is hard to see commonalities amid the twists and turns of their individual circumstances. They all had different reasons for wanting—or needing—to change. There were no set steps that they followed. There was no typical amount of time it took to make their life changes. They didn't even have to be unusually smart or unusually lucky. But it turns out they did have something very powerful in common: each of them used a set of specific skills—creative skills—to transform their lives. This book is all about those skills, and how you can use them to navigate the creative process of life change.

Today there is more interest than ever in making life changes. If you are part of the large group of aging "baby boomers," you probably have no interest in living your parents' version of the "golden years." Instead, you're likely anticipating a vibrant "third age" of life, characterized by health, longevity, and meaningful pursuits. And you're smart enough to know that it won't happen by accident. This book will help you understand how to reinvent your life so that your dream of a vital, enjoyable third age becomes a reality.

But it's not just boomers who are interested in life change. We've all been affected to some degree by the worst economic downturn since the Great Depression. Some of us have lost jobs and homes, while others of us who are more fortunate have just had to tighten our belts. Whether our finances have been affected a little or a lot, the majority of us are reexamining our values in these turbulent times. What's really important to us? How do we really want to spend our time? How can we take advantage of personal economic limitations to create a simpler, healthier, and more relationship-oriented lifestyle? How can we still dare to dream our dreams? We can never control every aspect of our lives, but we can always take actions that allow us to have a life that is deeply meaningful to us—no matter what our circumstances.

These broad social and economic factors are not the only ones giving rise to our transitions. Often change is activated by deeply personal circumstances. We lose a loved one. We get burned-out at work. An important relationship ends or a potential new one begins. We make a significant geographic move. We look in the mirror and see telltale signs of aging and wonder who am I really and why am I really here? We get a big idea and determine we must pursue it. A first-time child or grandchild comes into a family's midst. Change comes wrapped in a coat of many colors. Sometimes these changes are triggered as a matter of choice. At other times they are forced upon us.

As you read *Becoming a Life Change Artist*, you'll discover that your decision to embark on a journey of change puts you in the company of artistic greats such as Rembrandt, Pablo Picasso, and Georgia O'Keeffe. That's because you have three things in common with all the masters of art:

- The creative *process* used by the great artists is fundamentally the same as the process you will experience in making a life change.
- The creative *skills* artists use are fundamentally the same as the creative skills you need to make a successful life change.
- Even the greatest artists had to *learn* their creative skills, and you can learn them, too.

Let's look a bit more at these three things you have in common with the great artists.

The Creative Process

In Part One of *Becoming a Life Change Artist*, you'll see that life change is not an orderly, step-by-step march, despite what you might wish. Instead, your creative process of change will essentially be the same messy process that artists, especially the great ones, go through to create and develop their original work over the course of their lifetimes. That doesn't mean you can't make any sense out of the process. In fact, the creative process includes four specific dimensions that you can use to understand where you are in your own change process. For instance, as you will see, *exploration* is one dimension of the creative process. Anyone who has seen some of Claude Monet's twenty-five paintings of the same haystacks—captured at different times of the day and through all the seasons—can appreciate how his passion for exploring the visual nature of the haystack contributed to his artistic innovations. Similarly, anyone who wants a more fulfilling life must become an enthusiastic explorer. The subject of the exploration may be one's own life and the greater world around us rather than a stack of hay, but the outcome is the same—a life infused with freshness and meaning.

The dimensions we'll discuss are critical to the creative process, but they don't happen in a predictable sequence. Imagine that you are looking at a topographic map (one that shows characteristics of the territory) of the United States. The map shows mountains, rivers, lakes, and flatland. These dimensions of the territory are always recognizable. That is, we can always recognize that a river is a river. But what we don't see is any pattern to the placement of the dimensions. For instance, there is no set distance between rivers, and if we look from left to right, there is no sequence, such as: a lake is always next to a mountain, which is always next to a river, etc. Instead, different parts of the territory look very different because the dimensions appear in a unique and seemingly chaotic sequence.

The same is true for the dimensions of the creative process. There are four key dimensions, but we, like the great masters of art, move from dimension to dimension in our own unique sequence and in our own unique time frame. Even though we can't predict the order in advance (or *especially* because we can't predict the path of change), it's very useful to know what dimension of change we are experiencing at any given time, just as it's important to have a map when we're in unfamiliar geographic territory.

The Seven Creative Skills

The second thing you have in common with the great artists is your toolbox of creative skills. In Part Two of *Becoming a Life Change Artist*, you'll learn that the Seven Creative Skills an artist uses to produce a masterpiece are the same as those you need to create a more fulfilling life. In the literature on life change, there has been a lot of emphasis on *life planning*. Some people mistakenly think that if they can only figure out what they want to do, then it will happen. It's true that at some point it's very valuable to have a vision for your future life. In fact, there is research that shows we are more likely to accomplish our goals when we picture them clearly and write them down. But planning our new life is not enough. We may end up with wonderful ideas for our future that we don't have the will or ability to implement. To realize our vision for our life, we need to take action. And action requires skills. What's more, effective life planning itself requires certain creative skills. For instance, we may need the creative skill of *risk taking* to muster the guts to imagine a life that's really worth living. And we often need a creative skill, such as *embracing uncertainty,* to experiment with future possibilities that will give us the information we need before we are ready to plan a new direction.

Creative Skills Can and Must Be Learned

The third thing you have in common with the great artists is that you, like them, need to *work* on developing your creative skills if you want to fashion your best possible life. You're born with creative aptitude, just like you are born with intellectual aptitude. But just as aptitude for mathematics isn't enough to make a talented mathematician (you need to study mathematics), creative aptitude alone doesn't result in wonderful creative outcomes. We need to take our inborn creative aptitude and build on it through study and practice. No one would claim that artists such as Mary Cassatt or Henri Matisse didn't have considerable inborn artistic aptitude. But if art-making were just a matter of talent, no artist would have to study her or his craft. As you'll learn later, Matisse is a great example of the importance of creative skills development. When Matisse first went to art school, one of his teachers told him that his drawing was so bad, he was afraid to tell him how bad it was. It's up to us to practice the creative skills that will allow us to express ourselves as fully as possible—whether in a vibrant piece of art or in a vibrant life. No matter how old (or young) you are, and no matter what your life circumstances, you can develop the creative skills you need to have a meaningful life of your choosing.

Do You Want to Become a Life Change Artist?

Many of us are tempted to dismiss the idea that we have anything in common with the great masters of art. A good number of us don't think we're particularly creative at all. But if you are skeptical that creativity is an inborn talent, spend an hour in any kindergarten classroom, where artistic expression is routinely encouraged. When we're five or six years of age, we don't doubt for a moment our artistic or creative capacity. That fundamental belief allows five- and six-year-olds to give themselves completely and spontaneously to the creative process itself. The artistic expressions of five- and six-year-olds are colorful, unconstrained, and unconventional. No kindergartner worries that his drawing of his mother is the right color or has the correct proportions. It's only when we get older, and society, culture, and family send us messages that art, or wild flights of the imagination in any form, is frivolous, that we begin to worry that our art is not accurately representative, or even worthy of spending effort on. This inclination to undervalue all forms of artistic expression by the adult world finds voice in, at best, a tepid tolerance and, at worst, an outright dismissal of the "practicality" of such activity. Perhaps economic pressures cause school districts to decide that art classes are expendable, and that contributes to our sense that creativity is expendable. Whatever the cause, it's common in the United States to ignore that our birthright is to express ourselves creatively.

With all of these social and cultural obstacles to discourage us, it's understandable that we would find the idea of being any kind of artist daunting. But in fact, we all are artists. We may not be painting, sculpting, or writing, but each morning we wake to the canvas of a fresh day, with its own unique challenges. We instinctively call on our creativity to face even the most mundane of circumstances: How to look good when most of our clothes are in the laundry. How to get to work on schedule when our gas tank is empty. How to make time for our children and our aging parents *and* still have some energy left for things we really want to do. How to strike a balance between self, family, work, and community. How to make each day one that we can be proud of when we put our head on the pillow at night. And if these small daily hurdles require creativity, then it's clear that the challenge of how to make a major life change requires the skills of the artist. When people decide to change, they instinctively tap into their natural creative abilities to navigate the uncertainties of moving in a new direction. *Becoming a Life Change Artist* will help you reconnect with and unleash your inborn creativity and build on those natural skills to create a more satisfying life.

Why We Wrote the Book

For many years we have collaborated on two professional interests: business innovation and personal transformation. During that time we have learned that these interests are two sides of the same coin. One is focused on change in organizational settings, the other on change in people's individual lives. Our discovery of the seven core creative skills was initiated by Fred. As he pursued his keen interest in sculpting and painting, he began to notice a number of parallels between the creative challenges he faced as an artist and those he had faced as a business leader charged with innovation. Fred then partnered with Kathleen to better understand the creative process and the concrete skills used by the great masters of art. Our interest at that time was to explore in what ways the creative process and creative skills of the great artists could be applied to our work with leaders.

We began by studying the creative process employed by the great masters of art. We researched the development of many of the great artists, including Leonardo da Vinci, Artemisia Gentileschi, Johannes Vermeer, Rembrandt van Rijn, Francisco Goya, Camille Pissarro, Édouard Manet, Berthe Morisot, Claude Monet, Mary Cassatt, Vincent van Gogh, Paul Cézanne, Henri Matisse, Pablo Picasso, Paul Gauguin, Alberto Giacometti, Henri Gaudier-Brzeska, Käthe Kollwitz, Wassily Kandinsky, Chaim Soutine, Willem de Kooning, Richard Diebenkorn, Frida Kahlo, and Georgia O'Keeffe. This research was wide-ranging, entailing trips to museum libraries in the United States and Europe to access primary sources. Through content analysis of artists' biographical and autobiographical material (including letters and essays), we ultimately identified seven behavioral characteristics that the great artists had in common. These behavioral characteristics largely accounted for their sustained creative body of work. We subsequently labeled these seven characteristics "The Seven Creative Skills." What follows are brief definitions of each of the Seven Creative Skills:

- Preparation—Deliberately engaging in activities that help break us from our usual patterns of thought and feeling and prepare us for creative insight.
- Seeing—Having the ability to discern new connections, gain fresh perspective, and stay alive to new possibilities.
- Using Context—Understanding how the varied environments in which we work and live influence our thoughts and behaviors, and using that knowledge to make changes in our lives.
- Embracing Uncertainty—Acting on the opportunities, sometimes hidden, presented by change and uncertainty.
- Risk Taking—Acting without certainty of outcome.
- Discipline—Acting consistently whether or not one feels motivated.
- Collaboration—Engaging with others to help one make desired changes.

If these skills are indeed central to the creative success of the artist, we reasoned, they should be equally important to the success of leaders charged with creating innovations in their products and within their organizations. We began to teach these skills to leaders in numerous organizations, with great results for them and their businesses.

As we worked with business leaders, many of whom were coincidentally involved in making significant personal changes, we began to hear how they were using the Seven Creative Skills in all areas of their life. Our personal experiences, along with the experiences of our business students, led us to believe that the Seven Creative Skills could be useful to anyone going through any important change—business or personal. We wanted to find out if our initial thoughts about the broader value of the Seven Creative Skills were valid. So we began by studying the phenomenon of baby boomers who wanted to think more creatively about their next stage of life. We examined the existing models of life change and realized that those old models either had not fully factored in the vital role of creativity or had not taken the importance of creativity far enough in understanding successful life transition at any age. Erik Erikson offered a developmental model in which the closest he came to addressing creativity was in his idea of generativity. The late Dr. Gene Cohen did seminal research placing creativity as a central element in the later stages of adult development. However, Dr. Cohen's efforts were, sadly, cut short by his untimely death. To better understand the role of creativity in the process of life change, we conducted detailed interviews with more than one hundred people who had gone through a significant life transition. We wanted to hear in their own words what the experience of change was really like, and what skills they used to get where they wanted to go.

The people we interviewed cut across a wide swath of demographics. They ranged in age from twenty-seven to seventy. Ten percent fell within their twenties and thirties. Thirty percent were in their forties. Forty percent in their fifties. Twenty percent in their sixties. They lived in New England and the East Coast, Midwest, South, and West. They ranged in profession from neurosurgeon to pipe fitter, from executive to farmer, from ex–professional football player to carpenter, from CEO to Jesuit priest. Most of the interviewees were middle-class and white. Sixty-two percent of the interviewees were women.

More than one hundred interviews later, we made an important discovery: The process of successful life transition is indeed the same as the creative process that the great artists go through. Because the similarity is so strong, it inspired us to coin the term "life change artists," which we use to describe people who are deliberately working to create a more fulfilling life.

Over the past several years we have also learned from our own personal change journeys. We have each walked the path of life change artists in our own way. As a result we have deepened our appreciation about *how* the process of life change unfolds and *what skills* individuals call upon to successfully change their lives. We have taught these skills—the Seven Creative Skills—to thousands of people, including business leaders and baby boomers going through transitions in work and in life. We have done this through speaking engagements, consulting, and workshops called "Life Change Studios," in which ordinary people discover how creative they really are and how much more creative—and fulfilled—their lives can be.

We have met people in all walks of life and at all stages of their lives. We have worked with people beginning their work careers and those transitioning to their third and fourth careers in their "third age." We have met senior executives and house dads, activists from the sixties and single moms on food stamps, physicians and entrepreneurs, artists and salesmen, financial advisors and clergy. The list can go on. They were all about to begin or were well into their transition journeys. While they sought answers for themselves, they also sought connection and community with fellow travelers.

The various life change programs we have offered have been transformative for both the participants and the authors. We have seen people who never thought of themselves as creative tap into incredible reserves of self-insight and creativity. We have seen people face their demons and come out with courageous commitments. We have seen people come in confused and arrive at flashes of clarity. We have seen people continue to struggle but with a new level of hopefulness and connection. And, of course, we have personally been deeply touched by these experiences.

Becoming a Life Change Artist integrates what we have learned about the creative process from studying the great masters of art, with what we have learned about how ordinary people use those same creative skills to make meaningful life changes. We wrote this book to help you develop the creative skills you need to have the most rewarding life possible.

An Essential Tool: Your Sketchbook

I recorded everything, even mundane things, and discovered what was in my heart.

—JOANNE CANCRO, *life change artist*

Throughout the book we offer various tools you can use to support your change journey. All the tools mentioned are in this book, save one: a sketchbook. And none may be more important. We encourage you to purchase one.

Consider your sketchbook a confidant, a constant companion. Take it wherever you go. Develop the habit of noting your thoughts and impressions in it. Feel free to leave doodles and markings. You do not need to be a "real artist" to use a sketchbook. Don't worry about whether what you record makes sense or looks pretty. You might choose to record what you ate in a given day as Leonardo da Vinci did in his sketchbooks. Or record observations, thoughts, insights, feelings. Ideas come quickly and unexpectedly and they often take flight just as we are trying to recall them. Using a sketchbook allows us to capture the momentary insight. It might later end up being a passing thought but it might also be the seed of deep insight. The purpose of

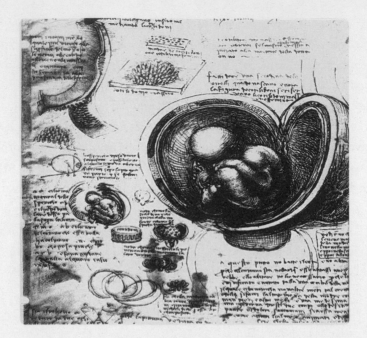

Page from Leonardo da Vinci's sketchbook

the sketchbook, however, is not to create a historical document. Rather, its purpose is to develop a chronicle of the inner life of your change journey where new patterns may emerge or identify themselves. It will serve to organize your thinking and be a source of important conversations with yourself and others. For instance, Mexican surrealist Frida Kahlo used her sketchbook in a way that goes beyond how most artists use their sketchbooks. Typically, artists will use their sketchbook for preparatory drawings or for working out solutions in a small format to be applied to a larger work. But Kahlo used her sketchbook, as did Leonardo da Vinci, much in the same way we are encouraging life change artists to use theirs: as a "repository" for feelings, thoughts, and images that arise in the course of your personal journey. Your sketchbook is a tool that supports the process of making sense of both your inner and your outer journey.

For you as a life change artist, a sketchbook is the single most important tool for staying focused on your transition work and developing your creative skills. There is a wealth of evidence that suggests that to be consistently creative, we need to transfer what is in our hearts and minds into the concrete form of writing or drawing. When we use our sketchbook, the point is not to produce great ideas or attractive drawings. The point is to keep our creativity flowing. Writer and creativity expert Julia Cameron, author of *The Artist's Way*, advocates the use of "morning pages" to remove blocks to creativity:

> All that angry, whiny, petty stuff that you write down in the morning stands between you and your creativity. Worrying about the job. The laundry, the funny knock in the car . . . this stuff eddies through our subconscious and muddies our days. Get it on the page.[1]

You can use your sketchbook in a similar way. Maybe your jottings will provide some insights. Maybe they won't. But it doesn't matter. What does matter is using your sketchbook every day to keep your ideas and images flowing. The value of daily creative work to the life change process cannot be emphasized enough.

Sketchbooks come in different shapes and sizes. You can find the most variety at an art supply store in your area (or on the Internet). Inexpensive sketchbooks are also available at craft and stationery stores. You want your sketchbook to be portable but not too small, so choose one that is at least six by nine inches. If you go smaller, it may be hard to be sufficiently expansive in your drawings or notes. Larger is great but may be more difficult to carry around. Avoid pricy hardbound sketchbooks with pages that don't lie flat. Spiral-bound sketchbooks are inexpensive and allow you to sketch on a flat surface. If you are left-handed, consider starting with the pages in the "back" of the sketchbook.

---

1. Julia Cameron, *The Artist's Way* (New York: Jeremy P. Tarcher, 2002), p. 11.

■ ■ ■

A note about the stories of the brave and wonderful life change artists who appear in this book: Most of the people you'll meet in these pages have allowed us to use their actual names. In a few cases, we've used fictitious names for reasons of privacy and comfort. But all were without exception enormously generous with their time, candor, and insights. They, and we, welcome you as a fellow traveler on the remarkable journey of becoming a life change artist.

Part One

. . . .

THE PROCESS

Chapter 1

The Dimensions
of Life Change

*It is the quest of our self that drives us along the
eternal and never ending journey we must all make.*

—MAX BECKMANN

I feel like I'm at the bottom of a river with the current raging around
me," says Andrea, a talented businesswoman and mother of two
teenage girls. "I'm working on a big project. I barely see my husband
and kids. I'm trying to get by on six hours' sleep, and I haven't been
to the gym in a month. I can't wait for this project to end, to reach
the shore and take a deep breath." The other women sitting around
the conference table nod their heads. They've been there. They understand. Then another woman pipes up: "I don't think there *is* a shore."
She adds, "I may be wrong, but my experience so far is that we are
born, we die, and everything in between is river."

Many of us yearn for the safety of that distant shore—whether in
our work or in our personal lives. But that shore is a mirage. We can't
stop the river and get off. We are all faced with constant change—a
continuously flowing river of transition, whether at work or in our
personal lives. The question for all of us is not "How do we get to an
imaginary shore?" but "How do we navigate the river of crosscur-
rents and continuous change?" Or, "How do we take advantage of
whatever river we're in to create a happier, more fulfilling life?" The

first step to answering those questions is to learn everything we can about the river. We need a map—a kind of navigational chart—to help us understand the experience of the life transition we're going through.

Old Maps of Life Transition

For a long time, psychologists have told us that change and transition happen primarily during specific developmental stages in our life. From infant to early childhood, from early childhood to play age, from play age to school age, from school age to adolescence, from adolescence to young adulthood, from young adulthood to adult, and from adult to old age. According to the famous psychologist Erik Erikson, each life stage is focused on a major life challenge. For example, during our infancy stage, our major life challenge is to learn to trust (especially those big people who are taking care of us). In our early childhood stage, we focus on the challenge of autonomy. Anyone who's been around a two-year-old knows how hard a young child works on that challenge.

According to Erikson, the quality of our lives depends on how successfully we make the transitions associated with each stage. If we don't master the challenge of one stage, we will likely have problems later on. You've probably run into people who seem never to have grown up. A life stage theory like Erikson's can help us figure out why and how that happens.

But Erikson's theory also presents a problem. Erikson devotes only three of his eight stages to adulthood, and of those, only two stages address life after age forty. In other words, with our life expectancy now approaching eighty, he assigns six stages to the first half of life and only two to the second half of life. There is a slight imbalance here since we know that life is a lot richer and the challenges more varied in the second half of life than Erikson suggests.

ERIK ERIKSON'S THREE STAGES
OF ADULT DEVELOPMENT

Stage	Challenge	Major Question
Young Adulthood (18–40 years)	Intimacy	How can I balance closeness with time alone?
Middle Adulthood (40–65 years)	Generativity	How will I create and guide the next generation?
Late Adulthood (from 65 years)	Integrity	What kind of life have I lived?

Stage theories do help us understand many of the predictable changes that happen to us, especially as children and younger adults. But they don't tell the whole story. For one thing, many people are living active lives much longer. The idea that at sixty-five we are primarily focused on "wrapping up" our lives, reflecting on what we've done and getting ready for death, seems premature to many people. Dr. Gene Cohen, noted psychiatrist, gerontologist, and author of *The Mature Mind: The Positive Power of the Aging Brain,* suggested that the second half of life contains more varied stages than Erikson originally described. Cohen identified four distinct stages that he called Midlife Re-evaluation, Liberation, Summing Up, and Encore. Clearly the notion of an Encore stage reinforces the idea that we have many possibilities for active engagement in life well into our older years. While stage theories of human development are useful, they do not emphasize many of the nuances and complexities of personal change.

The Complexity of Personal Change

Personal change can happen as part of the developmental stages described by both Erikson and Cohen. But change is by no means limited to those official life stage transitions. Life change is much richer, and much less predictable, than formal psychology tells us. Sometimes a transition is triggered by personal circumstances, such as retirement or a change in our health. Sometimes there are larger social or economic forces at work. A major economic disruption can cause a significant recalibration of personal plans. Sometimes change happens because of the choices we make; at other times the rug simply gets pulled out from under our feet. The triggers for change are varied and endless. In the chapters that follow, you will discover that life change is not a neat process. We do not move in an organized fashion from stage one to stage two, and so on. Our lives are messy. Life can be thrown at us from many directions at once and we often can't control the circumstances that surround our lives. Sometimes life delivers us gifts. At other times we get rotten tomatoes. What you will find within these pages are stories and insights of how individuals have built fulfilling lives from this messiness, lives based on the principle that *at its core, life transition is a creative process.* Transition and change bring us into the unknown—where creativity lives—and from this unknown, we can create in our lives that which did not exist before. We can initiate and respond to life-changing events or internal uneasiness with creativity and resourcefulness and create a life of meaning and purpose. So instead of fighting the currents in our river, instead of longing for the stability of the shore, we can flow with the river, finding our own unique way to make the journey.

The Creative Process

Art is born out of the tension an artist feels between what she has created up to that point and her desire to create something new and fresh. At the moment of beginning a painting, the artist faces a blank canvas. The canvas represents the unknown, and it poses a challenging question: Do I repeat what I have done before or do I try something different? This tension expresses itself in a *creative dilemma*: What am I trying to express? How can I express it? How can I do this in an original way? The artist may not have a fully formed vision of the painting, but she begins. When the artist commits to picking up the brush and dabbing the first stroke on the canvas, she has chosen to address this particular creative dilemma. But a painting does not flow from the imagination of the artist in a single, uninterrupted sweep of the brush. She *explores* various combinations of light and dark shades and color combinations. She adds elements and scratches them out. As she explores, she *discovers* things about the subject, about herself, and about the painting medium, for instance what a certain brush can or can't convey. The artist may think she has discovered a path to go down, but when she heads in that direction she is thrown into confusion or doubt and cycles back to experimenting again. There is give-and-take. The artist wrestles on the canvas with the subject, with the paint, with the light, with the design. She wrestles with many things in herself and in the physical world from which she takes her subject. And then eventually the artist senses that what she is aspiring to create is on track. The pieces begin to come together. She is now *integrating* all the elements into a cohesive whole, a whole that brings together not only the elements of a good painting but the true feelings of the artist.

The process has not been perfectly symmetrical. In fact, it has been quite messy. But it represents the experience of creating—not just for our contemporary painter, but for the great masters as well.

Imagine Rembrandt in his studio. He begins a self-portrait. He paints himself wearing a period costume with a plumed cap. He sketches himself holding a paintbrush to identify himself as an artist. He shapes his eyebrows in a raised fashion to project an impression of haughtiness. As an artist, he knows things others do not! But then he steps back from the canvas. He is not satisfied. He doesn't like what he has tried to express. He doesn't like the expression. After all, he is a man in his sixties. He has been humbled by life and by the task of creating art. He wipes out the raised eyebrows and paints in a set of eyes more subdued, vulnerable. He discovers that this is more consistent with the person he wants to portray. He steps back from the canvas again. Then he paints out the paintbrush. He wants to show himself as everyman, not as an artist. He wants the viewer to feel he is identifying with him. Then he turns to the plumed cap. "Too pretentious," he decides. He rubs it out and replaces it with a more modest cap, a simple white nightcap. Rembrandt began down one path. Like our contemporary artist, the great master experimented with the subject's expression, his clothes, and his posture. Then he discovered he did not like what was emerging on the canvas. He rubbed it out and began again. Even as great a painter as Rembrandt is immersed in the messiness of the creative process, its fits and starts. It is precisely because he gives himself fully to the creative process that the final versions of his paintings are so magnificent.

The Four Creative Dimensions

If the creative process just described sounds confusing, then you were paying attention. The creative process is not simple or linear. But it is also not chaotic. Within its complexity is interplay among four dimensions:

Creative Dilemma
The choice to act or not act on a particular tension in our lives.

Exploring
Searching for and experimenting with new directions.

Discovering
Using the raw material of our exploration to discern what is meaningful to us.

Integrating
Combining elements of our past life and experiences with what we have now discovered about ourselves into new ways of behaving and seeing ourselves.

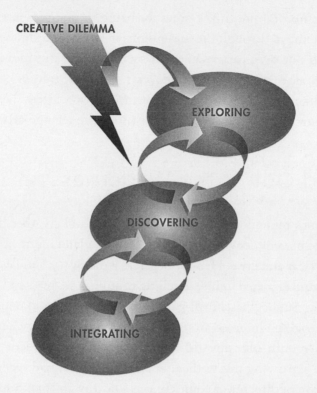

The Dimensions of Life Change

The creative dilemma is the personal force that launches the creative process. It motivates us to engage in exploration and discovery. When we explore, we experiment, like the artist, with new ideas and approaches. As we explore, we make discoveries about ourselves and our work. We keep exploring and discovering until we feel we have learned enough to integrate what we have discovered into a new painting, a new art, or a new self.

Like the creative process, life change is neither linear nor neat. There is an ebb and flow, emotional ups and downs, progress and lapses. We may be dissatisfied with our lives, but push the underlying tension aside because we feel we don't have the energy to deal with our creative dilemma. We may begin to explore new life directions, only to discover that those alternative pathways do not make sense.

There are no definite time frames for being in one dimension or another. We move through the dimensions in a totally unique way, each of us with our own pattern and our own rhythm. But move through them we do—exploration, discovery, and integration. Then we emerge, like a painting, different from when we started. We have re-created ourselves. We have become artists—life change artists.

In and Out of the Wilderness

Cyndi Jones remembers the exact date, time, and weather conditions when she entered the wilderness. The New England morning of March 19 broke clear and crisp. Her day began as it did every Sunday morning. Her husband engaged in his stretching routine as he readied himself for his regular Sunday basketball game. Her eight-year-old daughter and five-year-old son lingered around the kitchen table while Cyndi nursed her three-month-old baby girl. Life was good, if a bit hectic. Her husband had a growing psychotherapy practice. Cyndi had recently taken the position of director of counseling at a nearby college to spend more time with her family and to expand her own therapy practice. The family lived in a comfortable home they had just remodeled in a coun-trified Boston suburb. They had a wide circle of friends and seemed to enjoy balancing the many facets of their lives. Cyndi's husband kissed her goodbye as he scooted out of the house. Life was as it was. Un-extraordinary. Until the phone rang at eleven-fourteen that morning and brought the wilderness into Cyndi's life.

Her husband was dead from a heart attack at age forty. In the aftermath of this devastating event, she found herself with an outpour-ing of support and a sense that she was being "held by the world." Fifteen of her friends formed a group that met regularly, not only to give Cyndi a chance to share her sense of loss, grief, and anxiety but also to provide all members of the group an opportunity to express their thoughts and feelings about the impact of his life and death on them and the community.

Despite this ongoing support, Cyndi felt tested to her very core. She recalls this period as one characterized by bone-cutting weariness. Her life now felt like a house of cards on the brink of crumbling. Her son began to throw tantrums. Her older daughter withdrew in anger. With her infant by her side, Cyndi would lie on the family room floor half asleep from exhaustion. At work, she began to take ten-minute naps between clients. She was overtaken with the sense that she had no control. Should she attend to herself or her children or her job? She began to worry about everything: Will my children be permanently damaged? Will we be able to keep the house? How will we survive financially? Where will I find the emotional and physical strength? The questions came at her in an endless stream, and the answers seemed completely clouded by the haze of anxiety that surrounded them.

At times, Cyndi's sense of exhaustion became overwhelming. It seemed to seep into every bone in her body. But exhaustion, though real and debilitating, was, most important, a symptom. It was exhausting to hold tight to the past. She faced a *creative dilemma*. "Do I cling to the past, insist that only my husband can help me deal with all these life challenges, or do I find a way to re-create my family without my husband?"

Cyndi began to *experiment* with a different outlook. She began to chant a mantra wherever she went. *You can get through this. You can get through this*, she kept repeating to herself. But then she wondered whether this was, in fact, a positive mantra or simply the thin voice of sanity trying to hold her together, a desperate effort to convince herself that things would work out despite the immediate evidence to the contrary. To make matters worse, Cyndi discovered that the very way she was raised acted as an obstacle to change. She had been raised to be independent and self-reliant. On the surface these seemed to be admirable qualities. But then she realized that they were really holding her back from asking for the help she needed. This *discovery* startled her. She realized that she needed to allow others to help. She began to really let others in.

The three years immediately after her husband died were all about survival. In some sense, the future did not exist. She learned to compartmentalize. She gave no thought to what she could not control. Since she could not control the future, she did not allow herself to think about it. However, she could control what she ate, and she determined to eat a healthful diet. She could control physical exercise. She could put together a master schedule to coordinate her children's activities. She taught the children to respect "time out"—those times when she simply needed to take a moment and put her head on a pillow for a few minutes. She learned to multitask. By scheduling a walk with her daughter in a stroller along with a friend, she was able to get exercise, supervise her daughter, and maintain her social contacts. Cyndi quickly learned that these walks provided more than exercise and time to bring together friends and take care of her daughter at the same time. The walks provided perspective. She recalls arriving at insights that would never have come to her during the hectic rush of her daily life. The walks offered the opportunity to step outside the pressing demands of every day and find elements of physical and emotional renewal.

Slowly Cyndi began to allow the future to enter her thoughts. Her first step was to move from her countrified setting to a closer-in Boston suburb. Her friends rallied around to help her with the heavy lifting. She also acknowledged at a deeper level that she was no longer the person she thought she would be. Her life had not turned out as planned or expected. As she began to think about what she wanted her life to look like, one of her friends urged her to begin dating again. Five years after her husband died she still did not know if she was ready for such a step. It was not simply a practical matter of what to wear or who to meet or how to meet them. It was equally about trusting the world and the future. And she had every reason to question the assumption of trust. She trusted her friends, they had been there for her, but this future thing still made her uneasy. She still felt in survival mode.

Yet she had more than survived. She had *discovered* a capacity for creative responses to her new life. The year that she had no money to send her kids to summer camp, she wouldn't settle. She began to *explore* by calling camp directors around the region to try to obtain scholarships that would enable her kids to attend camp. To her surprise she received a positive response. This accomplishment made a deep impression on her. She *discovered* she could make change happen. She could imprint the future if she was willing to take risks. She began to see other things differently as well. And her different views in turn spurred her professional growth. She even helped organize and lead a successful psychotherapy practice of twenty clinicians.

Along the way, Cyndi took a class on the exodus of the Jews from Egypt and their wandering for forty years in the wilderness. She identified powerfully with the Israelites' fear of moving into the future and understood completely their yearning for the older, familiar ways. She realized that, like the Israelites, she had been wandering in the wilderness of her own survival. She recognized that to move into the future in a meaningful way, she would need to surrender her longing for what was familiar and comfortable.

Now, ten years after her husband died, and more open to the possibilities in her life, she decided to date again. By this time, she knew to ask for help when she needed it. So she hired a consultant to help her write an ad for the personals section of the local newspaper. Cyndi got her money's worth: her second date was with the man who became her current husband. Since her first husband had been Jewish, she raised her children as Jews even though she had never formally converted. With her second marriage, also to a Jewish man, she now took the step to formally convert. Looking back, she saw the last ten years as a study in contrasts. While the last decade had been full of loss, anxiety, and weariness, she had reshaped her future, and in doing so had given birth to aspects of herself she could never have imagined.

While the future was not guaranteed—and she knew this all too well—it was there nonetheless. The future was bound to arrive, whether she did anything about it or not. Her reflection time helped her arrive at a fundamental reorientation of her life, from one of impending tragedy to one of gratitude and possibilities. Her sense of loss was still never far away, but it was now cast differently, as something that had given her a sense of purpose. Several years ago, Cyndi established the Wildflower Camp Foundation, which provides camp scholarships for children who have lost a parent and cannot afford to go to summer camp. In a recent year, the foundation provided scholarships to twenty-seven boys and girls ages five to seventeen. She felt it was a way of weaving together and *integrating* the sense of tragedy and hope that her life experience had given her. Cyndi feels she has emerged from the wilderness. She can now look to the past, be in the present, and plan for the future in a way she could not or would not allow herself to do six years ago.

She acknowledges that deep personal change evolves over many years. There is a "layering of experiences," a building process. It's a long-distance run. She likens it to running a marathon. Now in her mid-fifties, Cyndi is continuing to rebuild her life. She learned to ski for the first time. She has taken up golf, also for the first time. She has opened up to new experiences and new people. She recognizes that accepting help is not an admission of weakness. She has become an explorer. Her youngest daughter goes off to college next year. She doesn't know with absolute certainty what will come next. But she is confident she will have a say in it. She trusts she will have a role in creating whatever comes next.

Like Cyndi's path, each of our change journeys is unique. We each express our essential selves through this journey. At the same time, each journey embodies the same creative process, with the same creative dimensions.

Cyndi's odyssey of change has a feel and texture unique to her. But her journey shares elements with all of our change journeys. We will each experience our transitions in a strikingly one-of-a-kind way. The pace may be different. The emotional experience may feel different. What we bring into the adventure and take out of it may be different. But there is no escape from the four dimensions themselves because they are the foundational elements of the creative process itself.

Cyndi's story embodies this essential truth. In some circumstances she was a reluctant and uncomfortable sojourner in various dimensions. For instance, it took her some time to act on her first creative dilemma. Overcome by exhaustion and the need to focus on the well-being of her children, she clung to an emotional reliance on her husband. Only after some time passed was she able to commit to re-creating her family without her husband. She found ways to call on her own emotional reserves to get through the rough spots and make decisions. But what surprised Cyndi perhaps most is that her transition contained more than one creative dilemma: Do I stay in my present community, or do I move to a new one? Do I tend to my own psychotherapy practice, or do I take on a leadership role in building a professional practice community? Do I remain a mother only, or do I risk entering a relationship with another man?

In some sense Cyndi's story is the narrative of how she chose to respond to these creative dilemmas. When she made each of these decisions, she subsequently stepped, sometimes anxiously, into the exploration and discovery dimensions. She explored various communities as possible places to make a new home for herself and her children. Once she discovered a suitable new town, she mobilized her friends to help her make the move. She experimented with different professional arrangements before determining that creating a vibrant professional community was essential at that point in her life. Her commitment to date did not happen at the first urgings of her friends. She had to explore the strange range of feelings that came over her as she contemplated such a move, and only after discerning that the time was right did she commit to begin dating again. When she looked back over this period of her life she could see how her journey through these dimensions naturally brought her into the integration dimension. The sum total of all these decisions, explorations, and discoveries contributed to who she now is—a combination of past and present. She is renewed and different and "more whole," in her own words, as a person.

Cyndi would hardly classify herself as a consummate life change artist. In fact, she would not call herself an artist of any kind. Yet she has created the ultimate work of art: a life of meaning and purpose imbued with hard-won self-awareness. There is something essential here. When we say that Cyndi is a life change artist, we are saying that her journey of change followed a fundamentally creative process—the very same one followed by the great masters of art.

Every Journey Is Unique

As Cyndi learned, life change is often a response to multiple creative dilemmas. In the same sense, when a great artist creates a body of work over a lifetime, he is responding not to a single creative dilemma but to a series of creative dilemmas. How he responds determines whether he becomes a great artist or simply one who repeats what he has done before. Similarly, in our personal lives we may fall into a creative rut. We may get stuck in patterns of behavior where we feel we are not growing or learning. Such patterns can be damaging to our self-image. It is here we can learn a great deal from the great artists. We can begin to see how they responded to their creative dilemmas and engaged in the dimensions of exploration, discovery, and integration in order to keep their art fresh and original. Through the creative process the great artists learned how to renew themselves and their art.

Henri Matisse appeared on his way to financial success and artistic fame when he confronted a major creative dilemma. At the age of twenty-seven he had won a series of national recognitions that put him on a trajectory to a life of security and public adulation. All that was required of him was to continue to paint in the same style that had earned him his early reputation. Should he follow this path or pursue

Henri Matisse, *Woman in a Hat,* 1905

an entirely different approach to his painting? Much to everyone's surprise, Matisse left Paris to enter the dimensions of exploration and discovery. He left fame behind for the sake of being true to his artistic vision. In the several years that followed he experimented with an entirely new color palette. This experimentation led to his discovery of new ways to mix colors and come up with vibrant combinations. His paintings began to be less representational. He developed a totally new visual "language" that incorporated wild color combinations and often partly abstracted images. This series of paintings culminated in a remarkable piece called *Woman in a Hat.* He entered this painting, still wet from his studio, in an exhibition in 1905 and the reaction was swift and devastating. The critics panned it. They claimed it was akin to a bunch of "wild beasts."

This was only one of many similar experiences that would raise a series of creative dilemmas for Matisse. These creative dilemmas came at different times in his life, but they all presented a similar choice: Do I continue to do what I have been doing, or do I step into the unknown territories of exploration, discovery, and integration that hold out the possibility—but not the guarantee—of creating fresh, original paintings? Time and again, Matisse chose to step into the uncertain world of the creative dimensions. When we look back on the evolution of his work we can see the results of his courage. His painting is characterized by great bursts of vitality and originality. He earned a reputation for being one of the greatest colorists in the history of painting. Yet his creative dilemmas would not let him rest. Even later in life, when his reputation was secure as one of the greatest living artists, he faced another dilemma. A heart attack had severely limited his ability to paint or even move about. Did he give up art altogether or could he find another way to express himself visually? Again, he stepped into the dimensions of exploration, discovery, and integration. He picked up a pair of scissors and colored paper and began to create art from paper cutouts. Some of his most brilliant work was produced after he could no longer paint and chose, once again, to reinvent his art.

The work produced by great artists is born out of the intense, messy, and demanding engagement of the creative process. This process broadly governs the birth of great art regardless of what stage the artist is at in his development. And it continues over a lifetime as the artist heeds the call of subsequent creative dilemmas. For Claude Monet, the father of Impressionism, the four dimensions were in play throughout a long and prolific artistic career as he shifted creative gears, overcame roadblocks, and continuously reinvented his art.

By the end of World War I, Monet, then in his eighties, was widely recognized as one of the world's preeminent artists. The prime minister of France commissioned Monet to paint one of his famous water lily paintings "for the French nation." Despite his failing eyesight, Monet agreed. He hung a huge canvas in a specially constructed

Claude Monet, *The Japanese Bridge,* 1899

Claude Monet, *Water Lilies, Green Reflection,* 1918–1923

studio and began to paint as he had other water lily works. But shortly he faced a creative dilemma. He understood this canvas was for the country he loved and that the public was expecting to see what they had come to expect from his previous work. Yet he could not allow himself to repeat what he had done before. Should he comply with the expectations of an adoring public or take the risk of reinventing his art even at this late age?

Monet responded by stepping boldly into the exploration and discovery dimensions. He began to experiment with new techniques and perspective. In his previous water lily paintings Monet brought the viewer to the edge of the pond, where she could observe the rich, varied nature of the water lilies. Now he tried to figure out how to create the sensation of actually being *in* the pond *among* the water lilies. There were fits and starts, frustrations and risks until he discovered the right spacing of the water lilies and right luminescent colors for the flowers. He painted and repainted. He scraped and painted over what he had already painted, until he discovered the intended effect. To stand in front of one of these water lily paintings is to be transported to the magical world that Monet brought into being through the creative process. You stand before a canvas and recognize the fully integrated mastery of the artist. And yet you also realize that this magic came about only because Monet was willing to step into the four dimensions of the creative process and fully give himself to them.

What is true for Matisse and Monet is just as true for the life change artist. You must be willing to confront your creative dilemma and step fully into the dimensions of exploration, discovery, and integration. Regardless of your age or the nature of your creative dilemma, the four dimensions are the common coin of your creative process.

The Life Change Viewfinder

> *I'm learning to be quiet with myself. The view is clearer through the stillness.*
>
> —CAROL FRANCO, *life change artist*

Life change artists, like the great artists, are often so absorbed in the creative process that it can be difficult to fully appreciate exactly where they have been or where they are headed. Because we move through the four dimensions in our own ways, we do not always have the perspective to trust that we are where we need to be in order to move ahead. Our progression through the dimensions can be maddeningly nonlinear. We can be fully absorbed in exploration, believing we have arrived at some meaningful discovery, only to find we are thrown back into exploration again. We may be well down the path of integrating everything we have discovered, only to find ourselves confronted by another creative dilemma.

- Where are you on your life change journey?
- Which dimension of change are you in?

The Life Change Viewfinder is a tool to help you get a quick read on these two questions. A viewfinder is a handheld tool that helps the artist frame the subject of a painting and more deliberately identify what is most important in a scene.

In the same sense, our lives sometimes become so crowded with "stuff" that we do not know where to place our focus. We do not see the elements of a good "life painting." If we want to create a well-designed life composition, what do we focus on? The Life Change Viewfinder can help us gain perspective. You can use the Life Change Viewfinder to identify which of the four dimensions of life change is most significant for you right now. Are you experiencing a creative dilemma? Are you exploring, discovering, or integrating? Are you engaged in more than one dimension? That is often the case when your explorations quickly yield exciting discoveries. Why does it matter knowing which dimension or dimensions are your primary focus? Knowing where you are can remove some of the feelings of confusion about being in a state of flux. They can help you understand that all the emotions you are experiencing about your life change are normal. The Life Change Viewfinder can also suggest what questions would be most useful for you to focus on within any particular dimension. For example, if you see that you've already been asking questions relevant to a particular life change dimension, you'll have not only a better sense of where you are, but reassurance that you are on the right track. Below, you'll see a photograph of the Life Change Viewfinder.

EXERCISE

A Reflection

If you are reading this book, in all likelihood you are personally going through transition, or are about to embark on a transition journey. Take a moment to reflect on the following questions.

• When you consider where you are in your life, how would you describe your dominant emotions? Jot them down. They do not need to make sense or be consistent. Be honest with yourself. Don't hold anything back. Do not be afraid to go below the surface. One of the first steps in becoming a life change artist is to acknowledge that we live our lives on many emotional levels. Jot down the emotions in play at the various levels of your life.

- Now consider the big questions you are currently asking yourself about your life. Again, don't hold back. Jot down not only the first questions that come to mind, but the ones that might be percolating below the surface.

- Now consider if there is any connection between the emotions you have noted and some of the questions you have identified. Do these connections suggest anything to you about where you may be in the dimensions of life change?

Chapter 2

The Creative Dilemma

The function of Art is to disturb.

—GEORGES BRAQUE

E very life change begins with a creative dilemma—that is, a situation requiring a choice between two difficult alterna- tives. When Shakespeare's Hamlet ponders, "To be or not to be, that is the question," he is articulating the ultimate cre- ative dilemma. Of course, not all creative dilemmas are expressed in such stark terms. They come in many different forms and many dif- ferent sizes and you do not need to be Hamlet to face one. We all encounter creative dilemmas throughout our lives. The only question is: Are we going to respond to them?

Mea, a stay-at-home mom for the last twenty years, tells us, "There are two *me*'s to fulfill." Should she remain a stay-at-home mom, or should she move forward with her desire to return to school? A suc- cessful attorney feels burned-out by his "adversarial" role. Does he continue to do what he's good at but no longer believes in, or does he pursue something with more social meaning? A corporate execu- tive realizes she is living according to what others expect of her, not what she wants for herself. Does she continue in the boardroom or does she embark on an uncharted journey of self-discovery?

Creative Dilemma

PURPOSE: *To disturb*

- Arises out of tension between our current reality and a sense that things can be different.
- Presents a choice between a known and an unknown.
- Poses the question: *Do I act or not act on this choice?*
- Is resolved by our commitment to create something in our lives that did not exist before.
- Launches us into the exploration dimension.

Creative dilemmas can be expressed initially in different ways, as witnessed by the comments of several life change artists.

Life Change Artists Speak About Their Creative Dilemmas

I was feeling broken, very sad. I didn't know I was this vulnerable.

—VAN LANCKTON

My purpose was to live my life with purpose, but I didn't know what my purpose was.   —NANCY IMHOLTE

Take a stand or lose yourself!   —MARTHA REDSTROM

There's one thing worse than a midlife crisis and that's not having one.

—JIM HIME

Common Creative Dilemmas

I lose my job. Do I seek another job in the same field or make a more significant change? Do I stay in a relationship or step away? Do I stay with what's familiar or do I listen to my inner voice? Do I pursue my passion or stick with financial security? Do I embark on a journey of self-discovery or hold on to what is comfortable? Do I stay with this career or explore another? A loved one dies. What's next for me? A creative dilemma is unique to each individual, but in practice, creative dilemmas frequently occur in these life areas:

Career and Work

We work for many reasons. Among the reasons is a sense of enjoyment, meaning, and contribution. Tension can form when our work does not provide these satisfactions. "Is it simply this particular job or is it the field of work I am in?" you may ask. "If I could really do what gives me a deeper sense of purpose, then I would be happy. But I am not sure what I really want to do." On the other hand, we may find ourselves out of a job for reasons beyond our control. A business goes under. Jobs are cut. The sense of urgency to find something else may mask the deeper sense that the work we were doing was not what we really want to be doing. Or it might present itself in the way it did for Cindy Carlson, a longtime corporate executive who slowly came to the realization that "what I was doing was not who I was." Her basic creative dilemma: Do I continue in my financially rewarding job, or do I explore more meaningful work, even if the pay is lower?

A Cause or Calling

Not everyone can identify a cause or a calling to which they feel immediately connected. For many, our calling does not emerge until we are engaged in the dimensions of exploration and discovery. But some of us may already be connected to a cause or a passion to which we have not yet given ourselves fully. Such a cause may occupy us part of the time or on a voluntary basis. For a variety of reasons we may hold off giving ourselves fully to it. Jenna Fletcher recalled her love of animals and wistfully lamented not pursuing it, but instead earning her MBA. After years in the corporate world, she felt a tension between her current career path and her earlier passion. The more she thought about it, the stronger the tension became, eventually forming into a creative dilemma: Do I remain in my current career, or do I pursue my love of animals and the environment?

Relationships

Relationships are a common source of creative tension in our lives. We swim in an ocean of relationships: spouse, family, friends, coworkers, community members, social and spiritual networks. Do I stay in a relationship? Get out of a relationship? Start a new relationship? Deepen a relationship? Change a relationship? These are all choices. For Maria, a young mother who had tried many times to save her marriage of nine years without success, her creative dilemma came down to: Do I remain in this marriage with its "known pain," or do I seek a divorce, with all the turmoil and uncertainty it will cause me and my family?

Place

So much is tied up in where we live: community, identity, familiarity, comfort, habits, family and friends, climate, access to work, health care, educational resources. Every aspect of our life is touched by where we live, and under what conditions we establish our place. Creative dilemmas related to our place tend to have a ripple effect in almost every other aspect of our lives. Meg Pearson had happily settled in Florida just a few years earlier, when she found out her pregnant daughter and son-in-law would be relocating long term to the Mid-west. Her creative dilemma: Do I move closer to my daughter and grandchild, or remain in my current community? For Steve and Kathy Connor, their creative dilemma was different. They were both artists who no longer wanted to spend so much time and money on the up-keep of their house. Yet they could not see themselves living in a traditional condominium. Their creative dilemma: Do we stay in our current home, move to a condo, or create an entirely new housing model for ourselves?

Spiritual Beliefs and Practices

We seem wired to connect to something larger than ourselves. For some of us, it may take the form of participating in formal religious communities and practices. For others, our spirituality may show up in a deeply personal but noninstitutional form. For still others, it may involve a kind of spiritual journey in which we experiment with and integrate a variety of spiritual experiences. An unanswered spiritual call can produce a tension in our lives that rises to the level of a cre-ative dilemma. At the age of fifty-three, a prominent entertainer to the Hollywood rich and famous experiences a powerful spiritual call that crystallizes into his creative dilemma: Do I continue to entertain and get paid very well, or do I become a rabbi?

Health and Well-being

Few people aspire to ill health. Yet we often do not do the things we need to do to live a healthy life. After all, it's often easier to drift into bad health habits. Eating what we enjoy may seem easier than eat-ing well. Not exercising may seem easier than finding time to work out. Stress, we rationalize, is "part of the territory." Then we're jolted by news of someone who has fallen ill. Or we begin to feel sluggish or overweight or overly stressed out. After Thad Stevens ballooned to almost four hundred pounds, he confronted a creative dilemma: Do I change my eating and exercise habits, or risk major health problems? For Catherine Blanton, her creative dilemma came wrapped in a bundle. The fifty-six-year-old first-time grandmother couldn't look at her grandson without wondering whether she would be around to celebrate his confirmation. Her creative dilemma: Do I continue "my couch potato, TV-watching existence," or do I start paying attention to how I can get myself physically and mentally sharp "for the long haul"?

Lifestyle

We're often surprised at how crowded our lives have become. We have social commitments. Work commitments. Community commitments. Committee commitments. And commitments breed more commitments. There may be children. Parents and other relatives. Friends. Interests and hobbies. Professional development. Vacations. Soccer moms. Coaching dads. The list goes on. And then in a flashing moment we wonder, "What about me? How do I get time for myself? How do I create balance in my life? How can I simplify?" A successful business executive at the peak of her career wants to spend more time with her grandchildren. "Will they be teenagers before they get to know me, before I get to know them?" she wonders. And then her creative dilemma takes shape: Do I continue to structure my life around a well-paying and demanding career, or do I create more time for my grandchildren?

Learning and Creativity

For many of us, creative dilemmas form around a yearning for personal expression. When we are learning and tapping into our creativity, we feel alive and energized. When we are not learning or using our creativity, we feel stagnant. A mother of four in her early forties who never finished college feels unfulfilled. She realizes she faces a creative dilemma: Do I remain at home and continue to be a full-time mom, or do I return to school? A pediatrician in practice for thirty-plus years has learned to read auras from a Native American medicine man. He faces a creative dilemma: Do I continue to practice medicine in the conventional Western way, or do I incorporate elements of nontraditional medicine into my practice?

Mortality

For some, a deepening sense of our own mortality stirs the what's-really-important and the what's-yet-to-be-done questions. A new sense of urgency wraps itself around these questions as we wonder whether the life we are living is enough, is right, is true to who we are and how we wish to be in the world. We play with new assumptions. If we only have a day to live . . . ? A month . . . ? A year . . . ? Only five more years . . . ? We become more tuned in to the cycle of life and realize we are closer to the cutting edge between life and death, leading to this creative dilemma: Should I spend my precious remaining years in the way I have been living, or should I change my life?

Tension: The Mother of Invention

Our creative dilemmas come in many forms. Whether and how we confront them shapes the trajectory of our lives. When we turn away from these creative dilemmas or try to deny them, the underlying tension takes on a subterranean life of its own, often surfacing in physiological symptoms or outward frustration at the direction of our lives. The great artists show us how we can leverage our creative dilemmas to realize breakthroughs not only in art but in our lives.

Creative dilemmas are sources of innovative breakthroughs in art as well as in life. Without them the history of art would be a series of boring reproductions rather than the lively bursts of expressive originality. Our lives, too, would take on the familiar but boring patina of repetition if it were not for the uncomfortable but necessary tensions that give rise to our creative dilemmas. When we understand creative dilemmas as the entry point into the creative process, we are more likely to face them for what they are, even welcome them, as unsettling as they may be, as opportunities for personal growth and reinvention.

One of the values of looking at the great artists is that their creative dilemmas come in sizes large and small. Sometimes they arise from major decisions about the direction of their art. Sometimes they present themselves as smaller challenges on a given canvas.

What we need to keep in mind is that creative dilemmas represent choices. How we respond to our creative dilemmas shapes our personal narrative. When we consistently deny our dilemmas we can be overtaken by a sense of letting ourselves down, of giving in to fear, of missing opportunities in our lives. Our narrative turns negative and that often amplifies the tension. When we decide to respond to our dilemmas, however, we develop a narrative that emphasizes our sense of personal agency. We can feel more self-empowered.

It was precisely the commitment on the part of the great artists to take on their creative dilemmas that led to their mastery. Along the way, they may not have felt like masters of their fate or of their medium, but they continued to step into the four dimensions of the creative process because they knew it was an essential part of their quest for mastery and the full expression of what was inside them.

The great Mexican artist Frida Kahlo (1907–1954) could have easily given up before she even started had she not had the courage to confront a major creative dilemma. At the age of eighteen she was in a life-threatening trolley accident that left her bedridden and in a full-body cast. She had planned to study medicine and become a doctor, but now immobile and near despair, she had a choice: to surrender to the debilitating effects of her accident or to find another means to express herself. Her mother constructed a special easel and Frida began to paint. No sooner had she started than she faced the dilemma of subject matter. She had little interest in the traditional subject matter of painting, such as still lifes or landscapes. Dare she paint what truly interested her? The art world was not used to images of women's or-

Frida Kahlo, *Without Hope,* 1945

gans or miscarriages. But Frida decided to make her body and her suffering the subject of her art. She decided to paint her own reality. "I paint myself," she wrote, "because I am alone. I am the subject I know best." Her commitment to face her creative dilemma gave us a body of work that forces us to face the realities of women and their bodies in entirely new ways.

Frida Kahlo's response to her creative dilemmas brought her into risky territory. Her willingness to accept risk has rewarded all of us. The truth is that risk is an essential element of facing our creative dilemmas because there is no guarantee that we will eliminate the tensions we feel in our lives when we enter the dimensions of change. Yet without risk there can be no breakthrough in art or in life.

We have seen in the previous chapter how the great artists were prepared to face the risks inherent in their creative dilemmas, even in their advanced years. Monet was in his eighties when he reinvented his water lily paintings. Matisse was in his seventies when he took up paper cutting. Yet the pattern of facing creative dilemmas was formed much earlier. The great artists showed early indications that whatever subsequent dilemmas they faced, they were prepared to confront them.

This is exactly what Monet did in his early twenties when he put his easel on his back and hiked into the countryside to engage in "plein air" painting in his early twenties. He did so in response to a creative dilemma: Do I paint the traditional way the Académie des Beaux-Arts expects artists to paint, thereby gaining public acceptance, or do I paint "Truthfulness, Life, Nature, everything that moved me"?[1] He was determined to overthrow the official art of the day, and years later emerged from the countryside with paintings that revolutionized art. Today we call it Impressionism. As Auguste Renoir claimed, "Without Monet, who gave us all courage, we would have given up."

Courage, risk, uneasiness, fear, self-doubt. These are among the experiential realities that characterize our creative dilemmas. We can understand, then, why the purpose of our creative dilemmas is to disturb us. We can also understand why for many of us the choice to confront our creative dilemmas takes a little longer.

The Voice of Knowing

The day Donna Krone sold her financial planning practice after nineteen years was a day she thought would never come. After all, she personally had been the most powerful impediment to making it happen. She was stuck in a web of emotional restraints, mental roadblocks, and the advice from others that told her point-blank she would be crazy to make a change. Many people told her she had a lucrative practice, she had the respect and loyalty of her clients, and she valued the scheduling flexibility it provided in raising her two children. She internalized it all. Each time the thought of doing something different arose, she allowed herself to lapse back to the familiar status quo ante. She would silence her own voice.

---

1. Karin Sagner-Duchting, *Claude Monet* (New York: Taschen, 1998), p. 16.

Donna had not started out expecting to be a financial planner. Nursing had been her original calling until a back injury at age twenty-seven forced her to look in a different direction. She attended a career seminar on financial planning. The prospect of building long-term relationships and helping others achieve their goals appealed to her. She made the shift and her intelligence, caring, and natural listening skills made it easy for her to connect with clients and gain their trust. She dedicated herself to learning the intricacies of the profession and earned her certified financial planning designation. As her practice grew, however, she became increasingly aware of a need within herself that was not being met through her practice. She realized the financial planning discipline placed invisible barriers around the relationship. Donna cared about the whole person and helping her clients navigate the major transitions in their lives. She did not want to be limited to addressing her clients' financial goals.

Donna had been raised with the view that "life is supposed to be a struggle." Such an outlook, she came to recognize, threatened to "normalize" her current situation without the need to change it. It was okay to be in struggle. In fact, being in struggle meant you were living your life the way it was supposed to be lived. Of course, such a worldview suggests that *any* struggle is good. To make matters worse, Donna felt she needed to ask permission to make changes. When permission wasn't given, she became overwhelmed with a sense of guilt because she believed she needed to please everyone.

Things came to a head when she decided to seek the help of a personal coach. During their meetings, her creative dilemma crystallized in a powerful way. During one meeting she blurted out, "Why, it's me that's the dilemma. It's not my situation. It's up to me to make the choice."

Over the next year and a half, Donna experienced a process she describes as reconnecting with her "true self." She shed the feeling that "no matter where I was, I was supposed to be somewhere else." She recognized that she had the power to make choices without the permission of others, because no one knew her as well as she knew herself. Her "inner knowing" began to find a voice and a direction. She took small, uneasy steps. She enrolled in coach training and immersed herself in numerous workshops, seminars, and supervised coaching opportunities. She came to discover and appreciate her gifts and how to manifest them with others. She believes the greatest gift is the one she has given herself: permission to choose her own struggle. She reached a milestone. She sold her practice. She feels freer. Despite the difficulties of building a coaching practice, she knows that this work is aligned with her true calling, to make a difference in the lives of others, to give voice to her "inner knowing" and to those of others.

Though a creative dilemma typically forms around a specific area in our lives, the consequences of acting upon it radiate out through many areas of our lives. Donna could not have foreseen the ways in which her decision to make changes in her work positively impacted the quality of her relationships with her children and husband or with her new and old friends. She perhaps did not foresee the ways in which the changes helped her step into new roles in her community and in her new work. She did not know that her decision to change would affect her physically, transforming her former weary demeanor into one of excitement and adventure. By first defining her creative dilemma, Donna, like a great artist, began to create a new art form out of her life and to infuse other aspects of her life with fresh energy.

The Texture of Creative Dilemmas

Creative dilemmas first speak to us through our emotions. The tension that gives birth to our creative dilemma speaks in many emotional tongues. Sometimes it can come in the form of a gentle uneasiness about our life situation. Sometimes we may feel anger, resentment, or frustration building up. Sometimes the tension expresses itself through our physiology. We have low energy. We get heart palpitations. Our blood pressure rises. And sometimes the tension may show up through "unexplained" behaviors. "I just haven't been myself lately," you say to a friend. But then you recognize the illogic of that feeling. "Who else have I been? Of course I have been myself. Only I'm speaking to myself in a language I do not fully understand."

Creative dilemmas unsettle us. That is their purpose. By their nature, creative dilemmas are anti–status quo. They are disruptive. They disturb us by stirring our emotions or influencing our behaviors or triggering our physiology. Creative dilemmas have their own Morse code. They are signaling us to pay attention. Do we keep doing what we have been doing, or do we travel down a different path? What makes this choice a dilemma? Like all dilemmas, each alternative carries risk. If we choose to keep on living in the same way, we will continue to experience tension. We may grow emotional calluses to cover up these feelings, but they will remain below the surface and they will continue to produce feelings of dissatisfaction at some level. If we decide to move toward other possibilities, we risk losing the familiarity and security of our current lives, without any assurance that a change will work out well for us.

Signs of a Creative Dilemma	
YOU MAY FEEL . . .	YOU MAY BE ASKING:
Uneasy	What's going on here?
Drained	Why am I feeling this way?
Helpless	What's the source of my tension?
Empty	How did it come to this?
Demoralized	Do I really have to do this?
Disheartened	Should I talk to someone about it?
Isolated	Do I need to ask permission?
Irritable	
Confused	

What makes this dilemma a creative one? Creating means bringing into existence that which did not previously exist. In that sense,
being creative means tapping into a source of energy that grows things
where nothing existed before. By its nature, being creative means stepping into the unknown and the unfamiliar. All creative processes lead
us to invent something—a painting, a poem, a new life, a new set of
skills—that did not exist before. Every dilemma features dicey alternatives. A creative dilemma is even more challenging because it asks
us to choose between the known and the unknown. It asks us to go
down a different path without necessarily knowing where that path
will lead and what the dangers might be along the way.

It's hard to overemphasize the difficulties involved in responding
to a creative dilemma. Discontent with our current life is often not
enough to propel us into an unknown future. We often have good
reasons for "deciding" not to change. But our emotions seem not to
have "gotten the memo" about our decision in favor of the status quo.
We try to quash those feelings of dissatisfaction, but tension keeps
rearing its ugly head. In some cases the tension actually seems to dull
itself and lose its sense of urgency. But it remains nonetheless. Many
of us take months or even years before we take a step toward change.

At sixty-four, Don Cucinelli had maintained the muscular frame
he first developed as a state trooper in Massachusetts. It's hard to think
that this physically powerful man had never faced the creative dilemma that sat at the core of his identity.

Since childhood Don had been pulled between warm memories of
growing up in a densely populated Italian neighborhood in Beverly,
Massachusetts, and a great curiosity about his family roots that ran deep
in his ancestral home of Pescina, Italy. But he had become estranged
from his family, and for decades his curiosity had stopped at the ocean's
edge. At least until his daughter received a cryptic email through her
Facebook account from one of the "Pescina Cucinellis," inquiring
whether she had family ties back in this ancient town. Don felt the
tension boil to the surface again. Do I continue to live my life "as
though I didn't come from somewhere" or do I pursue my family his-

tory? This time Don could no longer hold down the tension. Once he reunited with his forty living relatives back in Pescina, he felt he had come home. He felt he had reclaimed his identity, which he now traced back to the year 836, when a branch of his family landed in Naples from Spain. Today, Don is buying a house in Pescina. He plans to live there for several months with the very real possibility he will make a permanent return. "I realized there had been a gigantic hole in my heart. I didn't know how big it was until I went to Pescina." Even if it had taken some time.

The Good News About Tension

Though tension is uncomfortable, it is our first ally in making positive changes in our lives. Tension is the psychological equivalent of pain. It is a signal that something is wrong. Without physical pain, we would not know that we need to take steps to address the underlying problem. Similarly, tension tells us that something is off kilter in our lives. If it were not for tension, we might never take that first step to making the changes we ultimately choose to make.

Some of us have little tolerance for tension, so we confront our creative dilemma soon after we begin to feel it. Others of us find ways to squelch the tension for long periods of time. Everyone has his or her own timetable for change. But for most of us, it is not possible to eliminate tension without actively addressing our creative dilemma. So the sooner we choose to confront our creative dilemma, the sooner we can rid ourselves of the nagging discomfort associated with it.

We do not, however, confront our dilemma simply to get rid of the tension. After all, what would we replace that tension with? The real reason we confront our creative dilemma is to bring forth within ourselves what we truly want to express that is not being expressed, to bring forth aspects of ourselves that are crying out for attention and nurturing. Like the great artists, we aspire to express what is truly inside us.

Hanging On to Tension

If tension is such a good thing to dispense with, why do we hang on to it? What stops us from confronting our creative dilemma head-on? Often, we hold on to tension because we carry in our heads a set of constraining assumptions. We may *overestimate* the magnitude of risk we might take in changing our lives, and *underestimate* our personal ability to successfully navigate such a change. Many of us also mistakenly believe that we must fully understand and be happy with the potential financial consequences of a life change. And that belief also causes us to assume that we need to know in advance our exact life circumstances if we are to make a change. None of these constraining assumptions is true.

Confronting Our Creative Dilemma

Confronting our creative dilemma means making a decision to explore the possibility of living differently in some way. That does carry certain risks. It's highly likely that you'll feel uncertain, or fearful, or even incompetent, as you experiment with new activities, skills, or ways of thinking. It's probable that along the way you may confuse loved ones or even lose certain friends as your interests diverge from theirs. And it's possible that the choices you ultimately make to recreate yourself could have an impact on your standard of living or the nature of your personal relationships. But none of those risks is unmanageable, and none of them will happen simply because you have decided to explore a different path. The risks of change may indeed materialize, but most risks, with the exception of feeling foolish or incompetent, don't come into play until you are well down the road to making a life change.

Instead of letting constraining assumptions hold you back, you can create a "risk-free" zone called "exploration" for experimenting with new life possibilities. Deciding to confront your creative dilemma unlocks the key to exploration. While you are exploring, you are not nearly ready to commit to the life changes that could indeed be risky. And once you make the choice to confront your creative dilemma by beginning to explore, you'll find that most of the risks you feared evaporate. And that you are more than strong enough to tackle the risks that may remain.

EXERCISE

What Is Your Creative Dilemma?

The following statements are typical thoughts and feelings of people who have a creative dilemma.

Put a check mark () next to any statements that are true for you.

___Sometimes I wonder if my current life is "all there is."

___I find myself dreaming about a career that I did not pursue.

___I lack the enthusiasm about life that I used to have.

___I envy people who seem to be doing what they really love.

___I would like to change my life in some way, but I'm not sure what I really want to do.

___I have an idea about what I'd like to do differently, but there are things getting in the way.

___I feel obligated to continue in my life as it is, even though it is not the life I want.

___Those close to me would be upset if I decided to make a significant change in my life.

___I've had a recent experience that has caused me to question the meaning of my life.

___I worry about the financial consequences of making a major change in my life.

If you checked any of the statements above, you probably are experiencing a creative dilemma.

A creative dilemma gives us a choice between two alternatives: continuing our current life as is, or making changes in some way.

In the space below, try to express your creative dilemma as specifically as possible.

I have the opportunity to . . .

_____

OR I can continue to . . .

_____

Chapter 3

Exploration and Discovery

Creativity is allowing yourself to make mistakes. Art is knowing which ones to keep.

—SCOTT ADAMS

Once you've acknowledged your creative dilemma, you can begin to confront it. Resolving a creative dilemma begins by engaging in the two dimensions of exploration and discovery. This chapter focuses on both dimensions together because they are highly intertwined, working interdependently and synergistically. One does not occur without the other. We explore—that is, we try out new experiences—and those experiences in turn help us discover more about ourselves, including what we like and don't like, what fits and does not fit. What we discover can then help us realize that there are other things we want to explore. People who go through life change usually bounce from exploration to discovery and back, constantly experimenting and gaining deeper insights into their own lives and the choices they have made.

The essence of exploration and discovery is presented below:

Exploration

PURPOSE: *To learn*
- Searching for and experimenting with new directions.
- Reconnecting with an earlier interest or passion.
- Expanding our sense of what is possible for us.
- Open-ended.
- Becoming aware of old emotions and experiencing new ones.

Discovery

PURPOSE: *To discern*
- Uses the raw material of our exploration to discern what is meaningful to us.
- Challenges old assumptions.
- Leads to new insights about ourselves.
- Focused and evaluative.
- Often sets off a new cycle of exploring and discovering.

Beginning to explore is not easy. Taking those first steps requires a creative mind-set. We need to believe in our own creative ability, believe in our ability to experiment with the new and unknown, and believe that we can discover important things about ourselves if only we are willing to take that step into the unknown. But many of us lack that basic belief in our creativity, so fundamental to successful exploration and discovery. We're all born with creative ability, but often we are conditioned over time to believe we aren't creative. To illustrate, think about your own childhood experiences with art. Did you enjoy it? Were you "good" at it? How did you figure out whether you were good at art, or not so good?

"I remember when our second-grade art teacher, Mrs. Brown, came to our class each week," recalls Barbara Henley, recently retired from her job as an accounting manager with a state agency. Barbara continues:

> One day, Mrs. Brown asked us to draw a picture of our favorite character from a story we were reading. There was a horse in the story and I was crazy about horses at the time. I grabbed my crayons and drew the horse—a large animal with huge eyes, a spiral tail, and striped with various shades of pink and purple (my favorite colors at the time). I can remember really enjoying drawing that picture. Then Mrs. Brown stopped by the girl next to me and couldn't say enough about how wonderful her drawing was. When I looked at my classmate's picture, I knew immediately that hers was "better." She had drawn a princess with a dress that could have been sketched by a fashion designer. Of course, Mrs. Brown made a point of saying how nice my drawing was, but I could tell from her voice that she was just trying to make me feel better.

Like Barbara, most of us learn early that art is supposed to be about rendering what we see as precisely as possible. And when our early efforts did not pass muster, we concluded we were not very good at art. As adults we often morph this perspective into the sad belief that "I am not very creative because I can't draw worth a lick." Barbara's unintended drawing "lesson" pertained specifically to one of the visual arts, but the sad truth is that many of us experience similar unintended "lessons" in all the arts: dance, poetry, music, and so forth.

Happily, the great artists do not share this view about art or creativity. Art is not about copying or rendering. It is about exploring, discovering, and expressing ourselves. "I begin with an idea and then it becomes something else," Picasso tells us. He is letting out the dirty little secret of great art. It is not born out of a fully conceived idea and then executed through a few precise brushstrokes. It is not about copying. Great art is realized through imagination, experimentation, trial and error, discovery, and expression. The battle takes place in the head, heart, and hand of the artist and on the canvas. In the case of life change, the battle for living a fully realized life is fought on the uncharted waters of the exploration and discovery dimensions.

During Exploration You May Feel . . .		
Energized	Introspective	Unsure
Expansive	Anxious	Impatient
Elated	Absorbed	Restless
Curious	Uncertain	Self-conscious
Alive	Doubtful	Puzzled
Excited	Suspended	Conflicted
Hopeful	Frustrated	Regretful

Sometimes the dance of exploration and discovery happens with surprising speed. Cindy Carlson, a successful senior executive, no sooner began to explore ways to simplify her life, than she discovered how unfulfilling her marriage was, which sent her on a sidebar of further exploration. Ron Mortara, forced for health reasons to leave his medical practice, suddenly got the urge to explore his attic and immediately discovered clues to his future direction. He found an old camera his father had given him as a teenager. This led him to explore further by signing up for workshops in filmmaking. At other times the process of exploration and discovery is uncomfortably slow. There were periods when Cindy felt like she was "floating in a void without direction or insight." Ron often felt as though his transition to whatever was next felt like moving through a "pot of syrup." For Nancy F. Mills, an Emmy Award–winning former television journalist who is "trying to make sense of what comes next," the experience is "slow, hard, and painful."

During Discovery You May Feel . . .		
Excited	Optimistic	Tentative
Exhilarated	Vulnerable	Determined
Enthusiastic	Overwhelmed	Reconciled

In fact, it is not unusual for there to be a decoupling between how quickly or slowly we *feel* time is moving and how quickly or slowly it actually is moving. Ron Mortara may have felt that time dripped like a thick syrup, and Cindy may have felt that it buzzed by too quickly, but in truth, the same number of months had gone by on the real calendar for each of them. The sense of time passing is a function of our emotional clock more than it is an objective measure.

In addition, there is no prescribed amount of time one spends in these dimensions. Part of our creative mind-set must be to trust that these dimensions of exploration and discovery, however they play out, are serving their purpose in our particular process of change.

Listen to the voices of life change artists. How do they reflect your own experiences?

Life Change Artists Speak About Exploration

For a while it felt like flying blind, flying in a fog, feeling lost.

—RON MEDVED

I'm a risk taker. It doesn't always feel good. It's not always graceful.
But it's necessary to live the life I want. —SHARON SOKOLOFF

I was living the American Dream and then I just jumped off that track.
Why aren't I more scared and anxious? Am I out of my gourd?

—MARY KOMORNICKA

For me, it's been like living in parentheses. I'm not sure how to get out of it
or how to complete the sentence. —MARIA YUNIS

Being a woman was helpful. It meant I could be vulnerable and not be told there
was something wrong with me. —ELLEN GLANZ

If you show up, things will show up.   —JOHN RICE

You have to be fearless in exploration. The more confused, more fearful, more anxious the more likely the end result will mean something.

—BETSYANN DUVAL

Life Change Artists Speak About Discovery

Once I learned my body had its own language, my head began to listen.

—SUSAN KULLMAN

Lots of tears and fears.   —HEIDI WISE

Once I knew, I knew.   —D. MAJOR COHEN

I'm capable of a lot of things.   —SUSAN ROSENBERG

I gave up a lot of my ego. I got the most benefit when I didn't make myself the center of the universe.   —ELIZABETH COOK

It was hard for me. I value order and predictability.   —DOUG MCGRAITH

There were always people ready to tell me I was crazy.

—LINDA BERTENTHAL

As I let myself become more of myself, I discovered I liked me.

—PAUL FRAGALA

In some sense, we are always in transition and therefore always exploring and discovering. For Berthe Morisot, the great French Impressionist, the dimensions of exploration and discovery not only yielded a unique place in the male-dominated art culture of the day, but also left a legacy of innovation we still see in the work of contemporary artists.

Too Bad She's Not a Man

To understand the challenges Morisot faced as a woman artist, we need go no further than a comment from Édouard Manet, one of the leading painters of his day. Manet claimed, "This woman's work is exceptional. Too bad she's not a man." His comment reveals how strongly the odds were stacked against women artists in the 1860s and 1870s when Morisot was struggling to make her way as a painter. Women were not allowed to attend art schools. Yet Morisot's talent allowed her to join a group of artists, including Auguste Renoir, Claude Monet, and Edgar Degas, who would later become famous as the "Impressionists."

Morisot set off on her own journey of exploration and discovery. She was guided by her own words: "Real painters understand through the brush." Morisot meant that theories did not count, nor did pre-conceived ideas about what a painting should. The only thing that mattered to her was direct painting, using her brush as pathfinder and pioneer. Breaking with tradition, Morisot rarely pre-sketched on the canvas, preferring to place paint directly on the canvas with her brush. Her creative process fully embraced the exploration and discovery dimensions. She left evidence right on the canvas for all to see how she bounced around its surface as she experimented with different kinds of brushstrokes and thinly applied paint to build up her images until she discovered the right combinations. She believed that this led to greater spontaneity and allowed the painter to convey her emotional response to her subject more fully. Morisot used rapid strokes, some-times changing them by wiping, thinning, and blotting. She inten-tionally left her mistakes and corrections clearly visible. One of her great innovations was to leave a history of the painting process for all to see right on the canvas, evidence of the "pitched battle," as she

Berthe Morisot, *Girl with a Greyhound,* 1893

referred to her efforts to paint.[1] In this way modern art is directly indebted to her. Before Morisot, artists were loath to leave evidence of "mistakes."

One of her most poignant paintings shows how her commitment to experimentation and discovery led to continuous innovations. Painted just two years before Morisot died at age fifty-four, *Girl with a Greyhound* is a haunting work. In it, Morisot's daughter, Julie, sits on a couch. She is painted in a vibrantly rendered blue-black dress. All the other elements seem to be painted in pale, ephemeral colors. A greyhound faces toward what appears to be an unfinished chair. The chair represented Julie's father and Berthe's husband, Eugène Manet, who had died a few years earlier. The unfinished chair not only had symbolic value for the painting but was part of a larger debate Morisot had ignited. When is a painting complete? For the traditionalists, Morisot represented the breakdown of painting as it had been known. She reg-

1. Charles F. Stuckey and William P. Scott, *Berthe Morisot, Impressionist* (New York: Hudson Hills Press, 1987), p. 189.

ularly left whole parts of a painting unfinished, hinted at—she let the viewer envision what was unseen. For Morisot, this was another example of how art and life are united. A painting can never be finished. Neither can a life. Both are part of the never-ending creative process.

Some Guiding Principles

Morisot's creative experiments and artistic innovations were entirely her own. In the end, her journey provides three important lessons for life change artists who are ready to step into the dimensions of exploration and discovery:

> *Choose what you pay attention to; do not let others choose for you.*

Morisot was sometimes criticized for almost exclusively painting women. That is the subject she chose even though others thought she should expand her range. For life change artists to fully realize themselves, it is equally important to listen to our inner voice. We may not fully know what we want. But no one else does, either, even if some may claim they do. We are the only ones who can determine what is true for us.

A key is to understand that we do not need to know the answers to all of our life change questions when we respond to our creative dilemmas. After all, that is precisely the purpose of the exploration and discovery dimensions—to get us there as part of the creative process. The point is to begin, and we begin by making a choice regarding what we, as life change artists, choose to pay attention to.

Where, then, do we go to get an idea of what to pay attention to? A good starting point is our creative dilemma. Our creative dilemma reveals the sources of tension in our lives and leads us to what we must pay attention to. The more clearly we articulate our creative dilemma the clearer our point of focus becomes.

Exploring happens by doing; discovery happens by exploring.

Since exploration is action–oriented and discovery is reflective and evaluative, it makes sense that there is a strong interdependency between the two dimensions. Morisot would not have discovered the effects of leaving parts of her paintings unfinished if she had not first taken the steps to try out such effects. The same is true for life change artists. In some sense we do not know what we do not know and the only way to discover what we do not know is to actually experiment with things we are not familiar with. In other words, we need to step into the forest.

There are many ways to enter the exploration dimension. At a minimum we can read a book on a subject about which we have little understanding but about which we may be curious. We can stretch ourselves a bit further by taking a course, workshop, or program in an area we would like to explore. These are small ways of exploring. Or we can be more adventuresome and travel to unvisited places, serve an internship or do volunteer work in a field we find interesting. We can identify individuals who are engaged in areas we would like to learn more about and whose interests we might like to probe over coffee or lunch. A key to all of these steps is that we must get out of our normal routines. We need to commit to spending a significant portion of our time differently from how we have in the past.

You are never finished.

One of Morisot's insights about the creative process is that a painting is never done. This is true of life change as well. As creating human beings, not only are we constantly creating things, we are continuously creating and re-creating ourselves.

This means that becoming a life change artist requires that we develop enduring skills that can be adapted to the surprising array of creative dilemmas we will encounter over our lifetime. Life change artists never retire, because our creative dilemmas keep coming long after an official "retirement age." The great English sculptor Henry Moore warned that "there's no retirement for an artist, it's your way of living so there's no end to it." And so it is with life change artists.

Staying Afloat on a Sea of Change

Cindy Carlson's journey through the dimensions of exploration and discovery confirms these principles. For Cindy the experience of being in these dimensions has been transformative even though she has not yet arrived at a clear destination. "I sometimes feel like a sailor. I've sailed to some deep places and visited a number of ports, but I haven't found a safe harbor yet. I'm trying out a lot of things."

During a twenty-year career, Cindy rose through the corporate ranks of a major financial services company. She earned the reputation of getting things done. She was particularly astute at organizing businesses that required sophisticated technology systems. Despite her outstanding performance, however, she began to pick up internal signals that things were not all right with her. At first she thought she simply needed to change jobs within the company. The company was ready to accommodate her. But then a start-up venture presented itself. The new company came after her pretty hard, and although she was not a hundred percent sure this was the answer, she jumped at the opportunity. Shortly after that, she got her first jolt. It came in the form of a voice as she walked down the hall at work. The voice said, "More is expected of you." At first, Cindy paid no attention. But three months later, she received another jolt. This time it was physical. It literally "knocked me against the wall." And the voice repeated, "More is expected of you." "Okay," she answered this time, "I'm listening."

Cindy didn't realize she had already entered the exploration dimension when she accepted her new position with the start-up company. But the very fact that she was exploring a new job was another signal that she needed to pay attention. With this second jolt she finally acknowledged her creative dilemma: "Do I continue to do what I have been doing, or do I try to understand what the voice meant when it said, 'More is expected of you'?" And whose voice *was* it, anyway?

Cindy began to experiment in earnest through what she described as an "emptying" process. First, she began to empty her house of years of accumulated "stuff." Then she insisted she and her husband downsize from their large house to a smaller one. Their oldest daughter was in college and their son was in high school. Perhaps, Cindy thought, she might discover what was really important by removing from her life anything that was not important. Before too long, Cindy came to the painful realization that this need to empty things from her life was a diversion from the real emptiness—her marriage. Never one to shy away from tough decisions, Cindy soon filed for divorce.

She remembers the period after this decision as a "dark void," like "being in the open seas without a rudder or compass." In some sense, Cindy was now empty inside and out. She left the start-up company she had joined so precipitously. She had no job. She had no husband. Her friends seemed to have disappeared. "All the sources of my identity were gone," she recalls. "I was learning that none of them fit me anymore. My old identity went AWOL."

In order to cope with this "dark time," Cindy took up bike riding. She went on long rides, sometimes sixty or seventy miles at a time. She walked everywhere. And she began to read. With the exception of business reports, she had never been a reader. Now she spent hours in bookstores and in the library. She seemed pulled toward books on spirituality and healing. One book led to another. Cindy came to realize that her life up to this point had been about filling herself up with things, but not with what was important. She was not entirely sure what *was* important at this point. She thought perhaps joy needed to be in her life. But even that was not clear. Where would this joy come from?

After a while, Cindy became aware that new people were appearing in her life. They were going through the same "spiritual shifts" she was experiencing. She also noticed that the majority of these people, like herself, had been "brought to their knees" through some major life disruption. Illness, bankruptcy, divorce, job loss. Even though in many respects she was in the same spiritual flux as they were, many of these people started coming to her for support. She found a new level of honesty in her interactions with people as she shared something she had never been able to before—her own vulnerability.

Cindy explored further by participating in a series of workshops on healing. One in particular had a profound effect on her. She attended a weeklong retreat in the Ozarks. There was no electricity, no running water. She took long, quiet hikes into what once had been Native American land. She began to sense that not only was she being healed, but that she had healing powers.

Cindy has discovered a path. She still does not know where it will lead. Although she is in her late forties, she does not know how she will earn a living from this new direction. She recently received a job offer in the corporate world but turned it down. She is grateful that her talents are still in demand. She wonders how she can combine her knowledge of the corporate world with this new healing gift. She is committed to exploring where that may lead. When she looks back, she is convinced, "If I had had a plan for my spiritual growth, I would have missed it." It was her very openness to trying new things that brought her to this place. She may still be on open waters but at least she feels she has a rudder.

Like Morisot, Cindy explored by doing. She pushed herself to try things she had never tried before. She chose to focus on spiritual healing. This was not what others might have thought she should focus on. The new direction took her away not only from her old identities, but from old relationships, too. She had gained deeper levels of self-insight. Equally important, she has learned new skills. Not just healing skills but navigational skills. She learned how to float in the open seas without any land in sight. While she continues to deepen her self-understanding, Cindy also recognizes that her work has just begun.

In her formative years as an artist, Berthe Morisot received special permission to set up an easel in the Louvre in order to copy works of the great masters. This was a commonly accepted practice used to hone one's skills and learn different techniques. But it was a practice viewed only as a stepping-stone to discovering one's own creative voice. The only thing considered worse than copying the masters was to copy oneself. "To copy oneself is more dangerous than to copy others. It leads to sterility," Picasso observed. Morisot, Picasso, and Cindy understand this in relation to life and to art. They understand that in order to avoid such a fate, life change artists need to give themselves fully to entering the dimensions of exploration and discovery and be open to what these dimensions have to offer. We should also count Ron Mortara in this circle.

". . . Then Who Am I?"

Ron was at the top of his game when he found out he had a heart condition that would no longer permit him to practice neurosurgery. He was working at the cutting edge of medicine and technology. He was on call 24/7 and performed under extreme pressure. Life and death hung in the balance. This was Ron's world and he loved being in it. But stress triggered heart palpitations and caused dizziness. Ron's world had suddenly been flipped upside down. He had become the patient. Ron determined that if he could not perform surgery, he did not want to practice medicine at all. Within two weeks he closed his practice and wondered what would come next.

The first thing that struck Ron was "how quiet it can be, how slow and syrupy the day can be." He spent his initial "freedom" throwing away a lot of "stuff." He cared for his ill mother. He had always been intensely goal-oriented, but now the future appeared "covered with sand in all directions." Having chosen to leave the medical profession entirely, he felt without purpose and wondered who, in fact, he was or "what I was worth."

He also realized that at the age of fifty-eight he could envision a hundred different lives. He loved science. He loved adventure and toyed with the idea of sailing the world. He loved the arts. As he spent time visiting art galleries and museums, he recalled how his father would chronicle the family travels on film and how much he personally enjoyed movies. He vividly remembered making a 16-millimeter movie with friends when he was sixteen years old. Coincidentally, he noticed an article in the newspaper promoting a series of open studios by film and video artists. At one of the studios, he picked up a bulletin that offered courses in the technical aspects of filmmaking. Ron decided to try out a workshop. This course led to several others, and he began to wonder whether filmmaking would be a hobby or could become a more substantial life commitment.

But other things seemed to be going on at the same time. Despite the excitement that came from learning about a new creative field, Ron continued to be haunted by occasional dreams of being in the operating room. In these dreams he could actually see the patient, see himself poised to begin the operation, only to be overwhelmed by a sense of embarrassment that he could not go on. His life seemed caught in a riptide between a past identity and an unknown future. "If I am no longer the neurosurgeon in that operating room, then who am I?" he wondered. "It's nice to think I have a lot of options but right now I'm defined more by who I used to be than who I am."

Ron continued to take filmmaking workshops. As he experimented with learning how to develop techniques, he decided to buy his own equipment. He also noticed he was meeting new people with different interests as he was losing touch with his former medical colleagues. This shift in his relationship center of gravity was not without some uneasiness. His medical colleagues had been one of his primary sources of professional and personal identity. Yet Ron may never have reconnected with filmmaking with the same passion and commitment had he not actively cultivated these new relationships. The nature of their conversations was different from the ones he had with his old medical associates. The ideas they explored together were different. Ron's new circle of colleagues broadened his context. It provided him with the support and inspiration to develop the new technical skills he needed to push his confidence to try new things and take risks. Ron began to discover there were stories he wanted to tell through film. He began, like his father, to make documentary films of his family. These trial runs acted as small stepping-stones into a larger project. Ron has begun to talk about filmmaking not only as an activity but as an identity as well. Filmmaker. He talks about his latest project almost as a debut—a documentary about steel-band music. "I'm not only the filmmaker," he says, "I am also the producer."

Today, several years after leaving medicine, Ron acknowledges that he "hangs" with only a handful of his former colleagues. When he thinks of the medical world he is struck by a sense of returning to a high school reunion. He feels he has grown, changed. Still, he sees the future as a mystery. He has come from one direction—medicine— where the road was secure and predictable and where his place in the world was known. He now travels in a very different world—the world of filmmaking—where the outcomes are far less certain. He is living not only the life of an artist—even though he calls himself "a novice all over again"—but the life of a life change artist. He has entered the integration dimension.

Rather than see the "bad luck" of having to leave medicine, Ron turned it into an opportunity to discover and elevate new interests. He actually applied elements of his surgical training to his transition. He brought the dispassionate perspective of a clinician to his journey. He did this by experimenting with a variety of things during his exploration and discovery journey. Not needing to come up with an answer immediately allowed his dispassion to reconnect with an earlier passion. He monitored his emotional responses carefully. He may have felt like he was floating in syrup rather than on salt water, but that enabled him to identify a direction that ultimately has led to landfall.

■   ■   ■

While Berthe Morisot's, Cindy Carlson's, and Ron Mortara's creative journeys through the exploration and discovery dimensions share a number of common elements, each of their journeys reflects their uniqueness. The particular form and content of their journey in the exploration and discovery dimensions varied. What we learn collectively from them is that discovery can occur simultaneously with exploration. Discovery can also take a long time. More often than not discovery comes about through lots of experimentation. If we expect to "swing for the fences" by testing one thing and thinking we will receive full enlightenment, we are likely to be disappointed. Through Morisot experimenting with ways to apply paint or through Cindy reading a variety of books and attending a range of workshops or through Ron learning the benefits of floating with uncertainty, we come to appreciate that the most important thing we can understand about the exploration and discovery dimensions is that their timing and rhythm are a function of the individual going through them. There is no pre-installed rhythm built in. Our travels through these dimensions are uniquely our own.

EXERCISES

1. Helpful Questions During Exploration

Take some time to reflect on any questions below that resonate for you.

Why do I feel uncertain and confused?

Who am I really?

What are my core values?

What do I care most about?

What are my gifts, talents, passions?

What have been my sources of joy in the past?

What is my vision of the future?

Where can I get support in figuring this out?

- What other questions do I have while I am exploring?

2. Helpful Questions During Discovery

What are the implications for me?

- Financial?
- Identity?
- Social?
- New skills?

What (if anything) is holding me back?

- How can I find like-minded people or communities?

Chapter 4

Integration

In a successful painting everything is integral . . . all the parts belong to the whole. If you remove an aspect or element you are removing its wholeness.

—RICHARD DIEBENKORN

I t is no accident that the words "integrate" and "integrity" come from the same Latin root that means "wholeness," or "undivided." The integration dimension always moves us closer to personal wholeness, bringing us more in alignment with our values. The integration dimension helps us develop and incorporate new skills, new viewpoints, new relationships, and new identities into the way we live day to day. It also allows our past experiences to inform our current perspective through the presence of growing wisdom. We may never be complete, but when we integrate, we are more whole. We are not finished, but we are more fulfilled.

The great artists teach us that becoming a whole person is a lifelong quest. It is a process of ongoing exploration, discovery, and integration launched from our creative dilemmas. In that sense, the integration dimension is the key dimension of creativity that moves us closer to wholeness. Nathaniel Webb speaks of how at the age of sixty-three he learned to read for the first time. He had worked as a pipe fitter for the city of Cleveland for more than forty years, after dropping out of school in the ninth grade. Why did he decide at that point to go through the painful and embarrassing process of learning to read?

Grandkids and great-grandkids. Thirty of them. Nathaniel describes his experience of integration like this:

> For the first time I feel like a whole person. It really changed my life. It's not just reading to the kids. I walk differently. I talk differently. I think of myself differently. It sure changed my relationship with my grandkids and my greats, even with my kids. Can you imagine! Just the other day one of the grandkids told me I don't have to spell EVERY word for them. They already know how to spell. Imagine that!

We can enter the integration dimension at any age. The skills and perspectives Picasso integrated into his art during his famous "Blue Period" in his early twenties were different from those he integrated into his work during his "Portrait Period" when he was in his fifties. Nathaniel was in his sixties when he entered the integration dimension in relation to learning how to read. Having done so, he was awed by how learning to read had a ripple effect throughout almost every aspect of his life.

Integration

PURPOSE: *To fulfill*

Combining elements of our past experiences with what we have now discovered about ourselves into a new way of living our lives, including:

- new capacities
- expanded emotional range
- new forms of personal expression
- new public and personal identity
- a sense that we are becoming more whole

In important ways, the integration dimension is where the rubber meets the road. It's where lasting change happens. It's about translating all our explorations and discoveries into tangible changes in our lives.

Yet there is also a sense that life change artists are now becoming more of who they were meant to be. Who they were meant to be was inside all the time. We can hear it in their voices.

Life Change Artists Speak About Integration

I've crossed over to the light.
—BARBRA VOGEL

I didn't change. I allowed more of myself to come out.
—RON MORTARA

The older you get, the more like yourself you become.
—JIM HIME

All my life I cared more about what others thought. That no longer mattered. That's when I was free.
—MARTHA CARLSON

I don't have to play a role anymore.
—LAURA WHITEHORN

I am an unfinished piece of work.
—RON BROWNE

I am becoming more of who I am.
—MICHAEL LOTKER

Maybe I am who I thought I was.
—CAROL FRANCO

One of the indicators of being in the integration dimension is a sense of greater personal richness. Integration combines what is new with what is old, what we are learning with what we have known, how we now feel about ourselves with our older emotional touch points. We are able to appreciate a wider range of viewpoints because, as a result of moving through exploration and discovery, we have tried different perspectives ourselves. Perhaps the artist who best showed us how various viewpoints can come together into a harmonious whole is Paul Cézanne.

Painter of Harmony

There are those who consider Paul Cézanne (1839–1906) the single most important artist of his generation—including Monet, Manet, Renoir, Degas, Pissarro, Morisot, van Gogh, and Gauguin. Both Matisse and Picasso, who represented the next generation, referred to Cézanne as "the father of us all." More than any other artist, he built the bridge into modern art.

Cézanne did not start out as an Impressionist. But he befriended the venerable Camille Pissarro, who took on the role of father figure and mentor. Initially, Cézanne used a lot of black and gray in his paintings. He also applied paint to the canvas with a palette knife rather than a brush. The overall effect of these techniques was to make his paintings appear thick, dark, and somber. But then Pissarro and Cézanne began to paint together. They set up their easels side by side in the fields. Under Pissarro's influence, Cézanne began to experiment with brighter colors. He began to experiment with shorter, crisper brushstrokes rather than using his palette knife to thickly lay on paint. Pissarro also encouraged Cézanne to pay attention to the effects of light and to infuse his paintings with emotion. Cézanne eagerly absorbed all that Pissarro could teach him.

Cézanne believed art was about creating "harmony that runs parallel to nature." His painting began to take on a decidedly geometric quality. His brushstrokes became short and left a series of small, painstakingly applied geometric impressions. Cézanne was the first artist to introduce multiple viewpoints of the subject in the same painting. In the process, he revolutionized the whole idea of perspective and thereby laid the groundwork for what was to become abstract art.

Although it was painted sometime between 1880 and 1890, *Still*

Paul Cézanne, *Still Life with Fruit Basket,* 1880–1890

Life with Fruit Basket is a strikingly modern painting. Cézanne has integrated all the techniques and devices he learned from Pissarro, as well as his own experiments with color and perspective, to create a remarkably deceptive work of art. On the surface all seems innocent enough. Cézanne loved painting fruit, especially apples, and there is a variety of fruit liberally and richly rendered throughout the painting. Some fruits are on the tablecloth, some in the basket. We see a large bowl almost in the center of the painting and perhaps a sugar bowl and creamer on each side. In this painting, though, the fruits are mainly pears. When we look more closely at them we see that the thinner stem heads of the pears are pointing in a variety of directions. The ones in the lower left are uncomfortably pointing upward and slightly to the right. The large pear all the way to the right on the table just under the basket is pointing straight up. Then there is the pear snuggled into the left edge of the basket pointing toward the left and slightly upward. Why are all these pears in different parts of the painting pointing in different directions? Cézanne is leaving us with clues of what he is trying to do in the painting. Just as the pears are pointing in different directions, Cézanne is integrating different visual perspectives.

When we look more closely at the painting, we see even more evidence of how he has integrated his earlier experiments into a completely innovative visual experience. The frontal perspective of the painting gives the impression of *looking up* into the scene, yet the bowl in the middle of the table is painted from the perspective of *looking down* into it. In addition, parts of the tablecloth do not seem to bend with the edge of the table. Is Cézanne playing tricks on us? In some ways, he is. But does the painting hold together despite these tricks? Does it provide a harmonious whole? Here we would also have to say yes! Cézanne has achieved his aim. He has integrated all the parts into a harmony that parallels nature.[1]

Cézanne helps us appreciate the power of the integration dimension in art and in life. It was not enough for him to work side by side with Pissarro, or to experiment with the ideas and techniques of Impressionism. In order to fulfill his artistic vision, Cézanne had to integrate those experiences and lessons into a new and distinctive art. In that sense, Cézanne's art provides essential lessons for life change.

It's important to understand that integration is not an ending point. It is not a point of arrival. Integration is a dimension in the continuous creative process. As with the other dimensions, there is no prescription regarding how to move through the integration dimension or how long we will be in it. As our life change artists quoted earlier in the chapter suggest, we do arrive at a sense that we are becoming more whole, more in touch with who we want to be. That we are tapping into parts of ourselves we have perhaps neglected. At the same time, we recognize we are not finished. One of the aspects of the integration dimension relates to a deepening sense of being simultaneously more whole and still incomplete. Being able to live with this dichotomy contributes to an appreciation of our growing wisdom and humility.

---

1. Erle Loran, *Cézanne's Composition* (Los Angeles: University of California Press, 1943), pp. 76–77.

Yet there are as many experiential variations of the integration dimension as there are people who move through it.

Skydiving into Change

Pat Usner was willing to break with the past in order to pursue a life of greater harmony and wholeness. If she had not jumped from an airplane at five thousand feet, she would not now at the age of fifty-five be living in a three-room apartment in San Francisco Heights, working for a nonprofit and earning a fraction of what she used to make. Pat remembers vividly the feeling of terror just before leaping into the wild blue yonder for the first time. Now, almost five hundred skydiving jumps later, and six years since her last jump, she still feels the fear claw at the pit of her stomach. Jumping out of a plane for the first time as an "I can see my whole life in front of me" moment. "Are you ready?" shouted the jump captain. "No way," she thought. A moment later, she was hurling through space.

During Integration You May Feel . . .		
Relaxed	Tentative	Overwhelmed
At peace	Grateful	Optimistic
Happy	Wonder	Insecure
Productive	Wiser	Perseverance
Growing	Empowered	Satisfaction
Learning	Purified	Contributing
Calm	Anticipation	

Pat's current frugal life began innocently enough with a trip to Ecuador in 1989. She had been working in Philadelphia in the health care field for some time, primarily in marketing as a vice president. While she did not find this particularly fulfilling, she had not found a worthwhile alternative. At one point when she was between jobs, she and her husband took a trip to Ecuador. They traveled deep into the forest and encountered native people who had limited contact with the rest of the world. She was fascinated by the way they lived in relation to the forest and their environment. This experience touched something deep inside her. She returned to Ecuador the following year. When she came home this time, she decided she needed to do some "inner work." She started keeping a journal and she enrolled in a series of personal growth workshops that heightened her sense of being in a creative dilemma. "I am not happy in my work," Pat realized. "Do I stay in my current job or do I find more meaningful work?" These workshops also helped her explore what caused her to respond so powerfully to her Ecuador experience. So after almost twenty years as an executive at a large hospital and various health care companies, she decided to leave her job and establish her own consulting firm focusing on strategic marketing and public relations. Pat continued to meet with professional success, even though she remained unfulfilled.

Pat and her husband returned to Ecuador several more times. Pat began looking for an organization that did volunteer work with the indigenous people there and came across the Pachamama Alliance, based in San Francisco. She became a contributor and began doing volunteer work for them. When she received a general distribution email announcing that the Alliance was looking for an operations manager, Pat dismissed it. But on a western camping trip to Yosemite, only a few hours' drive from the Alliance office in San Francisco, she found herself sitting for an interview for the operations manager position. Leaving the office, her head and heart were racing a mile a minute. For the next week, while hiking through Yosemite, she agonized about the position and a possible move. There she was, living in a six-bedroom home in Philadelphia and earning a good income. She and her husband were far from financially independent, and the Alliance was offering a salary equivalent to what she had been earning twenty-five years earlier. Housing prices in San Francisco were astronomical. But Pat could hear the voice of her jump captain years earlier: "Are you ready?" "No way!" she thought. Then she reflected on all the inner work she had been doing. She thought about being in scary situations and her ability to survive and thrive. For example, she had never broken a bone in all her years of skydiving. She recalled when her father abandoned her family when she was eleven years old how she and the rest of the family survived. She knew she had developed the business skills that would help the Alliance. Pat brought all these perspectives into the big picture. It was as though her life were now a Cézanne painting. She saw herself from multiple viewpoints and together they added up to the possibility of new harmony in her life. She knew this was it. She just knew this was what she wanted to be doing. Then she jumped.

Pat is fully in the integration dimension. She believes she is doing what she is meant to be doing. This does not mean it has been easy. For the first two years after the move, she alternated between second-guessing her decision and gratitude that she is living a life she is meant to live. Pat feels some sadness about leaving family and friends back East. Yet she marvels that she could ever love work the way she does now. It's as though "all of my background led me here." Pat now has a new position at Pachamama as director of communications and is heading a new global communication and awareness campaign. She is integrating all of her explorations and discoveries into her present life: Her executive skills. Her sense of adventure and risk taking. Her commitment. She is grateful that she can apply her business skills to a mission of great meaning. Her work is about empowering indigenous people to decide how they live in their environment. It is about sustainability. It is about making a difference.

Pat recalls an exercise from one of the workshops when she was doing her inner work. She was asked to identify the key drivers in her life. She listed self-expression, learning, adventure, fun, personal growth, making a difference, and creative expression. She can feel the presence of these drivers in her life every day now. No matter from what perspective you view her life, it is adding up to a more fully realized picture.

How do life change artists know they are in the integration dimension? The truth is that it varies from person to person. But at a broad level we can refer to the exhibit at the beginning of the chapter.

If we have a sense that we are beginning to tap into and apply new skills and capabilities, if we are connecting with old emotions or expanding familiar ones, if we are accessing new ways to express ourselves, if we are beginning to form new identities and we are beginning to feel more whole and authentic, then we are in the integration dimension. We do not need to experience all these elements simultaneously, and it is likely we will experience them in different combinations and to different degrees. We may even feel that parts of ourselves are like the pears in a Cézanne painting—pointing in different directions. But the whole picture of our life is becoming more harmonious with who we really are. Whatever the precise mix, we have a sense we are growing as a person.

The integration dimension ripples into all aspects of our life. Sometimes, the changes we make may initially appear to impact only a small part of our lives. Nathaniel Webb, however, learned that developing a relatively targeted skill such as reading profoundly transformed all aspects of his life. On the other hand, Pat Usner knew her decision to join the Pachamama Alliance and move to San Francisco was huge. And it proved to be the case.

Ultimately, though, integration is not limited to picking up some new skills or even making a physical move. Integration is about developing a deeper self-awareness and manifesting this awareness through how we behave in our daily lives.

From Ambition to Humanity

Perhaps no other artist in history has brought viewers in touch with the humanity of his subjects as has Rembrandt van Rijn (1606–1669). Nor has any other artist left a more powerful chronicle of personal change than Rembrandt. He did this through eighty painted portraits executed over his lifetime. By looking at two of these portraits, we can deepen our understanding of the integration dimension.

Rembrandt was prodigiously talented. By the time he reached

Rembrandt, *Self-Portrait*, 1640

eighteen in 1624, he had set up his own studio and taken on students. When he moved to Amsterdam from his native Leiden a couple of years later, he quickly began earning portrait commissions from the emerging well-heeled mercantile class. By 1634 he had married into an affluent family and shortly thereafter bought a large house in the Jewish Quarter of Amsterdam. When he painted the self-portrait of 1640, he was at the pinnacle of his success.

In many ways, this painting can be seen as Rembrandt's expression of his ambitions.[2] He commonly dressed himself in historical costumes in his self-portraits. This particular outfit dates back to a full century earlier and represents the attire of the well-to-do Italian class. The technique of the painting also employs Rembrandt's "smooth" style, where the paint is layered in with thin coats. It looks finished. But

2. Christopher White and Quentin Buvelot, eds., *Rembrandt by Himself* (London: Thames & Hudson, 1999), p. 173.

most important is what Rembrandt conveys of the person being por-
trayed. His right eyebrow is arched, his eyes seem at first to stare directly at the viewer, but then they gaze beyond toward something else
requiring their attention. What can be more important than the
viewer? This is a portrait of a man who has achieved a certain station
in life. One can even say the rail that separates him from the viewer
is there to emphasize his special standing. Rembrandt would never go
so far as to position himself as arrogant. But he does call for recognition in this self-portrait.

Despite his success as a painter, Rembrandt's life was marked by
personal tragedy. His beloved wife, Saskia, died only eight years after
they married. Only one of his four children lived to adulthood. Rembrandt himself liked to live well. He bought a house he could not
afford and he spent extravagantly on an art collection. This lifestyle
caught up to him in 1656, when he had to file for bankruptcy. In order
to survive financially he was forced to sell his house and collection.
Although he continued to be revered as an artist and gain significant commissions, this episode chastened him. In 1669, the year he
died, he painted a remarkable self-portrait. How he has changed! Not
simply because he is older but because he is so much more accessible.
There's a lot going on here both technically and personally. For one
thing, Rembrandt initially painted himself with a paintbrush in hand.
Then he painted the paintbrush out of the picture and left his hands
simply folded together. Gone is the artifice and protection of portray-
ing himself as an artist. Also gone is the wooden railing separating
Rembrandt from the viewer. And gone is the costume and beret that
conveyed the pretensions of wealth and success. He is simply dressed.
His head covering is a modest cap. Technically, the colors are warmer
than the earlier portrait. He has applied thicker layers of paint, called
impasto, to emphasize certain elements of the painting. There is a
touch of sadness around Rembrandt's eyes. He shows himself to be
more vulnerable. "Yes, I have made mistakes. I am chastened." Yet the
set of his mouth suggests a touch of a smile, an intimation of energy
and liveliness. Chastened but not defeated. "I am not done yet," he

Rembrandt, *Self-Portrait*, 1669

seems to be saying. There's more to come from this old boy. And in fact, this was not his last self-portrait. In this painting, though, there is no doubt Rembrandt is looking directly and fully into the eyes of the viewer. There is nothing beyond the viewer, nothing calling his attention as in his earlier self-portrait. The eyes hold us as he is asking us to hold him. "Here I am, older, wiser." Everything is brought forward in the self-portrait. Rembrandt's extraordinary technical prowess is united with the full flowering of his humanity.

Rembrandt's lesson for life change artists is that the integration dimension provides the opportunity to unite our technical skills with our deepening self-awareness. We bring together competence and wisdom. We become more whole. In Rembrandt's self-portrait not only is he more whole with himself and shows less of a need for pretense but he has opened himself to being more whole with the viewer.

The integration dimension is critical to the creative process because it builds our confidence to move through change in the future. We are less fearful of our next creative dilemma. We've been through it. The next dilemma is likely to be different, but having navigated through the territories of exploration, discovery, and integration before, we have a better idea of what to expect; we better understand our strengths. Once we have experienced the reality of becoming more whole through the creative process, we no longer need to rely on earlier pretenses or affectations about ourselves. This is one of the great insights Rembrandt has given us through his art. In many ways, it is a biblical insight: vanity is a pretense that stands in the way of becoming a full person. The courage to "paint ourselves as we really are," that is, to align our lives with what is truly inside us and to allow others to see us in this light, is the ultimate creative act.

From Piety to New Possibilities

In some sense, Ted Welch's life seemed the antithesis of wholeness. He often felt divided against himself. There was more than one of him. Growing up in a devout Catholic family, he attended a Catholic grade school and a Jesuit high school. By the time he reached eighteen he was ready to commit to becoming a Jesuit priest.

Ted was deeply moved by spiritual practice. He loved the commitment to study and service. Over the next eighteen years he fully devoted himself to the life of a Jesuit. He spent many years in remote areas of Brazil, working to better the lives of those living in small communities. Returning to the States between long missions in Brazil, he earned a bachelor's and a master's degree in English and philosophy, respectively. He had always loved Shakespeare and these studies seemed to awaken a part of him that had never been nurtured before. Back in Brazil, he ran a community center during a period of particular instability and narrowly escaped death when a gunman attacked the center. By then he had developed an interest in pursuing theatrical studies. The arts held a long-venerated position in the Jesuit order, so Ted moved to Cambridge, Massachusetts, and earned a second master's degree in communication arts. But something else had begun to percolate. The arts started to call to him more and more clearly. He became torn be-

tween the spiritual appeal embodied in the Jesuit order and the opportunity to explore and express parts of himself through the theater.
He took a leave of absence from the order and moved to Los Angeles,
where he joined the Community of Jesuits in Hollywood.

On one level Ted thoroughly enjoyed being part of a like-minded
community. Yet at another level he could not hide his anguish. He
could easily accept the Jesuit vows of chastity and poverty. But the
vow of obedience weighed heavily on him. When he next met with
his superiors, he saw they had fully parsed out his next five years for
him. In fact, "I could see my life being completely mapped out for
me." He champed at the bit. He had never really lived outside the
security of the Jesuits, yet he could not bring himself to submit to a
life plan in which he had no say. He realized he had been on two
journeys: one aboveground, expressing itself through the outward
garb of the Jesuit order, and the other below the surface, expressing
itself through an intellectual and emotional awakening. With great
fear and trepidation, Ted told his superiors he could not take his final
vows, and he stepped out into a new world wondering whether his
new life would provide the kind of spiritual fulfillment he had found
within the order.

In important ways, Ted is in the same integration dimension that
led Rembrandt to drop the pretenses of his earlier ambitions and show
the world a more whole person through his painting. In one of his last
portraits, Rembrandt showed us a more accessible and vulnerable self.
He showed us a depth of wisdom that had no need to hide behind the
posturing of period costumes. He brought together the dazzling skills
he had developed with a self-awareness that conveyed a sense of deep
humanity. Ted, too, has come to realize that just as Rembrandt did
not need costumes, Ted does not need the structure of the church to
realize his full spirituality. Since leaving the Jesuits, he has participated
in groundbreaking theatrical productions for the UN in Bucharest.
He has organized theatrical programs to address issues of poverty,
women, health, and children in New York. Looking back, he understands that the Jesuits moved him along the path of engagement. For

this he is grateful and still refers to an "essential Jesuitness" in himself. Having spent so much time under the protective cover of the order, he feels he will always be catching up. But most important, he realizes he is not made up of two separate selves battling within. It is really two aspects of the same self, embarked on a single journey of integration and wholeness.

Changing *in Place*

It may take a while to notice that we have been engaged in integration. Often the results of our exploration and discovery come in small and gradual bits. Almost without knowing, we have been subtly changing who we are, how we see ourselves, or what we do. Even at times when integration seems to happen quickly, it is often the result of years of internal changes that suddenly become visible to the outside world. Whatever type of integration we achieve, it is only a pause before we feel the tug of the next creative dilemma. So we pull out another canvas and begin anew.

We do not necessarily have to change careers in order to become a life change artist. There are many instances of life change artists who remain in the same careers or locations or relationships. Yet they develop the skills to authentically move through the dimensions of change to refresh themselves, their careers, or their relationships. They continue to grow and learn, remaining open to new possibilities. They fulfill their potential and purpose while remaining a doctor or teacher or executive or cop or carpenter. They become life change artists *in place*. They may work in the same environment, live in the same community, and maintain the same networks. But they address their creative dilemmas and move through the dimensions of change within the framework of these associations: The pediatrician who practices for forty years but always manages to bring freshness and new skills to his doctor-patient relationships. The teacher who is loved by generations of students because she always appears young in ideas and enthusiasm and humor. The executive who always finds ways to innovate. Becoming a life change artist means creating alignment between the internal and the external, between our core values and the life choices we make, between our key motivators and how we live our lives. It means becoming masterful in the creative skills that allow us to create our optimal lives. For some of us, becoming a life change artist means we continue to do what we've been doing, but do it differently. For others, it means moving in an entirely different direction. Creative dilemmas are a fundamental in our lives. We will always have at least one creative dilemma tugging at us at any given time. Whether or not we become a life change artist is a function of how we respond to them.

EXERCISE

1. Helpful Questions During Integration

Take some time to reflect on any questions below that resonate for you.

- What is my new vision of my life and of me?
- What do I hold on to, and what do I let go of?
- How will I rebalance my time?
- How will I implement change?
- How do I cultivate new relationships?
- How do I describe myself to myself and to others?
- How do I continue to grow and learn new skills?
- What have I learned and how do I use it to live a good life?

Part Two

· · · · · · ·

THE SKILLS

Introduction

Part One sets out the four dimensions of life change and shows how they parallel the creative processes of the great masters of art.

Part Two describes the Seven Creative Skills a life change artist needs in order to navigate these dimensions. These are the same skills the great artists themselves developed and applied to their creative journey.

We invite you to take a self-assessment—the Creativity Calculator—as a way to evaluate where you stand in relation to these skills. The Creativity Calculator is in Appendix A on page 254 and is self-scoring. You should be able to complete the Creativity Calculator and scoring in approximately fifteen minutes. By taking the assessment before reading Part Two, you will have the opportunity to reflect on your personal level of creative skills as you read the book.

You should also feel free to dive right into Part Two without first using the Creativity Calculator. If you take the Creativity Calculator assessment after you have read the entire book, you will have the opportunity to bring all that you have learned into your understanding of your current level of creative skills.

Chapter 5

Preparation

I dream a lot. I do more painting when I'm not painting. It's in the subconscious.

—ANDREW WYETH

Try this experiment: Think of the last creative idea or insight you've had. Once you have it in mind, recall where you were physically located and what you were doing when you had that idea. Maybe you were taking a shower; riding a bicycle; going on a walk; playing golf; washing the dishes; meditating; listening to music; gardening; at church, mosque, or synagogue; playing with children; in a museum; or driving the car. One thing is certain about where you were: you were *not* at work. This is because work is a place that generally rewards highly logical, sequential, and analytical thinking. In addition, work environments tend to be high-stress, and sustained stress can wreak havoc on creativity. Creativity, on the other hand, is about divergence, not convergence; incongruence, not congruence. When you remove yourself from the work environment and its expectations about how to think, you are free to let mental play and intuition be part of the way you process data. You are free to let nontraditional sources of information enter your thinking and sensing.

Thinking about where you tend to have your best ideas is a good starting point for understanding the skill of preparation. Preparation means *deliberately engaging in activities that help us break from our usual patterns of thought and feeling and prepare us for creative insight.* Whatever you were doing when you had that last great creative idea probably served as a preparation activity for you, even though you may not have realized it, or done it deliberately.

During preparation, we:

- let go of the need to come up with an immediate solution.
- believe we can be more fulfilled in our lives if we engage in activities that stimulate creative insights.
- engage in some physical or mental activity before considering our problems.
- engage in some mind/body practice or practices on a regular basis.
- engage in a *variety* of creativity-triggering activities.

There are many forms that preparation activities can take. The critical attribute of a preparation activity is that it helps you get outside the familiar, exposes you to different stimuli, and takes you away from the normal way you might think of approaching a problem.

Whenever the great fifteenth-century artist Leonardo da Vinci found himself with a particularly intractable problem, he would take his quill, ink, and paper and go someplace where he could put himself in a quiet state of mind. Leonardo deliberately placed himself in a meditative state to support his creative process. He would close his eyes and allow images to rise to the surface of his awareness. Leonardo believed this was his subconscious speaking to him. As the images rose he would make marks on the paper—figures, symbols, markings. After a period of time, he would open his eyes and draw lines connecting his various jottings in order to make previously un-thought-of associations. This would help him break through an impasse and come up with new possible solutions, sometimes to problems he was not even immediately focusing on.

Other great artists routinely engaged in preparation activities that

were decidedly not artistic, but which helped them solve artistic problems or do their most original work. The great Abstract Expressionist
painter Willem de Kooning (1904–1997) got on his bicycle each
morning after breakfast and pedaled to his studio. De Kooning was a
workaholic, and the only break he would allow himself, especially
when his work was going badly, was a long bike ride on his Raleigh,
often to Louse Point, three miles from his studio on Long Island. He
loved Louse Point for its shifting atmosphere and because it reminded
him of his native Netherlands. According to de Kooning biographers
Mark Stevens and Annalyn Swan, nothing dramatic happened on
these bicycle excursions, but "they were probably as important to him
as any lover." The bicycling became like "a form of meditation" for
him, a way "to refocus himself upon what was important." It is probably no accident that during this period he entered a remarkable burst
of creative freshness when, in his own words, the paintings "poured
out of me like water."[1]

The French Impressionist Paul Cézanne would go on long walks
in the countryside surrounding his beloved Aix-en-Provence in southern France. Georgia O'Keeffe walked every morning through the
Taos, New Mexico, landscape before beginning her painting. She was
known to sit in the open high sierra watching a sunset for long stretches
of time.

In each of these diverse cases, the artists built these practices into
a routine that acted as a stepping-stone into their creative efforts.
These practices collectively reflect the creative skill of preparation. Of
course, artists throughout the centuries did not call such rituals "preparation." They simply understood that by engaging in these ostensibly
non-creative activities, they achieved better results in their work.

The great artists understood that creativity is not some mysterious
force that may or may not show up when we want it to. Creativity

---

1. Mark Stevens and Annalyn Swan, *De Kooning: An American Master* (New York: Alfred A. Knopf, 2004), p. 467.

begins by intentionally and regularly incorporating preparation practices into our daily lives. Herbert Benson, M.D., former head of the
Mind/Body Institute at Harvard Medical School, and William Proctor have documented myriad preparation activities in *The Break-Out
Principle*.[2] The activities listed below represent only a sampling:[3]
As you can see from the variety of activities, one person's preparation
practice may be another person's poison. The trick is to find the activities that help you feel relaxed and focused but which take you away
from your daily routines, including work.

- Spiritual Triggers, such as prayer or meditation
- Musical Triggers, such as listening to your favorite music
- Cultural Triggers, such as viewing a work of art, for example a
  painting or sculpture
- Water-Related Triggers, such as soaking in a bathtub or hot tub or
  taking a shower
- Athletic Triggers, such as walking, bicycling, or performing any
  other repetitive exercise for at least 15 minutes
- Repetitive-Movement Triggers, such as needlepoint
- Nature Triggers, such as sitting quietly in a garden
- Housework/Yardwork Triggers, such as doing the dishes
- Surrender Triggers, such as relinquishing control over a personal
  or a job problem
- Animal/Pet Triggers, such as sitting quietly with your pet
- Altruistic Triggers, such as becoming involved in helping others

It's ironic that scientists have only recently begun to figure out
what artists have known all along. But scientists are also helping answer
questions about how preparation fosters creative work. A big part of
that answer is that preparation activities literally change our brains.

---

2. Herbert Benson, M.D., and William Proctor, *The Break-Out Principle* (New York: Scribner, 2003).
3. See Benson and Proctor's complete list of triggers in Appendix D.

Creativity and the Brain

Over the past two decades a growing body of research has examined the relationship among the mind, the body, and creativity. One of the most astounding discoveries by neuroscientists is that *we can change our brain by changing our mind*. We have known for some time that the brain is made up of neurons. But a mere fifteen years ago, the idea that the brain is always creating new neurons was unthinkable. Neuroscientists believed that brain cells—in contrast to every other type of cell in our bodies—did not divide; they believed we were born with a fixed number of brain cells. Scientists also believed that the number of neurons declined throughout an adult's life, and that this loss of neurons partly explained the effects of aging.

Over the past two decades, however, research has totally flipped these ideas on their head. Today, scientists have demonstrated that we do have the capacity to create new brain cells ("neurogenesis"). They also have shown that the brain is "plastic," i.e., flexible. This flexibility, which scientists call *neuroplasticity,* allows us to use the brain cells we already have in new ways. Thanks to neuroplasticity, we can make new pathways in the brain that in turn can not only change our physical brains but also enhance our capabilities and skills. Neurogenesis and neuroplasticity together represent very good news for folks in midlife and beyond who want to become life change artists.

Dr. Gene Cohen, author of *The Mature Mind,* analyzed the growing body of research on neurogenesis and neuroplasticity. He concluded that the brain "actively grows and rewires itself in response to stimulation and learning" *regardless of age*. But Cohen did not stop there. He went on to indicate that additional research showed that the older brain is an emotionally more balanced brain. That is, "the capacity to ride out emotional storms more flexibly and resiliently is one of the great fruits of aging. This is partly due to learning, experience, and practice, which stimulate the growth of new dendrites and sometimes entirely new neurons."[4]

A good example of this kind of brain learning can be seen in the rare breed of London taxi drivers. Brain imaging research found that the cabbies have an enlarged region in their hippocampus—the area of the brain used for navigating in three-dimensional space. Anyone who has personally tried to negotiate London's streets in a car or taken a taxi through them would certainly appreciate this incredibly complex navigational challenge. The actual experience of having to negotiate the maze of streets and memorize the London map provided a virtual workout for that part of the brain, resulting in its growth.[5]

The enlargement of the London taxi drivers' brains is no small matter. The implication is that the enlargement was not simply a matter of physical change. It raises the question of what actually caused the physical change. Here scientists are coming to a profound realization. Change in the brain (neuroplasticity) occurs "only when the mind is in a particular mental state, one marked by attention and focus. The mind matters."[6] In other words, the physical brain cannot physically change itself. Through focused attention, we change our brain. *Our mind* changes our brain. When we focus our mind on developing a new skill or a new habit or new insights, such as the London taxi drivers did, we imprint new neural pathways to support the new skill or habit. And that's where the creative skill of preparation comes into play. When we regularly engage in preparation activities, we are using our minds to put down new brain pathways that predispose us to creative insight. Preparation is all about changing our brains to be more creative. And as you'll see in Susan Kullman's story, changing your brain through preparation activities takes persistence and focus. But her new life would not have been possible without preparation.

4. Gene Cohen, *The Mature Mind: The Positive Power of the Aging Brain* (New York: Basic Books, 2005), p. 17.

5. Ibid., p.7.

6. Sharon Begley, *Train Your Mind, Change Your Brain* (New York: Ballantine Books, 2007), p. 130.

Preparation in Practice

Growing up in a highly emotional and abusive household, Susan Kullman learned at an early age to guard her feelings. She became the funny one, the deflector, the one who helped diffuse disaster. Her older brother took the brunt of the physical abuse. Her older sister buried herself in books and became the student, "the smart one." Susan became the comedian and "the pretty but dumb one." Along the way she covered up her own feelings until they seemed pretty much to disappear. After all, it was more important to survive than to feel. So not showing her feelings was a sign of strength. And not feeling her feelings was an even greater sign of character.

It was only natural, then, that Susan would be attracted to, and eventually marry, her high school sweetheart. He was Irish and emotionally steady, predictable. She was Italian but hated to admit it, since in her mind Italian meant emotional and emotional meant hysterical and hysterical meant violent. He, on the other hand, believed that squashing feelings was a badge of honor, that "if you don't suffer, you won't go to heaven." To Susan, this was an affirmation of her own embargo on feelings.

During the sixth month of her first pregnancy, Susan discovered a lump the size of a walnut in her neck. By the next month, she was experiencing pain in her back. But in typical fashion she minimized her anxieties and chalked it up to a pulled muscle. The wake-up call came when she found herself unable to breathe. At first, doctors thought she might have lymphoma. But then they determined that she had a large cyst, which turned into a blood clot in one of her lungs. Susan remained in the hospital for another month, until doctors delivered a healthy son one month prematurely. They quickly removed the clot.

Soon everything was falling apart. Within six months of delivering her first child, Susan became pregnant again, followed by a miscarriage. When she still felt fatigued, a CAT scan revealed a cyst on her brain. Doctors diagnosed the condition as "thoracic syndrome," brought on by her blood flow being cut off when she engaged in intense exercise, thereby triggering a series of electric-like shocks up and down her side. Her asthma returned with a vengeance. After ending up in the hospital several times, she wondered whether this was her end of days. Trying to get used to the idea of dying, Susan began reading *The Tibetan Book of the Dead*. If she could not control her body, at least she could embrace death. It was then that Susan took up the practice of Pranayana Yoga with its emphasis on breathing. During her yoga practice she came to the realization that she needed to get reconnected to her feelings. It was not death with which she needed to become intimate but life, life without her emotions tamped down.

The question was how could she do this without unleashing the furies she so feared? She did not know how to connect with her emotions without being overwhelmed by them—as her parents had been. To complicate things further, Susan was overtaken by an urgent need to get out of her marriage. Her high school sweetheart, who had seemed such a perfect anchor of emotional steadiness, was now totally ill-suited to her growing need for emotional authenticity. He was predictable and fatalistic. She now needed to explore the new, unpredictable seas of her inner terrain. She needed to go on a voyage of emotional discovery. He did not want to leave port.

Susan's yoga practice set the stage for connecting to her feelings in an entirely new way. "I became acutely aware of their textures in my everyday life, and then deeper down I realized my feelings were really speaking to me. I had never really listened before." All kinds of insights began to spill out of her yoga practice. She realized she had much to overcome from her childhood. She had come to accept certain notions as core beliefs: I am pretty but dumb. Showing emotions is a sign of weakness. Suffering is good. She began to actually chuckle at her old self. Yoga practice acted as "the gateway to me, who I really was."

Now Susan began to "read and read and read." She discovered that she had not only a brain but also a voracious appetite to learn. She also had to learn some life basics. She had to learn how to speak about her emotions when she was experiencing them, without letting them overwhelm her. She had to learn to acknowledge vulnerability without feeling weak or inadequate. She had to learn intimacy.

Susan also relearned how to laugh, not in the role of the "comedian," but to laugh a good, hearty laugh from the gut, as when she realized that "when I was younger I hated the idea of being Italian because 'we are so emotional,' but now I love to boast I'm Italian because 'we are so emotional!'" That's stuff you don't find in too many books. Susan claims it comes when "you create your own truth."

When Susan tapped into the power of self-insight through yoga practice—leading to her personal transformation—she was actually applying the broader, multifaceted creative skill of preparation, of which yoga is one form. Of course it is one thing to gain self-insight; it is an entirely different thing to actually change behaviors and develop new habits. Susan's yoga practice provided the "attention and focus" to change her brain in ways that enabled her to make the external life changes she desired.

Using Preparation to De-Stress Your Life Change Process

Change is not easy, either in the brain or in our habits. There are barriers to creativity and change. One of them is the presence of stress. This shouldn't come as a surprise. Given the fact that we are born in stress and have accumulated a lifetime of experiencing a wide range of stresses, our minds and bodies have developed habitual yet highly personalized mechanisms for dealing with stress. At the conscious level, we are probably not even aware that these mechanisms are at work on our behalf. According to Dr. Eva Selhub of the Benson-Henry Institute for Mind Body Medicine at the Harvard Medical School, and author of *The Love Response: Your Prescription to Turn Off Fear, Anger, and Anxiety to Achieve Vibrant Health and Transform Your Life,* ninety percent of our response to stress is unconscious. The stress may be physical. For example, we may feel cold. The body responds to this stress unconsciously, triggering a physiological rallying cry that signals we are cold. We begin to shiver. In response, we put on a scarf. Or we may experience emotional stress, such as not feeling loved, which causes us to become defensive, mimicking the sense of being under attack. In Selhub's words: "The unconscious mind speaks to the conscious mind through physiology."[7] When the mind and body are under stress, "negative physiology" takes over and we become self-focused. Stress cuts off our ability to do higher cognitive thinking such as problem solving because "it's about me," and we cannot solve problems effectively if we are predominantly focused on "me."

Princeton neuroscientist Elizabeth Gould has provided physiological proof of Selhub's psychological findings on stress. Gould, who has done pioneering research on neurogenesis, has demonstrated that the structure of our brain is powerfully influenced by our surroundings. Put a marmoset monkey under stressful conditions, and its brain begins to starve. It stops creating new cells. As Christian Mirescu, one of Gould's postdoctoral students, put it, "When a brain is worried, it's just thinking about survival. It isn't interested in investing in new cells for the future."[8]

The irony is that some stress is needed for creativity. The creative dilemma that sets us on a course of life change is typically marked by some degree of tension or stress. If we allow ourselves to stay in stress or tension, however, we risk being cut off and isolated from ourselves and others. On the other hand, when we engage in activities that help us reconnect with positive emotions, we get tuned in to our creative selves. Positive emotions produce a physiological reaction that breaks us out of our self-protective stress response and allows us to process experience and information in a much more open way.

As noted in earlier chapters, negative emotions often accompany

---

7. Eva Selhub, personal interview by Fred Mandell, April 30, 2008.
8. Jonah Lehrer, "The Reinvention of the Self: A Mind-Altering Idea Reveals How Life Affects the Brain," Seed, February 23, 2006.

the tension we feel about the status of our lives. We feel anger or anxiety or depression or frustration. These negative emotions not only are signals of a creative dilemma, but may act as physiological barriers to accessing our full creative capabilities. In other words, negative emotions can be both our ally and our enemy. The good news is that we have the power to change our negative physiology.

Recent research at Princeton shows that laboratory rats that exercise are less susceptible to stress. As reported in *The New York Times:* "Scientists have known for some time that exercise stimulates the creation of new brain cells (neurons) but not how, precisely, these neurons might be functionally different from other brain cells." Rats that engaged in regular running exercises reacted more nonchalantly to stressful situations than rats that had not engaged in running exercises. When we combine this research with our growing understanding of creativity, we can begin to see how altering our behaviors by engaging in preparation practices can enhance our personal creativity.[9]

This is important for life change artists because many of us harbor a nasty little secret: As dissatisfied as we may be with the current status of our lives, we may be even more unwilling to give up the attachments and judgments that hold us to it. Even under the best of circumstances, change can be difficult. While we often express a desire to make different life choices, we find ourselves paralyzed to act. We are more inventive in coming up with reasons to remain in our current state than in figuring out how to make the changes. This secret can express itself in different ways, but it typically forms around the *how to change* question and the *what to change* question.

We may have a good sense of which direction we want to go in, but we just don't know *how* to get there. Or we may want to change our current situation but do not know in *what* direction we wish to go. While these represent different stress points, the physiology is the same. In both cases we are stepping into the unknown, which often

---

9. Gretchen Reynolds, "Phys Ed: Why Exercise Makes You Less Anxious," *The New York Times*, November 18, 2009.

triggers stress-producing beliefs or questions: "I can't do this." "I'm not good at that." "What will others think?" "I'm too old to do whatever!" According to Selhub, we allow "judgments, attachments and self doubt" to get in the way. These dynamics trigger negative emotions and we become less able to creatively open up to new explorations and discoveries, or to see new possibilities. We have difficulty in detaching from what is familiar, even if we are not satisfied with our circumstances. The sense of uncertainty shoves a detour sign in front of us and leads us down the boulevard of negative physiology.

But by deliberately engaging in preparation, we summon our physiology to establish favorable conditions for accessing higher cognitive insights. We call those insights "new connections," "breakthroughs," or "aha" moments. Those insights are the meat and potatoes of creativity. Those are the self-insights you can build on—as Susan did—to change your life.

But hold on, you might say. How can I find the time in an already crazy schedule to add *another* thing to the long list of things I have to do each day? This is a common theme given the demands on our life. But there is good news here, too. It's not about doing more. It's about doing things differently.

Most people acknowledge they are not functioning at their peak ability because of the multiple demands on their time. Our emotional and intellectual reserves get called on once too often and we find ourselves trying to cope with diminished resources. We rarely, however, pause to think about how much time we are wasting by repeating this same overstuffed pattern of living. Wouldn't we be more creative, save time, and accomplish more tasks more efficiently if we were able to tap into a renewable source of creative energy? We know the answer is yes. Yet we cling to our old patterns. So the question is not whether we have more time to do more. No matter what kind of math you use, there are only twenty-four hours in a day. Of course we don't have more time *as long as* we maintain our current habits. The real question, then, is how can I afford to continue to live the same way over and over again?

Preparation is very different from "not working." Preparation is not substituting one thing we "must do" at the expense of another. Preparation is doing "all of the above," but doing it all *differently*. We tend to equate doing many tasks in a short period of time with being productive. But such an attitude does not speak to the quality of the activities. In reality, doing different but higher-yielding creative-inducing activities in the same time period offers better-quality results. Doing things differently means emphasizing quality over quantity. Engaging in preparation practices develops sharper self-awareness and enhances our ability to solve problems more quickly and creatively, and with greater energy. We become more effective at doing the things that are most important!

Preparation can help us replenish ourselves over time and it can also help us get unstuck with shorter-term challenges. Susan Kullman came to this realization over time. She was able to apply it to facilitate major changes in her life. Don Koenig came to realize the shorter-term benefits one afternoon when he thought he had reached a dead end at work. Don, a marketing executive, called Fred to see if there was a way to get unstuck. Fred advised Don to write down the problem he was trying to solve in the form of a question he needed to answer and then to put the piece of paper in his desk drawer and to go to the local art museum for an hour and lose himself in the paintings on the walls of the museum. Fred then instructed Don not to think about business while at the museum. That's when Don lost his patience. "Now, how the hell am I going to do that? I've got meetings!" Don quickly realized he could reconfigure a couple of meetings that day and off he went at noon, a sandwich in hand for lunch. The next day, sounding out of breath, Don called to report the results. "I only lasted forty-five minutes. I really got into the painting, the different ways the artists looked at things and then ideas began showing up. I had to hurry back to the office to start writing them down."

This is not a story about a problem-solving technique, although this particular use of preparation does serve that purpose. This is really the story of a beginning. With this experience, Don enrolled in a drawing class. At first, he wasn't too good. But he found the class taught him how to look at things from different angles. He also found the drawing class acted as a kind of centering space where other aspects of his work and life gained new perspective. After several months he reported he was finding more creative ways to solve some of the problems he was facing at work. He had more energy. Some of the problems were actually fun to work on because he brought his drawing training to the challenge. Don chuckled at his initial resistance to "take time out" to go to the museum. But then he caught himself. "I guess it wasn't time out. It was really time differently."

Now the solution to every problem is not a visit to the local museum. It's not even taking a drawing class. The key point here is that Don found a way to regularly engage in preparation that seemingly had nothing to do with his work or his life in general yet which helped him break with his everyday patterns of thought and feeling, which positively affected both work and daily living.

Engaging in preparation practices can contribute to both long-term and short-term breakthroughs. A visit to the museum helped Don come up with new approaches to a pressing business problem. Katie Longwood is a research scientist who insists that regular walks around the lake are "prerequisites for research." Katie doesn't care what stage the research is at because she always builds "my walks" into every stage. She is convinced her walks enhance her mental sharpness because they "secretly incubate ideas."

Will Prest, an executive vice president of a start-up business in a major financial services company, initially thought playing tennis at six a.m. several times a week was for the pure enjoyment of the game. He noticed, however, that when he didn't play for large stretches of time, his stress level increased significantly. But when he returned to the game he also discovered that tennis provided "the perfect metaphor for thinking creatively about my business challenges."

Engaging in preparation practices can also trigger longer-term change. Ron Browne, a former teacher and marketing professional, recalls that he had never been an athlete as a kid. But for reasons he could not explain he began running in his thirties. Until that time he had been "living in the fast lane." To his surprise, once he started running, every aspect of his life began to shift. "I changed physically and spiritually. I became more focused and less anxious." Ron acknowledges that running "underlies my whole story" because it's not about running. "It's about how running opens me up, humbles me, and makes me receptive to the universe." Running as a preparation practice has been a remarkable source of self-insight and personal breakthrough. Today Ron is a community activist and works in the area of helping adults age productively and creatively. He believes running has also become a form of spiritual practice.

Preparation and the Four Dimensions of Life Change

Preparation plays a vital role in each of the four dimensions of life change. Each dimension has its own challenges and can throw roadblocks our way. We may acknowledge our *creative dilemma* but not know how to break out of it. We may find *exploration* does not immediately yield the answers we seek. Our *discoveries* may not fully add up to a clear path. And during *integration* we may still find ourselves trying out new things or developing new skills, friends, networks. Even when we are changing in a new direction by choice, we encounter frustrations and detours. We can get sidetracked and become weary. The preparation skill not only provides perspective during these challenging periods, but also acts as a source of renewal. Preparation brings fresh insights into our awareness. Through the exercise of our mind it increases the capacity of our brains to incorporate new learning and habits. By enabling a positive physiology, preparation opens us to new experience and information. Artists such as Leonardo and de Kooning understood this. That is why, even after they had achieved a high degree of mastery over their techniques, they continued to apply their preparation skill by meditating or riding a bike.

Preparation does not simply act as a launching pad. It underwrites the entire enterprise of life change. Preparation is a source of continuous creative energy.

The French have a wonderful phrase: *L'appétit vient en mangeant*. Appetite comes while eating. And so it is with preparation. The more you do it, the greater the appetite for it.

Practicing Preparation

The first rule of preparation is to let go of the need to come up with an immediate solution. Instead, we step back and engage in some mental or physical activity before actively considering our life options or engaging in some aspect of exploration and discovery. And in order to be able to access the full power of preparation when we need it, it's important to engage in preparation practices on a regular basis. By practicing preparation regularly, we create the new pathways in the brain that will lead to creative life changes. The exercise below will help you select the preparation activities most suited to you and make them a regular part of your new creative life!

EXERCISE

1. Review the list of preparation practices in Appendix D.
2. Choose one preparation activity that you will commit to practice daily for twenty-one days. Don't be afraid to choose something out of your normal habits. For instance, reading a book that is not in your professional field, taking a guided museum tour, or listening to a kind of music that you normally don't listen to.
3. Write a commitment statement in your daily planner/calendar/ scheduling device. For example: I commit to practicing _____

regularly through _____ (twenty-one days later). If possible, make an appointment with yourself to engage in the practice at a particular time of day.

4. Share your commitment with one other person who is part of the working or living environment in which you intend to practice.

5. Keep a record of any thoughts or feelings that arise whenever you engage in this preparation practice.

6. At the end of the second week, add a second preparation practice and repeat prior steps. Keep doing the first preparation practice. Consider an activity that is unrelated to the first one; e.g., if you started practicing meditation, add gardening or a brisk walk. Different activities create different brain pathways that will empower you even more.

7. Notice how you feel at the end of the twenty-one days, by which time the preparation practice should be a habit. How is it affecting your personal and/or work life? If you're not finding benefits, or it seems like drudgery, congratulate yourself for having experimented with it and try a different practice.

Chapter 6

Seeing

Are we to paint what's on the face, what's inside the face or what's behind it? Isn't that the great question?
—PABLO PICASSO

I n many ways, Joanne Cancro's life was working out just as she had expected. With her smarts and dedication she quickly made her mark in corporate marketing, first at Bristol-Myers, then at Lever Brothers. She was living in New York City, where she had grown up and where her family was still close by. By the time she moved over to Revlon she was in charge of all sales communication. So why, she asked herself, wasn't she happy? The negatives were pretty clear to her. She had come to dislike the corporate environment. She felt closed in. She did not like the "sense of paranoia floating around." She wanted a more positive environment. She thought she might want to be her own boss. She knew she wanted to be talking about things that interested her. But that was as far as it went. She had no specific idea of what she wanted to do.

Joanne found herself in a situation not uncommon for many of us. We often know what we don't want better than we know what we do want. We know what causes tension in our lives, but not what would bring us true fulfillment. Joanne realized, for instance, that she wanted to be talking about things that interested her, yet she was not sure what those things were. For Joanne to truly determine what she wanted in her life, *she needed to learn to see herself in new ways and at deeper levels*. In Picasso's terms, Joanne needed to paint more than what was on the face of her work life. She needed to explore what could be "inside" or "behind it."

The Ultimate Creative Skill

In both art and life, seeing is the linchpin creative skill. The essence of seeing is *discerning new connections, gaining fresh perspectives, and staying alive to new possibilities*. When seeing, we:

- notice aspects of situations that other people don't seem to see.
- do not make assumptions before the full picture emerges.
- are aware of at least several ways of interpreting a situation.
- pay attention to what is missing or not obvious about a situation.
- detect connections between seemingly unrelated things or ideas.

In art, seeing means looking at something, say a human eye, and noticing what is really there, not our stereotype of what an eye looks like. We all *think* we know what an eye looks like. If you're like most of us, when asked to draw an eye, you might draw something like this:

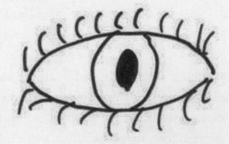

But of course, that's not what an eye looks like. An eye really looks more like this:

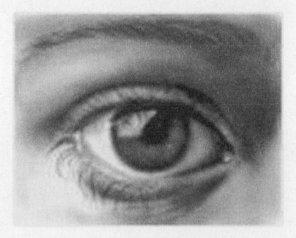

If you look closely at this second picture of an eye, you'll see that there really aren't even any lines, just patches of different shades of light and dark. In fact, there's no such thing as a typical or generic eye. It doesn't exist in nature. There are only particular eyes. To be able to draw a realistic representation of an eye, we must suspend our ideas about what an eye looks like and instead look for what is really there. That's the essence of seeing.

There's More to Seeing Than Meets the Eye

But seeing is not simply a visual ability. Seeing in the creative sense goes beyond physical stimuli registering on our retina. Seeing involves observing our own responses to various experiences and to the world around us. It involves being in touch with the range of emotions evoked by various situations. In other words, seeing is also a form of heightened self-awareness during which our emotional vocabulary is able to differentiate among a wide portfolio of feelings. In this sense, seeing means we are able to "see" our internal landscape as well as we are able to see the visible world of trees, houses, and oceans.

Rembrandt's Lesson

Perhaps no artist demonstrated the many layered aspects of seeing—physical, mental, and emotional—better than Rembrandt. Look at his painting, shown on the following page. Though you can't tell from this copy, the original painting is only ten by twelve and a half inches, one of the smallest pieces Rembrandt painted during his lifetime. Rembrandt painted this in 1629, when he was only twenty-three years old. The painting shows an artist in a spare, run-down studio. The scene is dominated by a huge easel and canvas that dwarfs the painter himself, who seems to recede into the background. A strange, soft glow emanates from the canvas as though it is the only source of light in the studio. While the artist fully sees the front of the canvas, the viewer actually stands outside the painting, outside the studio. The viewer is allowed to peek into this sanctuary of creative engagement yet is denied access to what the artist has placed on the canvas. The front of the canvas is reserved for the artist and only he can bathe in its glow. As you look at this painting, what impressions come to your mind? What might the painter be thinking and feeling? What do you think Rembrandt might be trying to convey through this painting?

Maybe Rembrandt is playing with us. Maybe he is trying to teach us about perspective. Where you stand, he seems to be telling us, determines what you see. What you see on the surface is only half the story. There are many layers to seeing. For us to engage in personal transformation, a humbling and daunting task, we, like the artist in this painting, must also face what is unseen by others.

Rembrandt, *Artist in His Studio,* 1629

We Are What We See

What makes the seeing skill so critical to personal change is that there are consequences to how well we apply this skill. What we pay attention to shapes our destiny by defining our choices and the way we frame them. To become life change artists we need to be able to see ourselves "inside" the face and "behind" the face in Picasso's terms, and in front of the canvas and in back of the canvas in Rembrandt's terms. We need to imagine ourselves as different from how we are now. Seeing differently pushes us toward creating new realities in our lives. William Blake, the great artist and poet of the eighteenth century, said that "the eye altering, alters all." That is Blake's way of telling us that when we change the way we see, *everything* changes. That is because we can now see a whole new field of choices.

Joanne's Journey of Seeing

So how did Joanne Cancro cultivate her seeing skill? She decided to keep "a little notebook." It was her way of beginning to visualize her future. Visualizing is a form of seeing in which you create mental pictures. When you visualize your future, you use your mind's eye to explore life possibilities. There are two main benefits of visualizing. One, when you're visualizing, you can do anything you want, and go anywhere you want—without cost or danger. You don't need to be constrained by practicalities in order to envision how you'd like your life to be. A second benefit is that visualizing a future life that excites you makes it much more likely that you'll achieve that future. Neuroscience research shows that your brain can't tell the difference between something you actually do and something you imagine you are doing. Imagining a future life creates the brain pathways that make it easier for you to actually make the changes you have imagined.

Joanne's approach to visualization was this: She decided to be truthful with herself and record what she saw as being important to her. She decided not to worry about what she thought she *should* want, instead to concentrate only on what she *really* wanted. She might not yet know what "it" was, what her new work would be, but she could begin to describe the elements to herself. She began to record everything she wanted in a new career. Everything. She saw flowers on her new desk. What time she would arrive and what time she would leave. How much sunlight would enter the workplace. She saw what she would be eating. Where the office would be located. What kind of people would enter the office. Who would work there. How she would talk to her customers or clients. How they would feel. How she would feel. Even what she would be wearing. She wrote down everything she saw.

The only problem was that Joanne still had no idea what she would actually do—what her actual work would be. In some sense this was because Joanne had not learned how to see in different ways. She consistently recorded the surface elements of work but had not yet

really journeyed "inside" or "behind." She was like the viewer in
Rembrandt's picture—looking in from the outside. She had not yet
positioned herself in front of the canvas, diving deep and endowing
that canvas with its magical glow. She had even begun to look at a
number of different fields such as women's studies, theology, and nutrition. Her friends laughed at her "career of the week." Undeterred,
Joanne kept her little notebook. What kind of building she would
work in. What her view out the window would be. How much money
she would earn. The notebook grew thicker with verbal pictures—all
potential clues to her future.

But it was not until two things came together that Joanne broke
through to a new level of self-insight. Both came serendipitously. A
friend told her about a group that consisted of six professional women
who met each week to discuss "living the life we want to live." During these meetings the women explored their values and gifts and
dreams. With the support of this group, Joanne came to see that wellness in the broadest sense of its meaning was important to her. She took
pride in caring for her own mental and physical health and fitness. If
she could help others live a healthier life then she could also have a
broader impact on society, one client at a time. It was in the flush of
these insights that she met a man at a seminar who seemed unbeliev-
ably happy in his work. He actually loved his life. He had a sparkle in
his eyes. He was aglow much like Rembrandt's canvas was aglow. During a lunch break, he told Joanne he was a "holistic chiropractor." This
meant he didn't simply crack bones. He paid attention to nutrition,
lifestyle, and general wellness. He helped her see a new set of possibilities for her future, possibilities she had never considered. Joanne
rushed home from the seminar and recorded her thoughts and feelings
in her notebook. But this time she went below the surface. She paid
attention to her feelings about how well external aspects of her desired
future suited her. She compared what she was writing now with what
she had written in the past. All kinds of connections began to spark.
All the notebook words seemed to fit with these new feelings she was
recording. The possibility of a career that was consistent with how she

saw herself and what she had envisioned in her notebook was incredibly exciting. It fit, it felt right. Her path became clear. She wanted to be a holistic chiropractor. When she shared her idea with her group, she was greeted with a chorus of "I think you've found it."

Leonardo da Vinci might have said that Joanne had developed the key creative skill to *saper vedere,* to know how to see. She had discovered what all life change artists know: In order to discover new possibilities for ourselves in the outside world, we must first explore our internal world.

If we don't know how to see, we are destined to keep repeating the current patterns in our life because we are imprisoned by what is familiar. Real change only comes from encountering what is unfamiliar, what is new and unknown. "Art is either plagiarism or revolution," claimed the French artist Paul Gauguin. In the same sense, we can live our lives routinely. We can copy ourselves over and over again, every day. Or we can step into the unknown. When we apply the seeing skill to our own lives, it opens potentially revolutionary possibilities we might never have imagined. Joanne's story demonstrates that we must learn to make new connections—learn to see inside as well as on the surface—in order to find a more fulfilling life path. Only after learning how to see at multiple levels did Joanne open herself up to insight and a new solution.

Blinded by the Familiar

Joanne's story illustrates the importance of the seeing skill. But if it's so crucial to life change, why are we not better at it? If it is so fundamental to setting us in the direction of positive change, then why as mature adults isn't this skill more fully developed? The great artists can help us answer those questions.

The remarkable Swiss painter and sculptor Alberto Giacometti (1901–1966) spent his most productive years in Paris during the forties and fifties. He is known for his excruciatingly thin, highly textured and agitated figures of men and women that offer a vision of physically and emotionally emaciated human beings. His sculptures seem to embody the tenuous, angst-drenched quality of the mid–twentieth century. As an artist he was equally agitated and finicky. His aggressive crisscrossing lines in a drawing or the way he vigorously wiped out and repainted portraits spoke of an artist who was insatiably dissatisfied with his efforts, whose visual explorations could never find rest. But despite his outward turmoil, Giacometti was the embodiment of the artist in quest of seeing with unbiased eyes. He wanted to capture the essence of what was seen, rather than draw an image in a preconceived way. Of course this made him irascible at times, almost comical at others. But no one ever questioned the integrity of his effort, which was characterized by a rigorous, almost ruthless search for what he truly discovered through the process of observation.

James Lord, an art critic and contemporary of Giacometti, described a series of portrait painting sessions during which he himself was Giacometti's subject. The artist told Lord that it would take only a few hours to paint his portrait. It ended up taking eighteen days. Day after day, Lord returned to Giacometti's studio and sat for between two and three hours. At the end of each session an agitated Giacometti would rub out what he had painted and say, "No, this is no good, you must come back." And so Lord returned. During each sitting, the artist lamented the impossibility of getting the head and the nose right. Sometimes the lament would rise to a torrent of invective and cursing:

> "Hell is right there," Giacometti groaned.
>
> "Where?" Lord inquired. "On the tip of my nose?"
>
> "No. It's your whole face." Lord laughed. And then Giacometti added, "The most difficult thing to do well is what's most familiar."

Although Giacometti was referring to painting, to the difficulty of capturing the essence of such a familiar thing as a nose or a face, he was in essence describing one of the most difficult aspects of developing our seeing skill related to life change. We often do not notice what is most familiar, what is right in front of us. The way we take in the world and ourselves becomes so ingrained that we have difficulty imagining our life being different. Our imagination muscles atrophy. We fail to see that our current life may be based upon assumptions that might not be true or relevant any longer. Giacometti understood that a true artist cannot succumb to such assumptions or stereotypes. The artist must not paint the idea of a nose because then one ends up painting a stereotype of a nose. Rather, the artist must paint what he or she truly sees. If that is done well, what will emerge is what we recognize as a nose, although it will be a very particular nose. In the same sense, when we observe our life and how we are living it, we must see it for what it is, not for what we hope it is or take for granted it is. Giacometti battled against the notion that we must accept ideas as given. "What's essential," Giacometti tells us, "is to work without any preconception whatever, without knowing in advance what the picture is going to look like. . . . It is very important to avoid all preconceptions, to try to see only what exists."[1]

Of course this is easier said than done, often because we are not even aware of our preconceptions. But preconceptions are powerful: they are the filter through which we make judgments about what is good or not, what is acceptable or not, what we can or cannot do or should or should not do. The tricky thing is that we can't, and shouldn't, try to get rid of all preconceptions entirely. They serve as a useful shorthand for making quick decisions. The only challenge is to discover which preconceptions are based on false assumptions. Giacometti could have painted a preconception of a nose and superimposed it on Lord's face, but it would not have been Lord's nose. In the same sense, when we are trying to figure out what we want to be when we grow up, it is dangerous to bring preconceptions of ourselves—fears, biases, or negative ideas about ourselves—into the process. When we

1. James Lord, *A Giacometti Portrait* (New York: Farrar, Straus & Giroux, 1980), pp. 67, 79.

allow ourselves to succumb to fears, biases, and self-criticism, we paralyze ourselves. We are unable to see new possibilities, and therefore to make positive changes in our lives.

Often our limiting ideas about ourselves come from others. We grow up in families ruled by powerful people called parents. When we're young, we're at their mercy. How they define us becomes our truth: *Emily is the smart one; James is the clumsy one; Pete is the adventurous one; Mary is the responsible one.* These assessments may be said in jest, yet they carry weight in our formative years. More often than not, we accept our family's version of us, and this acceptance makes it more likely that we'll buy into the roles that our spouses, children, and friends assign us when we're adults. To become a life change artist we need to see how others see us, and make a decision about whether others' views of us are consistent with how we see ourselves, or how we would like to see ourselves. We all know people who spend their whole lives seeing themselves, defining themselves, as others do. But to ensure that we live the most fulfilling lives for ourselves, we must be willing to shed others' expectations about who we are and how we should behave. That is the challenge that Carolyn Dunn, a seasoned journalist, faced when she realized that she had consistently made life choices based on her perception of what others expected of her: That she should get a job rather than travel after college. That she owed it to her husband to be a good mother and a good housekeeper. That she owed it to her children to sacrifice her career to their needs. That she owed it to her community to get involved in causes for which she had marginal interest. The shoulds kept adding up. Carolyn should do this and Carolyn should do that. The sad thing was that these were not bad shoulds in and of themselves. She wanted to be a devoted wife and mother and all-around responsible person. The problem was that there was no room for herself. The shoulds pushed her away from herself. There were things she wanted to do and express. There were things inside herself she did not fully understand but wanted to pay attention to.

Then one evening, at a group meeting of people who were in

transition, Carolyn's wire got tripped. She was talking about the possibility of moving to a different area when someone in the group said
she really didn't think she should do that. Carolyn had had enough.
"Listen, don't should on me," she shouted at no one in particular, yet
to the whole world. "I'm over that. I'm not should-ing on myself any
longer, and I'm not going to let anyone else do it to me, either." With
this new mind-set, Carolyn announced she was ready to explore new
possibilities in her life. She was no longer going to be held prisoner by
the shoulds imposed on her by others and by herself.

Carolyn had reached the point where she was ready to explore new
directions. She was ready to see things differently. It is in such an open
orientation to our lives that we realize that diversity of perspectives
adds to the richness of life. This is another way of saying that seeing
is not prescriptive. Today, Carolyn is on the move. She is holding fast
to her commitment to resist the shoulds. And she is relocating to a
whole new area of the country.

Cultivating Our Seeing Skill

It's important to consciously practice seeing. The more we develop
our seeing skills, the richer our lives can be. But no matter how much
we develop our seeing skills, we'll never see something exactly as
another person does. As the examples above suggest, seeing isn't easy.
Every day there are incentives to look at things in stereotypical ways,
and as we already know, there's much value in being able to see and
interpret information in a habitual way. Deep in our brain is the hippocampus, an area that houses our habitual ways of registering and
responding to information. It's very fast, much faster than the areas of
our brain where we register and react to completely new information.
When, for instance, we see a car heading toward us at great speed,
we immediately assume we're in danger. We don't try to view that
situation in a fresh way. We don't take time to notice that the car is a
new Toyota Prius hybrid. We just race out of its path. And our pre-

conceived notions about that situation save us. But when it comes to planning for life change, exploring new activities, or developing relationships with others, we have lots of opportunities to cultivate a new way of seeing. In the next section, you'll find four powerful ways to build your seeing skill. These seeing strategies are based on ones that artists use to enhance their creative efforts. They are also commonly used by individuals who make successful personal transitions.

Seeing Strategy 1: Stepping Back from the Canvas

Stepping back from the canvas means moving yourself some distance from your day-to-day life or work to gain a fresh perspective.

Mea Simanski's day-to-day life meant being immersed in a thousand and one things, every day. There were her four girls, each two years apart. There was her husband's contracting business that she helped out with. There were the three PTO committees, the charitable work, and the four-mile walks every day. And of course, friends and her extended family. She was like a painter slapping paint on the surface, feverishly working the brushstrokes, up close and personal with the canvas. She was nose deep in the work. She had the feeling that she was doing "a million little things that weren't adding up to enough big things." She felt a nagging need to go back to school, though she had been away from the classroom for twenty years. She had a bachelor's degree, and held a dream of one day earning a Ph.D. and writing a book. She had her husband's encouragement, but her youngest daughter wondered, "Isn't being Mommy enough?"

But Mea decided to jump in, going back to college for her master's degree. At first, she wondered whether she was "trying to eat a horse." Yet she believed she was called to pursue her education. There was a greater purpose at work here even if she did not yet know what that purpose was. She talked about how this sustained her during the ups and downs, the crunch times, the late nights and early mornings and "always feeling frazzled." She also talked about her walks with friends and how that provided breathing room and time for reflection and processing. These were the preparation practices she built into her day. But there was something else she talked about, a kind of lesson she was learning about placing things in perspective. "Write your commitment down," she counseled. "Look at it, walk away, look at it again. Keep perspective. Every day. Sticking with your commitment is everyday work. It can feel overwhelming. But step back. Keep it in perspective for the long term." The simple act of getting out of the house every day provided perspective. Her walking stimulated her creative thinking. This advice has allowed Mea to stay with her commitment. She graduated with high academic honors and completed two master's degrees before beginning her Ph.D. program. There are lots of other little things, only today, at forty-six, Mea feels all the "little things" are adding up to "some pretty big things."

Stepping back from the canvas means taking time to remove yourself from the intense day-to-day demands of your work or life. In some ways, stepping back from the canvas may sound like a form of preparation. It is, however, a discreet action that may precede a preparation practice, but it is not the practice itself. When we step back from the canvas, we are physically moving away from the day-to-day tasks that consume us in order to gain a better perspective. Leonardo da Vinci advised:

> Every now and then go away, have a little relaxation, for when you come back to your work your judgment will be surer. Go some distance away because then the work appears smaller and more of it can be taken in at a glance, and a lack of harmony and proportion is more readily seen.[2]

---

2. Michael J. Gelb, *How to Think Like Leonardo da Vinci* (New York: Dell, 1998), p. 54.

On the other hand, when we engage in preparation practices we are deliberately engaging in mental, physical, or emotional exercises that prepare our minds for creative insight. As we noted in the previous chapter, Leonardo also engaged directly in preparation practices such as meditation. Yet he distinguished the meditative act from his suggestion to "go away" from "your work." Although stepping back from the canvas may lead us into preparation, it is not preparation by itself.

While working on a painting, artists regularly step back from the canvas as a way of refocusing and evaluating their work. Often an artist is too close to the work to see if the design is right, whether the values (the relationship of dark and light) are correct or whether the colors are working. Only by stepping back from the canvas, away from the immediacy of the problem, can the artist evaluate what is working, what is not, and what adjustments need to be made. It is no accident that in *The Artist in His Studio,* Rembrandt shows the artist standing back from the canvas. This reinforces the importance of seeing, which is the major theme of the painting. Matisse was notorious for spending extended periods of time looking at his paintings as he reflected on what he had done and plotting his next stroke. He would hold his paintbrush at a distance from the canvas and move it slowly through the air to try out different movements before committing to the next stroke on the canvas. Willem de Kooning, the great abstract expressionist, would spend hours observing his paintings in progress from a distance before reengaging with the work. For Mea, stepping back from the hectic canvas of her life by simply getting away from the house every day allowed her to refresh the picture of her personal vision.

Seeing Strategy 2: Paying Attention to Negative Space

Paying attention to negative space means tuning in to thoughts and feelings we tend to avoid, deny, or undervalue.

Georgia O'Keeffe, *Brooklyn Bridge,* 1949

In art, negative space is the space that surrounds the primary subject. Negative space is generally contrasted with positive space, by which is meant the main subject in a painting. Negative space often appears less important because the main subject draws all of our attention. But, in truth negative space exerts a powerful influence on how we experience the main subject.

To see how strongly negative space can define what we observe, look at this picture of the Brooklyn Bridge painted by the twentieth-century American artist Georgia O'Keeffe. Our eye is drawn to the spaces between the structures of the bridge. Our impression of the bridge is formed as much by what is not the bridge, as by the bridge itself.

Leonardo da Vinci's famous *Last Supper* is another brilliant ex-

ample of the use of negative space in art. The work depicts the moment just after Jesus reveals that one of the apostles will betray him.
But the meaning of the painting goes well beyond the typical Christian Gospel narrative of the Last Supper. Readers familiar with the
bestselling novel *The Da Vinci Code* won't be surprised to learn that
there are symbolic messages "hidden" in the painting. In order to fully
understand the painting, the viewer must decipher the "codes" to find
the symbolic messages left by Leonardo da Vinci. What *The Da Vinci
Code* didn't mention was that Leonardo used negative space as part of
his code. As you look at the painting, notice how the shape of Jesus is
rendered as a large triangle. The "empty" area directly to his right
forms negative space in the shape of an inverted triangle—just the
opposite of Jesus' own triangular shape. The negative space helps define Jesus in ways that we may not notice, but were very apparent to
Leonardo's Renaissance contemporaries. Leonardo also used negative
space to represent certain symbolic themes that were popular during
the time. In the painting, Jesus is thought to represent the spiritual
union of seemingly contradictory elements—fire and water, matter
and spirit, male and female, body and soul. The fire element is expressed by the upward-pointing triangle of the Jesus figure. The negative space between the figures is rendered in a downward-pointing
triangle, a traditional symbol of water. When the two triangles are
overlaid on top of each other they form the "Seal of Solomon," or a
hexagram, one of the oldest and most universal spiritual symbols,
which represents divine union.[3] While the empty space next to Jesus
appears far less significant than Jesus himself, and far less important
than any of the apostles, in fact this negative space tells us more about
what Leonardo wanted us to understand than many of the "positive"
figures in the painting.

It is critical to emphasize that negative space is not negative in the
sense of being bad. Negative space simply exists in juxtaposition to

---

3. As discussed on the website at http://altreligion.about.com/library/davinci/bl_lastsupper.htm.

Leonardo da Vinci, *The Last Supper,* 1495–1498

the main subject. Nowhere is this truer than in *The Last Supper,* where Leonardo is conveying a larger message about negative space. He is saying we must pay attention to negative space because it contains vital information.

Turning Negative Space into Positive Energy

Paying attention to negative space is also an essential life change strategy. Judy Short might find it odd to be referred to in the same sentence as Leonardo da Vinci, but she actually called upon the same seeing strategy to transform her life as Leonardo used to bring power to his art. From the time Judy was a little girl, she loved playing sports. She played basketball, volleyball, and baseball. She swam, she ran. Judy was a good athlete, but not great, and didn't qualify to play on any official teams at the University of Massachusetts, where she went to college. Instead she played on intramural teams for her dorm, and every morning got up to run a few miles before she headed to classes. Her career plans were a little fuzzy, though she thought she might like using her business degree to do something related to professional sports management. Her father, a disabled former construction worker, urged her to get a more secure job. So she took the Massachusetts civil service exam, and soon found herself working as an administrative assistant for a state agency. Over the next fifteen years she was promoted steadily into a series of increasingly senior administrative positions.

But there was another Judy who lived in the shadows. Her mother, who had died from breast cancer when Judy was a teenager, had a fierce belief in making the world a better place, and she had instilled that belief in her daughter. Judy's desire to make a difference simmered in the shadows of her life, as she rose through the ranks of the state bureaucracy. She could not shake the feeling that she was not wholly who she was meant to be. And then, when a friend asked her to take part in a three-day walk to support breast cancer research, she began to see a glimmer of another Judy, someone who could make more of an impact on the world. When Judy participated in the walk, she realized how much she loved both the physical challenge and the chance to support a cause dear to her heart. By the time she reached the finish line, Judy had a feeling that this was part of what she had been missing for the last fifteen years.

For the next three years, Judy made a point of signing up for athletic events that supported cancer research. Soon it seemed that almost every weekend she was walking, or running, or biking for charity, and eventually she was traveling all over the country to compete in charitable races. Sunday evenings after a race she would feel exhausted but exhilarated. On Monday mornings when she went back to work, she felt like a different person, a paler version of the weekend Judy.

Judy had spent many years ignoring the negative space in her life. Now she began to wonder if she could turn her love of athletics and her commitment to cancer research into a "real job." She began to feel more and more uneasy that she had defined herself professionally in terms of security rather than purpose. Her creative dilemma was beginning to take center stage in her life. Do I continue my safe job as a state administrator and keep doing my charitable work on the side, or do I redefine myself by turning an avocation into a full-time commitment? Could she turn "weekend Judy" into the real Judy? She began to think that she might apply her administrative skills to a more meaningful purpose than keeping the wheels of state government turning. Maybe she could even use those skills to help cure the disease that had taken her mother's life. She knew it was time to bring "Weekend Judy" and "Administrator Judy" together into a new, exciting, more meaningful life. Judy networked with coordinators of charitable events in which she had been involved over the past few years. Within a few months, Judy had found a new home for her skills and her passions as full-time director of a consortium of charitable walk, run, and biking events. Judy still remembers the look on her father's face when she told him she was quitting her safe and secure state job. She had feared that he would feel she had betrayed his advice. But he could see a new, impassioned look of determination on his daughter's face, and he understood the cause to which she had become committed. It was as though he was acknowledging the truth of who Judy had become. He nodded his approval. Judy is busier than ever, but almost every weekend, she still gears up for an athletic event that might someday help change the world as she has changed hers.

For a variety of reasons, many individuals do not pay attention to the negative space in their lives. When they ignore that negative space, they usually feel tense or uneasy. Only after they tune in to their personal negative space are they able to make shifts in their understanding of themselves. They begin to ask different questions: What are the things in my life I have not been paying attention to? What are these feelings that nag at the edges of my awareness? What am I afraid of? What do I really want to be when I grow up? What are the interests and talents I have been neglecting? What are the deeply held values I've been ignoring? It is not until they pay attention to the negative space in their lives that they are able to make the important changes that define them in new ways.

Seeing Strategy 3: Turning the Subject Upside Down

Turning the subject upside down means radically shifting perspective. It means turning the premise of our thinking completely around.

A number of years ago, Fred took a drawing class from Tim Harney, an outstanding artist and teacher, that involved the use of a live model.

> It was my first drawing class and I really struggled. The instructor noticed that I was floundering, but for some reason, he left me alone for the first class. During the second class he finally came up to me and asked: "What are you trying to do?"
>
> "Well," I said, "I see the model sitting over there and I'm trying to draw what I see on the paper as best as I can."
>
> "No, no, no," he scolded me, waving his hands emphatically as he spoke. "You do not see in order to draw, you draw in order to see." His words hit me like a ton of bricks. It created a revolution in my mind. It made me realize that drawing was not about copying the model perfectly, but about exploring and discovering what was really there.

Harney was saying the same thing Giacometti had said to James Lord decades earlier—and what great artists have said for hundreds of years: "You do not see in order to draw; you draw in order to see."

> Suddenly I felt much freer. I loosened up. I no longer had to worry about getting it perfect. I could really explore with the charcoal. I became almost giddy. I started noticing the way a lighted surface receded into a slightly darker surface and then plunged into a really dark crevice before popping up again into strong light. It was really amazing. I

lightened up my touch and then pressed down and really moved the charcoal around. At the end of the class a couple of the other students came up to my easel and said, "Hey, you really captured the fullness of her lips." I said, "Is that what you call them?" I had been so immersed in the creative process that I couldn't even recall the names of common body parts. But I was feeling really good.

Harney had caused a revolution in the way Fred approached his subject. As a result, he was able to break through his conventional understanding of what drawing entailed and come up with a fresh, distinctive picture. In essence, Harney turned everything upside down for Fred.

In other instances, artists literally turn their paintings upside down in order to gain a better perspective, to better see how the design holds up, to be sure everything is in balance. During life change, we are accustomed to looking at our lives and ourselves standing on our feet. We habitually see things right side up and that limits other perspectives. We get stuck seeing our lives from the same angle with the same old reference points. Allowing ourselves to be turned upside down, much as an artist might turn his painting upside down, can free us to see things in an entirely new way.

An Upside-Down Encounter

People are often surprised at how their lives have turned out. "It wasn't supposed to be this way," they say. "I had different dreams." "There were twists and turns in the road and it's as though I closed my eyes and now here I am." "My life has just turned out different from what I expected." "I'm amazed at how my life has evolved" may well have been Randi Carney's theme song. Randi was twenty-eight, divorced with two children, working as a waitress in a university section of Chicago and living on food stamps. "The only thing I had was my wits and sense of humor. I thought my life was going to be bleak, bleak, bleak. I mean, I was a failure personally, and I thought of myself that way." Despite her solid middle-class upbringing, this was the reality she faced. She had no financial means, she had graduated from high school with barely a C average, and her work experience was heavily weighted toward bartending and waitressing.

But Randi had not factored in an unexpected encounter. She had been waiting tables at a restaurant often frequented by academics. The university president would often be among the patrons. Randi occasionally waited on his table, and her energy and sense of humor caught his attention. After lunch one day, he asked her, "What do you plan to do with your life?" It just so happened that during that period Randi had been thinking about her deceased physician father and how he used to take her on rounds. So when the president posed that question, the words simply skipped from her lips: "I'm thinking of going to med school." She hardly believed the words had come out of her mouth, and she believed even less that such a thought had any real possibility. The president looked her directly in the eyes and said he believed she had it in her; he gave her the name of the academic dean at the university. "I was twenty-eight years old, and the only possessions I had were my children, a welfare check, and his belief in me."

It took a while for the full power of the president's words to sink in. It was not only what he said but who he was that forced Randi to take a fresh look at herself. To begin to think of herself in upside-down terms. Maybe, she thought, he sees things in me I do not see in myself. She wondered if she had been too focused on her current reality and on believing that that had to be her reality for the rest of her life. Maybe, just maybe, she could create a new reality.

Randi followed up on the president's referral and talked her way into the college. Today she is a physician setting up innovative medical clinics in underserved areas around the country.

Seeing Strategy 4: Cultivating the Mind of a Child

Cultivating the mind of a child means introducing a spirit of play and spontaneity into the way we look at things, unbound by rules. It means allowing ourselves to return to what gave us joy and energy without prejudgment.

Ron Mortara—whom we met in Chapter 3—had been a neurosurgeon until a heart condition forced him to leave medicine. A period of time followed that felt "like syrup." Time moved very slowly. Then he came across a video camera his father had given him as a youngster. He played around with it, remembering and experiencing the joy that shooting movies had given him as a child. Ron felt reenergized and enrolled in a series of workshops that led him to becoming a filmmaker. Looking back, he observed: "I didn't change. I allowed more of myself to come out. It was like being a child in a grown-up body."

Jenna Fletcher realized that she had stayed with her former career as a corporate executive because she thought that was the "grown-up" thing to do. But when she left that world to pursue a childhood love of nature by becoming an environmental conservationist, she realized that no one had given her points for squelching her passions. She announced: "I'm no longer pushing 'me' down. I'm a kid again. Only older."

"It takes a long time to become young," Picasso concluded in his later years. He was referring not only to a general outlook but to the way artists in particular need to look at the world. One of Picasso's contemporaries and greatest competitors, Henri Matisse, shared a similar outlook. He wrote:

The effort to see things without distortion demands a kind of courage; and this courage is essential to the artist, who has to look at everything as though he were seeing it for the first time: he has to look at life as

he did when he was a child and if he loses that faculty, he cannot express himself in an original, that is, a personal way.[4]

Both Picasso and Matisse are telling us that creativity requires one to
cultivate the mind of a child. In the Yoga tradition, this is referred to
as "beginner's mind." This means we see things with unencumbered
eyes. We allow a kind of innocence to guide us. We take in information as though it is the first time, as though anything is possible and
we are not bound by convention. We can say 2 plus 2 is 4. We can also
say it is 22. And why not say it is 2 over 2, or twotwo, or tutu? When
we see with the mind of a child, we can play and invent our own
rules. But somewhere along the way most of us lose that ability. Conventional thinking takes root. We follow the path of least resistance.
We allow the shoulds and should-nots, the that'll-never-works, the
I-can't-do-thats, the how-will-I-evers, the what-will-they-thinks to
shout down our more youthful instincts.

In a recent Life Change Studio workshop, Diane Sasson, a sales
manager, was asked to come up with a visual image that represented
her personal transition journey. A number of images came to mind,
but when she was asked to actually paint or draw one of the images
on a group canvas she balked. She expressed concern that others in the
group would negatively judge her effort. When asked whether she was
worried about *others'* judgments or her *own* judgment, she admitted
both concerned her. A double whammy! As a result, she had lost her
"childish" spontaneity.

When we internalize such feelings, we become deaf to the child
voice in us. The Japanese artist Howard Ikemoto tells us about a conversation he had with his daughter. "When my daughter was seven
years old, she asked me one day what I did at work. I told her I worked
at the college—that my job was to teach people how to draw. She
stared back at me, incredulous, and said, 'You mean they forget?'"

---

4. Henri Matisse, "Looking at Life with the Eyes of a Child, 1953," in Jack Flam, ed., *Matisse on Art*
(Berkeley: University of California Press, 1995), p. 218.

The great artists have a message for life change artists: Look at your life as though you are seeing it for the first time. Everything is possible. Play with the possibilities. Resist the adult mind dampening your fun. Stick your tongue out at it. The adult mind will tell you this is dreaming. It is childish. It is not responsible. It is unrealistic. And then remember Picasso's challenge: "Every child is an artist. The problem is how to remain an artist after growing up." Cultivating the mind of a child is the first step in reconnecting with what is true in our selves.

■　■　■

As you practice the four seeing strategies discussed in this chapter, be prepared at times to be both excited and unnerved. Kathleen recalls an experience she had driving down a beautiful tree-lined country road on the way back from a beginner's art class she took when in her forties. What had always before registered in her mind as a black road surface was suddenly transformed into a chaotic collage of varied light and dark, irregular shapes. Her sense of driving on something recognizable and solid evaporated. It was momentarily dizzying and frightening. What had happened? Was she hallucinating? Having a mental breakdown? The explanation turned out to be simple: in her art class she had been learning to pay attention to tonal "values"—the different shades of light and dark that make up any object. She learned her lesson too well, because in that disturbing moment, the normal driver's stereotypical view of the road was disrupted by her new way of seeing. Learning to see our lives in new ways can be similarly jolting. It takes courage to travel on a new road, one that may not feel solid when we begin our journey. But with seeing skills in hand, we can find all the information we need to create new possibilities for ourselves. So relax. And enjoy the ride.

EXERCISES

1. Stepping Back from the Canvas

- Sketch a portrait of yourself today.
- Allow it to be as spontaneous and primitive as you like.
- The next day, draw a portrait of yourself two years from now. Again, allow it to be as spontaneous and primitive as you like.
- Record your observations on how the portraits are different.

2. Paying Attention to Negative Space

How would you answer these questions about the negative space in your life?

- What in my life am I not paying attention to?

Example: *I am not really acknowledging that I am fundamentally unhappy in my work. I am afraid of losing my source of income if I allow myself to dwell on my dissatisfaction too much.*

- What is missing in my life?

Example: *There's something inside me that wants to get out. I'm not sure what it is but I think I have more to give, more to say, more to explore, more to express.*

- What don't I do that could make me more fulfilled?

Example: *I don't really look into moving in a different work direction or even starting my own business.*

3. Turning Life Change Upside Down

Gain a new perspective on your life by answering these questions:

- What change would you like to make in your life right now?

Example: *I would like to change an unhealthy relationship.*

• What roadblocks are getting in the way?

Example: *I am afraid of leaving.*

• How is my thinking contributing to that roadblock?

Example: *I'm assuming that I will be lonely, I won't have any money, and others will think badly of me.*

• How could I turn that thinking upside down?

Examples:
CHANGE *I will be lonely* TO *I will have an opportunity to meet new people.*
CHANGE *I won't have money* TO *I will be emotionally broke if I don't create the future I want.*
CHANGE *Others will think badly of me* TO *I will feel better about myself.*

• How could this upside down thinking affect my outlook and my actions?

Example: *I can see that there are other ways to look at my situation. There are real positives on the other side of the fear. If I focus on the positives, I can begin to imagine some new possibilities.*

4. Cultivating the Mind of a Child
• Recall a situation from your childhood when you were no more than ten years old that gave you a lot of joy.

Example: *Going to an amusement park with my second-grade class as an end-of-school celebration.*

- What was it about that situation that made you so happy?

Example: *The excitement of the rides. Bumper cars were my favorite because I felt so powerful to be driving. I liked the feeling. I felt free. I felt different than on any other day. And eating treats like cotton candy that would never be allowed at home.*

- What aspects of this experience could bring you more joy in your current life?

Example: *Doing something different from the everyday. Trying something where I wouldn't feel constrained or limited. Reconnecting with the feeling of being free and powerful.*

- What is one thing you can do in your life right now that would reconnect you to those feelings?

Example: *I could go on a weekend trip by myself to a place I haven't been before.*

Chapter 7

Using Context

Know what the old masters did. Know how they composed their pictures, but do not fall into the conventions they established. These conventions were right for them, and they are wonderful. They made their language. You make yours. All the past can help you.

—ROBERT HENRI

We live our lives in contexts. Every day we are influenced by our social, economic, cultural, and political context. Sometimes we are aware of these influences. For instance, when we call someone a baby boomer or Gen-Xer, we are defining that person by a demographic context. When we call someone middle-class, we are defining that person by a social and economic context. When we claim we are living in a "Google world," we are making a contextual statement about how technology shapes people's experiences and expectations. When we talk about living in a "post-9/11 world," we are acknowledging a global political context that affects where and how we travel, which leaders we elect, and to what extent we feel personally safe—or free.

Many times, though, we are unaware of our context. Context can be like the air we breathe, always there and taken for granted. When we don't pay attention to our context, however, it's very hard to change. If we're swimming in an ocean but don't realize it is an ocean, and that there are other habitats we might explore, we'll likely be stuck swimming around in the same body of water indefinitely.

We each can probably describe elements of each of these common contexts:

- Personal—our personal and family story
- Social—our friends, social network, and community
- Work/Professional—our work colleagues, environment, and associations
- Historical—the broader world in which we live and how it came to be

The list of contexts can go on. They can include cultural, economic, political, geographical, technological, and spiritual contexts. For life change artists, the particular contexts we inhabit are less important than how we learn to use our various contexts to facilitate life change. Life change artists, like the great masters of art, recognize that creating something new happens only in the context of where they are now and what has happened in the past. They use context in order to break with existing contexts. That is what makes the skill creative. Therefore they cultivate the creative skill of using context, which means *to understand how the varied environments in which we work and live influence our thoughts and behaviors and to use that knowledge to make changes in our lives.* When using context, we:

- pay attention to trends taking place in our areas of interest.
- pay attention to what's going on in society and the larger world.
- take social trends into account when making key life decisions.
- assess what's working and what's not working in our areas of interest when considering a new direction.
- understand how our social identity (professional, marital) can bias our thinking about options for change.

Trends

Trends make up a critical component of context. Knowing that someone is a baby boomer is just an interesting fact. *Understanding* trends, however, gives meaning to the facts of our lives; for instance, knowing that the large number of baby boomers is contributing to an aging demographic trend in the United States (and elsewhere). This demographic trend, in turn, has many implications. For example,

- Aging baby boomers may create higher demand for health and fitness facilities.
- Hospitals may become overcrowded with baby boomers who become ill as they age.
- Social Security funds may run out more quickly because so many people will be collecting it over the next few decades.
- Aging baby boomers who wish to continue working past normal retirement age may have to seek and define new models of work or career.
- Retiring baby boomers may find it difficult to sell their homes, because there will be fewer younger people to buy them.

These possibilities are only a fraction of the many implications of the aging demographic trend. And of course, there is a dizzying array of contexts in which each of us lives. How, then, do we begin to know which of these contexts we should pay attention to, or which questions we need to be asking related to our context? By looking at examples of how the great artists and life change artists use context we can begin to see how understanding context enhances any creative process.

Context in Action

The great artists were consummate context seekers. They understood themselves not only in the context of their artistic milieu, but in the context of the broader world in which they lived. This violates the stereotype of artists as individuals who work in splendid isolation, relying exclusively on some hidden, inner source for their creativity. Nothing could be further from the truth. It is precisely how great artists understand and use contexts that helps explain such remarkable freshness in their art.

Using Professional Context

"The Louvre is the book in which we learn to read," Cézanne observed. For many of the great artists, the Louvre offered a lesson plan on how to paint, and they eagerly soaked up everything they could from the work of the teachers on the museum's walls. This was the artists' professional context. They learned by setting up easels in the museum and literally copying the works of the masters who had gone before them.

Yet the great artists were not content to learn only from museums. They had to know what their fellow artists were doing as well. Whether it was Georgia O'Keeffe hanging around with Alfred Stieglitz and his band of avant-garde artists at Gallery 291 in New York, or the Impressionists gathering around small marble tables at the Café Guerbois in Paris, or even Rembrandt joining the Guild of Saint Luke in Amsterdam in 1634, artists came together. They not only learned what their immediate contemporaries were up to, but used these gatherings to hear about what artists beyond their immediate community were doing and what the trends were.

Even an artist as "eccentric" as Vincent van Gogh had a firm grasp on who was doing what among his contemporary artists. Generally thought of as isolated, van Gogh was actually a keen evaluator of his fellow artists. In a letter to his brother Theo in July 1885, he mentions the names of twenty-three different artists, many forgotten today, who were actively working at that time. Some he terms "little masters of today" and others "lesser ones." He refers to Greek and Renaissance painters, as well as many from the Old Dutch school. By doing so, van Gogh is "placing" himself—putting himself in context. He is trying to determine his artistic path in relation to other artists both great and small. A few years later, in another letter to Theo, he wrote that "the painter of the future will be a colorist such as has never yet existed." Here, van Gogh shows his hand. He is staking out what will distinguish him. But he does this in the context of his fellow artists and of all artists. Van Gogh is tuned in to the professional gossip of the day. He also knows his art history. He has used his contextual domain—that is, other artists—to define who he is as an artist. To this day, we think of van Gogh as perhaps the greatest colorist in the history of art.[1]

Using Historical Context

Monet Stops the Trains

The story behind Claude Monet's famous painting *Gare Saint-Lazare*, from 1877, is an intriguing example of how far some artists will go to get a good painting—and how they used their context to create art and interpret their world. Monet executed the painting in a period when the industrial revolution was sweeping across western Europe and many did not fully comprehend its profound implications. Nothing was more emblematic of this revolution than the railroad and

---

1. W. H. Auden, *Van Gogh: A Self-Portrait* (New York: E. P. Dutton, 1963), pp. 240-45, 289.

the locomotive. Both were powerful symbols of the machine and its intrusion on the agrarian culture and values of the time.

As an Impressionist, Monet was interested in capturing the moment in paint. What could be a greater challenge than capturing both the mood and the nature of the period than an imposing locomotive coughing out billows of smoke? How does one capture the impression of something as fleeting as smoke with paint! Never one to back down from a challenge, Monet hatched an outrageously daring plan that even his fellow Impressionist Auguste Renoir called "mad."

Monet donned his finest suit with ruffled lace at the wrists, grabbed his cane and presented himself to the director of the Saint-Lazare train station with a note introducing himself as "the painter, Claude Monet." The director was too embarrassed to confess ignorance of the arts, so he admitted Monet into his office, where "the painter" announced, "I have decided to paint your station. For some time I've been hesitating between your station and the Gare du Nord, but I think yours has more character." The director granted permission. Monet asked that all trains be delayed from departing for at least thirty minutes. The platforms were cleared, and the engines were crammed with coal in order to produce as much smoke as Monet could dream of. When he left, Monet had half a dozen new paintings.[2]

And what paintings they are! They are striking examples not only of Impressionism but also of a historical moment in time that conveys the full imposing threat of the industrial revolution through the plumes of smoke belching from two locomotives. Monet understood that he was not just using an artistic technique; he was chronicling an important shift in civilization in which a whole new set of technologies and values would come to govern our lives. He was telling us that our context would never be the same.

2. Sue Roe, *The Private Lives of the Impressionists* (New York: Harper, 2006), pp. 173–74.

Claude Monet, *Gare Saint-Lazare*, 1877

Reaffirming "Old-time Values"

Growing up in New York during the sixties and seventies, Charlie Finesilver had been deeply touched by President Kennedy's call to service. He had always thought of himself as an idealist, someone who wanted to make a difference in the world. But it seemed that life took him in a different direction. He accepted a job in corporate finance in Seattle but after eight years got burned out of the corporate world. He moved back East to Vermont, and for reasons that are not entirely clear to him, enrolled in a vocational education class—and was utterly surprised to find he loved plumbing. Solving problems with his head and hands gave him a great deal of satisfaction. For the next ten years Charlie ran his own plumbing business while his wife, Jeannie, worked as an occupational therapist in the local school district. Life was good. They built a home and established themselves in their community. Since they did not have children, they were free to travel and enjoy nice things. Charlie thought he had done okay for a kid from Bayside, New York.

But as Charlie thought back to an earlier time, when he had been moved by the idealism of the sixties, he couldn't help feeling that he had left something behind. He also sensed that the country today had drifted away from those "old-time values." Like Monet, he sensed a broad shift. Only this time the shift was away from values based on social engagement to ones based on self-interest. Monet expressed this shift through his art. Charlie Finesilver had a different way to express his concern about the shift in values in his own time. From time to time he and his wife had talked about the Peace Corps. True, the first decade of the twenty-first century was a very different time from the decades of the sixties and seventies, but he couldn't let go of the "durable appeal" of his youth. At age fifty-four, many might have shied away from the risks of being in an uncomfortable situation. But not Charlie. The idea of changing the world still counted, but now he also wanted to challenge himself to grow as a human being. He could not re-create the sixties and seventies, but he could still connect with the core values that resonated so deeply with the mood of that period. In a real way, Charlie was bringing a historical context forward into his present life.

So when Jeannie lost her job at the school, she and Charlie took it as a sign to make the move. It took them a year to apply and get into the Peace Corps program. Friends looked at them with "a combination of awe and pity" as Charlie sold his business and they sold their house and then shipped out to Mali, an African country of unimaginable poverty. During their two years there, Charlie taught business courses and worked with local villagers to start small businesses. Jeannie worked in a local health clinic. Charlie contracted malaria twice, and Jeannie broke her leg. But they stuck it out and believe they made a difference for the villagers and for themselves.

Today, Charlie and his wife live in South Carolina. Charlie is starting up a plumbing business again from scratch. Jeannie found a job at the local university. In some ways he feels he has been changed forever. In other ways he feels he has simply been given the opportunity to put his personal values into practice in a more direct way. Before joining the Peace Corps he had never done volunteer work. Today he remains connected to the Peace Corps. He raised money to build a mosque in the village where he lived and worked in Mali. He teaches business locally to disadvantaged youth in his South Carolina town.

While in Mali, Charlie befriended the village elder, a man called "Vieux" (French for "the Old One"). They talked for hours on end about Islam, God, faith, proper living, death. This Jew from Bayside, New York, and this Muslim from a remote village in West Africa built a friendship that has outlasted Charlie's time in Mali. They may not have changed the world, but they changed the village and they changed each other.

In some ways, Monet and Charlie Finesilver were moving in opposite directions. Monet chronicled the intrusion of modernity into a traditional culture. Charlie Finesilver wanted to find ways to resurrect old values and make them relevant to today. Monet the modernist, Charlie the traditionalist. Yet despite this difference, they both used context in the same way. Both led to creative solutions to their dilemmas. Monet introduced innovation into art. Charlie introduced innovation into his life and the lives of those in a remote African community.

Charlie Finesilver Uses Context

Creative Dilemma

Do I continue to run a successful business or reconnect with my earlier values of making an impact in the world?

Explore and Discover

Identify contexts affected by creative dilemma

Charlie understands he held on to the legacy social values of the sixties and seventies; and he resists his current social context, which tells him to "act his age."

Gather and assess information related to contexts

Charlie researches opportunities for midlifers to engage in social change.

Identify potential implications

Charlie reflects on consequences of such a dramatic shift to his future options. He considers risks relative to finances, relocation, and health care.

Experiment with responses

Charlie tests out his thinking with friends and family.

Integrate
Expand possibilities

After the Peace Corps, Charlie continues his involvement in community initiatives serving the poor. He had never done this before.

Using Social Context

Achieving "Bubbie-hood"

Sandy Johnson fully admitted to being a type A personality when it came to work. Actually, make that a "triple A" personality type. At least until a heart attack knocked her off her game at age sixty-two. Until then she had been the "Energizer Bunny," running several Human Resource teams in a large corporation. She was fully absorbed in the work. For her it was all about making a difference. She loved the challenges and her colleagues and comfortably thought of herself as a top-notch business manager.

At first Sandy thought she would bounce right back and pick up where she left off. But when her stamina failed to rebound she became less certain about her future. The thought of leaving her career gave her a sense of hanging on to the edge of a precipice. If I do not have my career, she wondered, then who am I? Sandy was wise enough to seek help in figuring it out. She worked with a coach to think through what made the most sense. She began to read and journal and reflect on the choices in front of her. This helped her become a heightened observer of her own social environment. In some sense the answer to the "Who am I?" question was all around her. She had been so focused on work, however, that she had never considered drawing a sense of meaning and identity from her broader social context. This came home to her one day while talking to Maggie, the youngest of her four grandchildren. Maggie told Sandy that they were having a "Special Person Day" in kindergarten and she wanted "Bubbie" (chosen term for grandmother) to be her special person. With sudden clarity Sandy realized she wanted to be around not only for the special day but also for when Maggie entered first grade and then second grade and for a long time to come. But if she did not change her life, she was unlikely to get there. Little Maggie helped Sandy shift the focus of her social context from work to family. "I realized that not only was I Bubbie in her eyes but I was Bubbie at my core." It fit. "Bubbie-hood is what I want to be about. It's who I am. I felt this unbelievable freedom that was given to me by my granddaughter."

Sandy is also taking better care of herself. She's enrolled in a meditation class. She goes on long walks almost every day. She volunteers at the Alzheimer's Association and YMCA Diversity Initiative. She's involved in her town's Visioning Project. She's still about making a difference. That will never go away. In some ways she feels she is the same person. In other ways she is more balanced, more relaxed, more fulfilled. So she has been told. She smiles and says she thinks she has "achieved Bubbie-hood."

Sandy Johnson Uses Context

Creative Dilemma

Do I remain in a lucrative corporate job, or do I redefine my role in relationship to family and grandchildren?

Explore and Discover

Identify contexts affected by creative dilemma

Sandy undertakes a full scan related to her work environment and its impact on her role and identity and her potential new role and identity outside full-time work.

Gather and assess information related to contexts

Sandy reviews her financial plan; consults with doctors related to her heart attack and long-term health; reflects on personal values and personal motivators.

Identify potential implications

Sandy does not fully know what impact full-time "Bubbie-hood" will have on her sense of self-worth and her desire to make a difference.

Experiment with responses

Sandy tries different volunteer community initiatives.

Integrate

Expand possibilities

Sandy embraces "Bubbie-hood" as a new identity; expands personal wellness practices; commits to engage in community activities.

Using Personal Context

Picasso Confronts the Horrors of War

Pablo Picasso is not known as a political painter. He was fiercely independent artistically and politically. His subjects tended to be highly personal and often erotic. Yet it was a deeply felt personal identity with his Spanish roots and family history that stirred Picasso to paint one of the most powerful political paintings in the history of art. Even though he had been living in France for more than twenty years, Picasso drew on this deep personal context to express a universal outrage at the horrors of war. In 1937, Picasso learned that the fascist forces of Francisco Franco, backed by the Nazi regime in Germany, had bombed his native Spain and massacred men, women, and children in the Basque city of Guernica. On May 1, the very day after this catastrophe, the fifty-five-year-old Picasso went to his studio in Paris and drew the first preliminary sketches for what was to become *Guernica.* Picasso threw himself at the huge canvas, standing eleven and a half feet high and twenty-five feet long. Over the next four weeks he left his studio only to eat and sleep. On June 6 he completed the work, and almost immediately, with the paint still wet, he installed it at the Paris International Exposition of 1937, where it dominated the entrance to the Spanish Pavilion. Crowds thronged to the black-and-white painting and were deeply moved by its portrayal of the horrors of war. Picasso had spontaneously and powerfully used the immediacy of his historical and personal contexts to paint a timeless work of art. Picasso died in 1973 at the age of ninety-one, and he had insisted that this great painting not be allowed into Spain until Franco was gone. In 1986, *Guernica* was finally brought to Spain, where it now hangs in a national museum in Madrid.[3]

---

3. Russell Martin, *Picasso's War* (New York: Plume, 2002), pp. 64–101.

Pablo Picasso, *Guernica*, 1937

A Survivor Uses Personal Context

"Memory brings you back. It reconnects you to your old world. For me, remembering that old world led me to my new path," Patricia Hinchey concluded in recalling a youthful, painful world. Her father had abused everyone in the family—her mother, her brother, herself. At age sixteen she had to testify against her father in court. After the judge slapped a restraining order on him, he returned to the house one last time, beat everyone up, and left for good.

After high school Patricia enrolled in a local college but dropped out after two years. She latched on to an executive assistant training program at Katharine Gibbs, which landed her a job with a hospital association. Patricia quickly learned she had a knack for seeing inefficiencies in the association's operations. She was put in charge of launching a group-purchasing initiative, and this led to enrolling hospitals throughout New England in a collaborative group-purchasing agreement. The cost savings were enormous. From there Patricia joined forces with the man she eventually married, to create a for-profit business which grew into the third largest health care group-purchasing company in the country. Patricia focused on business development while her husband built the business infrastructure.

Then the roof fell in. Patricia's husband filed for divorce and forced her out of the day-to-day operations of the business. While she retained an equity interest, she had no control and had to watch while the business fell apart. Under the divorce settlement she was able to sell her share at a dramatically diminished value. But the damage had been done.

Patricia was devastated. She fell into a deep depression. All options were on the table, including "the choice of all choices: Is life worth living?"

Patricia sought help in the form of therapy. She was able to see the pattern of abuse she had fallen into. Her father had physically abused her. Her husband had abused her sense of self as well as her financial stability. Yet she also realized she had not allowed herself to play the victim the first time around. And she was determined not to let that happen this time.

Patricia started her own consulting business in the group-purchasing arena. She also invested in a small but promising digital imaging company. But neither of these satisfied her. They had a "been there, done that" quality. Like Picasso, she chose not to ignore her roots. She went back to redefine her personal context. She began to recall some of the positive experiences she had had with her father when he was sober. She recalled how he had taught her how to take care of things, like her bicycle, how to give her best effort, how to believe that anything was possible, how to be a fighter.

Patricia now says, "I realized it's about how you use your history to define yourself. In my case it can be as victim or survivor. My history tells me I have something to offer. I refuse to be a victim. I am a survivor, but I want to be more. I want to be a thriver. Context is neutral; it's how you interpret your context that influences your choices." Today, Patricia has moved her energies to the nonprofit side. She is involved in several community-based organizations dedicated to preventing domestic violence against women. Patricia's powerful identity with her personal history allowed her to make a meaningful shift. By reconnecting with her painful family history of abuse she was able to find the strength and direction to make a difference in the lives of others. Both Picasso and Patricia found that our contexts sometimes contain imperatives from earlier in our lives that compel us to respond to our creative dilemmas in entirely new ways.

Patricia Hinchey Uses Context

Creative Dilemma

Do I continue to focus on traditional business opportunities, or do I do something about the pain of my childhood?

Explore and Discover

Identify contexts affected by creative dilemma

Patricia feels there is unfinished business related to her personal family history.

Gather and assess information related to contexts

Patricia begins to map out trends in social and institutional responses to the abuse of women and children in the nonprofit sector.

Identify potential implications

Patricia examines her personal finances; she also wonders how the nonprofit culture will react to her entrepreneurial instincts and experience.

Experiment with responses

Patricia interviews leaders in the community involved in abuse initiatives; she explores possible roles with specific organizations.

Integrate

Expand possibilities

Patricia affirms her core values; she has a sense of working for something greater than herself.

Using Context for Life Change

Life change artists, like the great artists, excel at using their contexts to launch themselves in new directions. Like Monet and Picasso, who used context to create new art forms, Charlie Finesilver, Sandy Johnson, and Patricia Hinchey used context to create new directions in their lives. The mode of expression may be different, but the skill is the same.

Developing the Skill of Using Context

Developing our skill of using context comes when we are explicit about our context and the influence it bears on our lives. Too often we neglect to fully appreciate how powerfully our context impacts the story we tell ourselves about ourselves and our history. Sometimes these narratives can play a positive role and other times a negative role. It is important to understand that the purpose of developing this skill is to expand our possibilities rather than to limit them. Mastering this skill opens our lives to creating previously unperceived opportunities. Monet used his historical context to concoct an original way of capturing how his world was changing. Charlie Finesilver followed Monet's example. He used his historical context to find a new life direction. Sandy Johnson used a freshly tuned appreciation of her context to define a new social and personal identity. Picasso used his deep personal connection to Spain to create one of the most moving political paintings in history. In the same sense, Patricia Hinchey's emotional work helped turn her painful family past into a springboard for service to abused women.

The best way to develop the using context skill is to follow a structured and reflective approach. In many ways, using context is the most analytical of the creative skills. The templates offered with the Charlie Finesilver, Sandy Johnson, and Patricia Hinchey stories show how to organize and examine the elements of our context. The more we use this template, the more effective we will get at the skill.

Though the using context skill may include a strong analytical component, that does not mean there are not powerful emotional dynamics in play. The exhilaration Monet must have felt upon completing his Gare Saint-Lazare paintings is matched by Charlie Finesilver's excitement at reconnecting with his old-time values. Picasso's wrenching decision to visually express the anguish of his countrymen matches Patricia Hinchey's pain at coming to terms with her family history. It is the very commitment to begin the process of examining our context in a dispassionate way that brings us to those compelling emotional realities.

As we can see from the stories in this chapter, it's not the particular context that matters, but rather the way we use our contexts that counts. Our creative dilemmas usually come packaged in a set of contexts that are as unique as our individual stories. It is this very rich brew of creative dilemmas and their contexts that make life change so varied and filled with adventure.

But context can also be a double-edged sword. It can trap us as easily as it can help free us. We may get stuck in our professional and social environment and have trouble seeing ourselves in different settings. This is because our current contexts often reinforce our current identity and assumptions. In other words, context can be a closed-loop system. We live in a context that carries its own values and beliefs. We in turn adopt those very values and beliefs as our own. One of the dangers of context is that we come to believe that the values and beliefs of our context are unchangeably our own. When this happens we can often be blinded to new ways of seeing both ourselves and our context. Consider these examples of potential contextual traps:

- Going every week for years to a church that does not nourish me spiritually.
- Putting aside my dream of world travel because I couldn't leave my children.
- Ignoring the urge to become a teacher because I have an expensive lifestyle to support.

This dark side of context makes it imperative that we examine context in a structured and thoughtful way. The example of the great artists serves us well here. They understood why it was important to refer to context to gain fresh perspective. They tell us that context is not determinative. Context is not destiny. As powerful as context can be in locking us into a certain identity, it also contains vital seeds of change, but only if we are willing to experiment outside our contextual comfort zones. And if we do, we'll discover, as one life change artist joyfully observed, "There's a wide world for me out there!"

EXERCISE

Exploring My Contexts

To develop a better appreciation of how your contexts may impact your ability to respond to your creative dilemma, use this worksheet. After you have completed the worksheet, discuss what you've learned with several trusted advisors.

Creative Dilemma

- My creative dilemma is:

Exploration and Discovery

The following contexts may influence how I respond to my creative dilemma:

- What are the characteristics/trends of these contexts?
- What are important implications of these characteristics/trends to my creative dilemma?
- What might be ways I could experiment with new contexts or new ways of responding to my contexts?

Integration

- What new possibilities may emerge for me as a result of understanding and playing with my contexts?

Chapter 8

Embracing Uncertainty

*Painting is damned difficult—you always think
you've got it, but you haven't.*

—PAUL CÉZANNE

ystery, suspense, and the unknown have always captured
the human imagination. But that does not mean we are
comfortable with uncertainty in our day-to-day lives.
We do not mind if the mystery and the unknown come
to us under controlled circumstances such as in books, movies, or even
in our religious experiences. But when it comes to the way we live
each day, most of us prefer the predictable and the familiar. We don't
like chaos or uncertainty. We long for stability in our finances, careers,
family life, relationships, and so on. But life rarely cooperates. Things
may settle down in one area of our life, only to destabilize in some
other area. As legendary singer-songwriter John Lennon's words
suggest, "Life is what happens to you while you're busy making
other plans."[1]

Like it or not, life is uncertain. Navigating life's changes requires
that we cultivate the skill of embracing uncertainty. Embracing uncertainty involves *acting on the opportunities, sometimes hidden, presented by
change and uncertainty.* When embracing uncertainty, we:

---

1. John Lennon (1940–1980), "Beautiful Boy."

- understand that constant change and uncertainty is a source of creative insight rather than an impediment to it.
- do not try to impose premature solutions.
- allow opportunities for change to unfold even though we do not have all the information we wish we had.
- actively seek opportunities in fluid situations.
- adapt approaches in midstream to help us move forward.

We live with constant change. We do not know when it will come or what form it will take. The question is not "How do I stop the many uncertainties from entering my life?" but rather "How do I navigate uncertainty in my life?" The beginning of the answer lies in reframing our basic attitude. Instead of looking at uncertainty as something to be eliminated or endured, we need to embrace it. When we embrace uncertainty, we agree to stop trying to manage it away; rather, we allow ourselves to "sit" with it, and eventually to trust that hidden treasures will bubble to the surface. Uncertainty affects our perceptions about "who we are" in three main areas:

- Our emotions
- Our bodies
- Our thoughts and language

Emotionally, we may feel confused and inadequate. Physically, we may feel stressed, bored, or fatigued. Intellectually, we may find that we have trouble finding words to express where we are and what we are going through. When we are in transition, the way we have described ourselves up to that point may no longer ring true or feel adequate. Our journey may even outpace the way some people describe us. In the previous chapter, Sandy Johnson's friends and former colleagues kept referring to her as a "former executive." They understandably had not adapted to her new self-professed identity as "Bubbie." In other situations we may be the ones who have difficulty in

coming up with a new language to express our identity. That is uncertainty at play. We know we are no longer who we were, but we do
not know who we will yet become. Yet as Ron Medved discovered,
despite the turmoil uncertainty may cause, it is an essential source of
creative life change.

Life Without X's and O's

How long can a professional football player live without a playbook?
How long can a fish live out of water? According to Ron Medved, it's
a lot longer than you think, even when there seems no end to the
uncertainty. But then again, it depends on what you mean by "living."
Not that many kids get to live their dream of becoming a professional
athlete. But Ron was driven. He embodied intensity, focus, and fierce
competitiveness—so much so that even his father worried about what
he saw in his son. He didn't like the hard edge. He didn't like it when
Ron called himself an "assassin." Ron, however, wore the rubric with
a sense of pride. He wore it when he played for the PAC 10 Conference in college, and he wore it for the Philadelphia Eagles.

That pride and hard work earned Ron five years in the National
Football League as a defensive back. He was never a star and he had to
earn his position every year. But he was tough, undergoing knee surgery
and then ankle surgery in his five years, until one day it happened—just
as in the movies. The team manager came up to him in the locker room
and said, "Coach wants to see you and bring your playbook." Just like
that. It was over. Now he was a fish out of water, a football player without the playbook's X's and O's to guide his next move.

Ron didn't realize that for the previous five years he had been
in denial. He had refused to admit that a professional football player's
career was brief. In those rare moments when he had contemplated
the end of his playing days, he assumed he would leave the game with
dignity and a sense of pride. He would make a smooth transition

into a meaningful long-term career. Instead, the end came suddenly and harshly. Now Ron was angry. He was in pain—physically and emotionally.

Ron was in denial about something else as well. He had become addicted to amphetamines. His addiction grew out of the need to stay driven and deal with the residual pain of his past injuries. His addiction intensified as the emotional pain joined hands with the physical pain. His football career was over and he had no real idea of what would come next.

Soon after he hung up his jersey, Ron went alone to the New Jersey shore for a long weekend. He was distraught about his future. The thunderstorms that rolled in from the sea seemed to parallel his own inner turmoil. He felt scared and depressed. He had seen other athletes leave the game and wallow in self-pity, bumping around without direction. Surrounded by uncertainty, Ron now wondered whether he would share their fate. Though angry and confused, Ron determined he would take a different path. He might not know what he really wanted to do, but he *did* know it would not involve living a life feeling sorry for himself.

During the football off-season, Ron had tried his hand as a stockbroker. So he now wondered whether he should pursue a financial career more seriously. While he had met with some success, he knew almost immediately that this was not his passion. Being a stockbroker was not who he really was. It certainly helped put bread on the table, but it bore no resemblance to how he thought of himself inside. The problem was he had no idea of exactly what could make him happy now.

Ron's life began to spiral out of control. His addiction worsened, and six months after he left football, he suffered a serious emotional breakdown. He hit rock bottom. He had to acknowledge he was an addict. He had to admit that his image of himself as a strong, competitive athlete who was "bulletproof" was a sham. He was, in fact, an angry person who felt betrayed by the game he had dedicated himself to. When the game was no longer available to him, he was adrift in ways he couldn't have imagined. He was afraid. Doctors now gave him other drugs to get through the day. Psychotherapy helped somewhat, but he still felt totally alone, wounded. He looked in the mirror and couldn't recognize the image staring back. He was flying blind. And he was not a very good navigator. He knew he had to begin at the beginning.

Ron began to read voraciously—philosophy, psychology, history, and religion. He began to keep a journal and write poetry. He even returned to sports for the first time, playing racquetball and basketball. As he learned to play for pleasure, his intense competitiveness seemed to melt away, and he found the pure physical movement therapeutic. He allowed himself to enter into the realm of "being lost" as part of a larger journey. He hoped to develop newly discovered navigational instincts. Ron began to think of himself as "working at the soul level." The further he traveled into this unknown territory, the more interested he became in "making the biggest transition I could make." He began to talk to others who were seekers and thinkers. In the process, he also reconnected with some of his youthful instincts, remembering the satisfaction he used to feel when he had the opportunity to make even a small difference in someone's life.

Still actively seeking, Ron moved with his family back to his hometown of Seattle. As he felt himself starting to grow into his change, Ron made contact with the Pacific Institute. The institute was founded in 1971 in Seattle with the vision of working with organizations all over the world in the area of performance improvement, professional growth, change management, and leadership development. Ron was impressed by the institute's belief in people's unlimited capacity for growth, change, and creativity. What could be more aligned with his personal journey? Ron joined the institute as project director five years after leaving professional football.

Helping organizations make deep change seemed the perfect context for facilitating his own growth and healing. Ron came to see life as a constant flow of transitions through uncertainty. Yet there was a price to pay. As he felt himself changing inside, he and his wife grew apart and divorced. After several years he left the Pacific Institute to set up his own shop as an independent consultant and then returned to the institute seven years later in a senior management position. He remarried. And so it has gone.

But it is at the deeper level, the "soul level," that the real transitions have occurred. What has sustained Ron is the recognition that there are crises at every stage in one's life. He now knows that we are not defined by our crises but by how we respond to them. Ron's story demonstrates the importance of "unlearning" what we thought was true but personal experience teaches us is not. We may not yet arrive at what is true, but unlearning helps us molt older, false assumptions about ourselves and our world. Ron had to unlearn the meaning of the term "tough" he had acquired while a professional athlete in order to allow himself to feel vulnerable and go deep. Unlearning may intensify our uncertainty, but it is necessary to go there and embrace it in order to come out stronger, wiser, and ready for the next dilemma. The external life of our crises is available for all to see. But Ron will tell you that it is within the private recesses of our soul that the real battles are fought, where the pain and fears cut deepest, and where the real healing and growth take place. Ron had to learn how to embrace uncertainty. In his words: "It's where the playing field is at its widest and there are no X's and O's to tell you where to go—that's where the real action is." And it was here that Ron finally found his new happiness.

Ron lived his life in the tradition of the great artists. Once he embraced the uncertainty in his life as a new starting point, he became a self-described "seeker" and found a new direction. In important ways, this makes Ron and Leonardo da Vinci soul mates.

Painter of Uncertainty

Many consider the *Mona Lisa* the greatest painting of all time. It certainly has been seen by more people than any other painting in history.

A certain aspect of the painting is familiar to us: that enigmatic Mona Lisa smile. Books, commentaries, research, and even movies have been inspired by her smile. Or is it really a smile? Perhaps it is a smirk? Perhaps it is saying, "I know something about you but you really do not know much about me"? Does she hold a secret she is not sharing? Is she coy? Smug? Comforting or judging? Is she simple or wise? What does she know? What is she hiding? Is she standoffish or inviting? Is this a painting about a particular woman, or is it a painting about women in general? The questions go on, the answers uncertain. If we look more closely at how Leonardo painted the portrait we learn that he employed a particular technique called sfumato. Sfumato literally means "going up in smoke." In painting, sfumato refers to the hazy, smokelike effect created on the canvas, where objects are rendered with

Leonardo da Vinci, *Mona Lisa*, c. 1505

a kind of fuzziness. There is an absence of sharpness or clarity to them. We can see how Leonardo used the sfumato technique for Mona Lisa's background. The trees, the water, and the general landscape appear hazy. As in many of his paintings, Leonardo is a master of technique and hidden clues. He loves conundrums. In the *Mona Lisa* he is playing both the master artist and the master magician. Through his rendering of the mysterious smile and his use of sfumato, he gives us a painting of ultimate ambiguity. It is as though he were saying, "Life is filled with uncertainty." And he has turned not only Mona Lisa but uncertainty itself into the subject of his painting. Like Ron Medved, Leonardo tells us that uncertainty is at the core of our lives. Embracing uncertainty then becomes a critical step on the road to self-insight.

Strategies for Embracing Uncertainty

Right now you may be thinking, "Embracing uncertainty sounds like a nice concept, but how do I actually *do* it?" How did Ron and Leonardo da Vinci actually embrace uncertainty and convert life's ambiguities into sources of creative insight? When life seems composed of so many moving parts, when the future seems so murky, when answers are so elusive, what do life change artists and the great artists actually do that can help us better make our way through the sfumato of our lives? Turns out, both use two important strategies for embracing uncertainty: *grounding* and *mindful floating*. As you'll see, grounding and mindful floating are in some ways opposites. Grounding techniques keep us centered, so we can float without floating away. Mindful floating gives us the tools to let go of the familiar and calmly explore the space between the "what was" and the "what will be" in our lives.

Grounding

Grounding refers to any number of techniques that we can use to feel solid and stable in the midst of uncertainty. Though we may not know the future, and though everything around us may seem "up in the air," grounding activities help us to stay in the present, keep our feet "on the ground." When we ground ourselves, we remind ourselves that though our roles and social identity may be in flux, there is an essential self that is unchanging and secure. Grounding has been used for centuries across many cultures as a way of centering individuals caught in the cross-currents of change and uncertainty in their lives. In Eastern spiritual traditions, grounding is often understood as being connected to earth energy. Traditional Indian medicine identifies seven energy centers, or "chakras," one of which is Muladhara, or root chakra. This energy center is believed to be located in the lowest part of our torso, in the genital area. It is traditionally related to security and survival. On the other hand, traditional Japanese spiritual practice identifies three energy centers, or "haras." The lower hara is believed to be located about three inches below the navel and deep within the abdomen. The lower hara is thought to contain earth energy that is "grounding," i.e., a source of stability and security. And when we examine the lives of great artists as well as contemporary life change artists, we find that all of them had their own way of centering themselves and relied on some form of grounding as part of their creative work. When the world seems to be spinning in many directions at once or even when our everyday environment holds no immediate answers, grounding provides a tool to steady ourselves and refresh our perspective.

The Power of a Mantra

When her husband of thirty years died of a brain tumor, Ronni Wadler looked toward the future with "something akin to terror." Ironically,

Scott had been a brilliant oncologist, and as painful as it was to watch him lose his mental acuity and emotional sensitivity over the two and a half years of his illness, Ronni at least felt that they were on the terrible journey together. Now that he was gone, she had to face the terror alone.

For Ronni, everything seemed to be up in the air. She felt extremely anxious about an uncertain future and the myriad decisions she would have to make on her own. The questions started coming, fast and furious: Should she stay in the house in the New York area or sell it? Where should she move? Her two children lived in Los Angeles, but her dear sister and her mother-in-law, to whom she had become very close, lived in New York. Would she have enough money or would she need to work? She had developed an interior decorating business over the past several years, but if she moved to L.A. to be near her kids, how could she start the business all over? What furniture should she keep and what should she sell? All this "noise" overwhelmed her. While Scott was dying, she could postpone decisions. Now they were upon her and she did not have Scott to help her sort through them. The only thing she had to hold on to was the memory of Scott's "quiet confidence." But even that memory seemed inadequate in his absence.

Then, serendipitously, Ronni came across the headline of a magazine article that read "Cultivating Quiet Confidence." The headline jolted her. Ronni instantly recognized it as the very quality in Scott that provided her with a sense of hope. She cut out the article and made dozens of copies. She taped the title of the article on everything: the refrigerator, the mirror in her bathroom, the car dashboard, the bookshelves. She carried a clipping in her wallet. She surrounded herself with the words "Cultivating Quiet Confidence." "It became my mantra," she says. "It had such a calming effect on me. It helped me breathe deeper. I had never done yoga before, or meditation, or anything like that, but I am a worrier and I had all these unanswered questions about my life. This mantra acted like a stand-in for Scott's quiet confidence. It actually gave me confidence that I would get through it one step at a time. It *centered me and calmed me* and gave me perspective." The mantra helped her realize that "I was much more capable than I ever knew."

Little Rituals amid the Big Questions

While Ronni grounded herself using a random headline that she adopted as her mantra, Pamela Morgan ironed napkins as a way to manage the uncertainties that surrounded her imminent death. At first, Pam thought the back pains were simply a pulled muscle. When the diagnosis came that she had pancreatic cancer, she and her family understood that everything had suddenly changed. In some strange way a kind of certainty had entered her life in the form of a terminal diagnosis. She did not deny it or resist it. Yet within this new certainty her life is now filled with uncertainties. What kind of day will I have today? How bad will the pain be? Will I have energy? How can I be sure my two sons will be okay? How will my husband manage the house when I am no longer here? What can I get done today? Will I be calm or will I start yelling at my family? Will I be able to plant a few flowers today? All these uncertainties!

And so she turns to ironing napkins. A soft, peaceful smile comes over her face at the prospect. Her head tilts toward the kitchen and her eyes widen. This is something over which she has some control. There is a beginning, a middle, and an end. She feels a sense of accomplishment. Not like the bigger questions such as the meaning of it all, or why me, or the big social issues of the day, which never seem to end. When she irons the napkins after she washes them she is allowing herself to float. She knows who she is. She understands her condition. She, the iron, the napkins, beginning, middle, end. From this perspective she senses the various undercurrents running through her life, her household, and her relationships. There is a calming rhythm to the simple task. It is familiar and reassuring and gives her the strength to face the bigger uncertainties in her life. She has reached a kind of wisdom, an acknowledgment like the one Paul Cézanne came to later in his life: "Painting is damned difficult—you always think you've got it but you haven't." Only Pam would substitute the word "life" for the word "painting." She understands what it means to be a life change artist. She has no illusions. Ironing the napkins offers order where there is none, something concrete to hold on to when she can see the abyss. She aims to iron them well, as she aims to live well amid the big and little uncertainties.

The great artists were also masters of grounding. Many of the preparation techniques discussed in Chapter 5 are also a way to ground ourselves. The preparation rituals used by the great artists worked on two interconnected levels: they helped free the mind of habitual ways of seeing, and at the same time, they accessed a reservoir of energy that kept them focused on their work while enmeshed in ambiguity. When de Kooning biked to Louse Point on Long Island and back, he was grounding himself. Pumping his legs and feeling the road vibrate through his body cleared his head and kept him focused. Georgia O'Keeffe's lengthy walks around Taos, New Mexico, infused her with the sense of the earth that was so essential to her paintings. Leonardo's meditative states helped him turn uncertainty into sources of creative problem-solving.

But grounding in isolation won't allow us to fully embrace uncertainty. For that, we need the complementary technique of *mindful floating.*

Floating Toward a Whole New Orientation

Mindful floating is a form of surrender to the inescapability of uncertainty. Mindful floating acknowledges the uncertainty surrounding the unknown by saying, *"I do not have immediate answers. I allow the uncertainty to be."* When engaged in mindful floating, we suspend self-judgment. We allow ourselves not to be tough on ourselves. We don't force a premature resolution to our situation; rather, we allow ourselves to follow the current, emotionally and intellectually. Imagine we were to find ourselves in the deep sea, where there is no bottom on which to secure our footing, and no land in sight, and the ocean undulating beneath us. If we fought that reality we would exhaust ourselves and not last very long. Most of us might follow the natural impulse to start swimming in a particular direction. Yet how would we know we were headed in the right direction? If we wanted to survive in that situation, there are things we would need to *stop* doing: We would stop trying to reach for the ocean floor. We would resist swimming frantically in random directions. Instead we would learn how to float.

But mindful floating is more than simply floating. It is, as the term suggests, intentional. When we learn to float *mindfully,* we use our body/mind to tune in to different things. We adopt a sensing mode. By contrast, when we react to a situation by immediately thrashing about for direction, we ask certain kinds of questions: Am I headed in the right direction? How long can I keep this up? Will I survive? When we are floating mindfully, we do not so much ask questions as tune in to the undercurrents, the ups and downs of the ocean swelling and receding, undulating. We pick up subtle changes such as the water temperature. We look skyward and notice the direction of the sun or moon and stars. We realize we can use the ocean's undercurrents to husband our energy and nature's reference points to identify possible directions. We are moving in tune with nature, not against it.

Henri Matisse and Willem de Kooning employed mindful floating as a specific technique in their painting process. Old films show Matisse literally holding his paintbrush above the canvas without touching the painting's surface. His hand guides the brush in circular motions above, trying to pick up the rhythm of the painting, rehearsing certain strokes before he commits his brush to the painting. De Kooning would stand some distance from a painting, staring for long periods of time, taking it in, then lifting his brush in mock strokes before bringing it in a deliberate yet energetic commitment to the canvas. They engaged in this mindful floating as part of the creative process. They understood the importance of this in-between time. Their art is an aggregation of creative choices they made in the uncertain space between what came before and what they were trying to create.

Mindful floating, though, does not mean being passive. Rather, it means we assume a different perspective from which to view the various parts of our lives. We see the uncertainty not as an obstacle, but as a source of new information. Mindful floating, then, is not only a tool for embracing uncertainty, but a tool that enables the creative skill of *seeing*. We begin to understand that the elements of our new life are all out there. We simply need to find a new way to make sense of them before we rearrange them. When we float in the open seas we become alert to the underlying currents. And so with the currents in our own lives. Floating mindfully helps us access information that can help us decide in which direction we want to swim. And so our ability to embrace the unknown in a mindful way opens our eyes to new perspectives about the directions we might take.

Of course it is not easy to surrender to the uncertainty in our lives. We have been programmed to resolve problems as quickly as possible. To tackle them head-on. We grow impatient with ourselves and our circumstances. Sometimes we internalize this into a sense of inadequacy or failure. Such impulses, while understandable, lead to missteps. The great risk in conditions of uncertainty is that we lose perspective or act prematurely. Even the great artists sometimes succumbed to the hazards of uncertainty.

Finding Treasure in the Garbage Heap of Uncertainty

"I work out of doubt," claimed Willem de Kooning, the great twentieth-century Abstract Expressionist painter. But despite de Kooning's claim, doubt can be exhausting. And doubt once led him to throw away one

of the most revolutionary paintings of the last century. Only the inter-
vention of a friend helped him recover this discarded treasure.

When de Kooning initially pinned a large blank canvas on his
studio wall in June 1950, he did not realize that it would preoccupy
him for two full years, before he finally threw it out in utter frustration. The painting landed on a heap of old newspapers and junk in his
back hall, ready for the dumpster. De Kooning had struggled with the
painting that would later be named *Woman I*. He wanted it to be too
many things. He slathered on paint, scraped it off. He overlaid charcoal drawing and plastered newspaper over it to keep the oil paint wet
until the next day, when he ripped the paper away and began his
struggle again. When he reached a point of being stuck he would go
on long walks, often in the wee hours of the night, to regain his perspective and fortify himself for his next go-around. When we look at
the painting today, it is gouged and scraped. You get the feeling that
he left parts of his own flesh on the canvas. Clearly de Kooning was
not floating. He was fighting. And in despair he threw it on the garbage heap on the landing of the back stairs to his studio, believing he
had failed.

The painting remained there for several months until an art-critic
acquaintance showed up at his studio unannounced. As luck would
have it, the critic came up the back stairs and noticed the painting in
the pile. He stopped to study the work in progress, and then told de
Kooning how impressed he was with it. They began to discuss it. De
Kooning became reenergized by the critic's fresh perspective and with
renewed energy finished the painting in a short period of time. Today
that painting (shown on the following page) hangs in the Museum of
Modern Art in New York.[2]

De Kooning's experience is a lesson less in failure than in human-
ness. Even the great artists need an outside perspective to regain their

---

2. Mark Stevens and Annalyn Swan, *De Kooning: An American Master* (New York: Alfred A. Knopf, 2004),
pp. 309–31.

Willem de Kooning, *Woman I*, 1950–1952

footing during times of struggle and uncertainty. The lesson is not in
the way de Kooning succumbed to the frustration but in the way he
opened himself to a different perspective. He acknowledged his judgment had become mired in his daily struggle with the painting. He
acknowledged he was not yet comfortable with the new visual language
he was trying to create in the painting. In that sense, de Kooning was
no different from the rest of us. We often succumb to everydayness and
to the weight of uncertainty that accompanies it. Our impulse may be
to give up, or to get down on ourselves because we have not yet found
a new language with which to express ourselves. But if we engage in
mindful floating, and the new ways of seeing that accompany our floating, we will soon be rewarded in our search for more vital, creative,
and fulfilling pathways.

EXERCISES

1. Grounding Exercise

- Sit comfortably in a chair or on the floor. If you are sitting in a chair, make sure your legs are uncrossed and your feet are planted solidly on the floor.

- Now begin breathing deeply and slowly. Breathe in through your nose, taking your breath all the way down into the center of your belly. Feel the breath travel all the way down to your core.

- As you exhale, imagine your breath leaving through your skin everywhere on your body, and feel your breath continue to move out into the space around you.

- Repeat this deep, slow breathing for five to ten minutes, each time taking your breath all the way down into your abdomen, and breathing out through your skin.

- If you become distracted by thoughts or worries, just allow them to gently move away, focusing completely on your breathing.

- You may also want to play some soft, quiet music that you find to be relaxing.

- When you have completed the deep breathing, take a minute to record feelings or images you may have experienced, and note how you are feeling at this moment following the grounding session.

2. Mindful Floating Exercise

- Place a single raisin in your hand. Take full notice of it. Turn it on its sides and look at the variations in color, texture, shape. Put it to your nose and breathe it in. Consider its smell. What do you notice through these engagements with seeing, touching, and smelling that you might not have noticed previously?

- Now gently place the raisin on your tongue, and then bring it to the roof of your mouth. Feel its skin, its dryness and moistness. Allow the taste to linger in your mouth. Feel the texture change as the raisin moistens in your mouth. Inhale its smell. Does it smell different from when it sat in your hand? Does it have one taste or several? How would you describe the combined sensations of taste and smell? What else do you notice that is going on with you?

- Now slowly, deliberately begin to chew on the raisin. What does your tongue feel? Your teeth feel? What is happening in your nasal passage? How would you describe the taste, feel, and smell of the raisin? What does it sound like?

- As you swallow the raisin, continue to tune in to your experience of the raisin and what is going on with you. What lingers? What changes?

- The better we become at tuning in to the moment with this heightened awareness, the better we are at mindful floating, embracing uncertainty and discovering many things we were not previously aware of, even in such a commonplace thing as a raisin.

Chapter 9

Risk Taking

I've been absolutely terrified every moment of my life—and I've never let it keep me from doing a single thing I wanted to do.

—GEORGIA O'KEEFFE

L ife is by nature a risky business. In life, we take risks all the time, even when we think we are not. Consider the challenge we face when we recognize a creative dilemma: Do I confront my creative dilemma and begin the journey of exploration and discovery, or do I stand pat, continue to hold the tension and avoid change? If we ignore our creative dilemma, we accept the risks that come with staying on the same path. Standing pat is a choice that may seem less risky, but which often over time causes even greater tension and pain. When we refuse to confront our creative dilemma, we also take the risk that events beyond our control will force some kind of unwanted change upon us.

Risk is a defining element throughout the life change process. During exploration, we voluntarily wade into uncharted waters, where the risks and rewards of what we will discover are unknown. And when we engage in integration—assuming a new or expanded identity—we accept all the risks of committing ourselves to a new path. In this chapter, you will discover how great artists approached risk taking and how you can use risk taking to make optimal choices as you navigate the journey of personal reinvention. Risk taking means *acting without certainty of outcome*. When taking risks, we:

- believe in the importance of moving in a different direction, even when the path is unclear.
- decide to do what seems right for us, despite possible negative consequences.
- manage the emotions (e.g., fear or anxiety) that could interfere with taking action (courage).
- take action even when others doubt us.
- convert mistakes into opportunities to learn.

Risky Choices

In our daily lives, risk taking is not an abstract concept. Rather, risks are associated with specific choices we are considering. For example, if I decide I want to sail across the Atlantic, a host of risks come into my mind: What will happen if I get sick far from medical help, or bad weather damages the boat, or I can't make it back home in time for the birth of my grandchild? Life change artists must confront five categories of risk:

- Financial Risk—Will I have enough money?
- Competence Risk—Can I develop the skills and perform the tasks required by my new direction?
- Social Risk—What will others think?
- Identity Risk—Will I be able to adopt a new identity with which I feel secure and which fits?
- Relational Risk—Will my family, friends, and significant others give me permission to make the changes I seek?

We can never know the answers to these questions before we make a choice. It's healthy to ask questions about potential risks. But in some cases, we use questions about risk as an excuse for inaction. We may create a towering list of so many risks, both plausible and improbable, that our courage collapses under the sheer weight of them all. In many instances it is easier to "awfulize" an imagined result than to take the steps necessary to understand and manage the risks toward a positive outcome. The risks of life change are inescapable, but they are worth it. When we embrace the uncertainties that surround life choices, and take action despite those uncertainties, we will be rewarded with a life that is truly ours.

The Matissean Vow

For the great artists, taking risks is essential to their creative process. Artistic innovators take risks every day on their canvases. Describing his working method, the contemporary master Francis Bacon offered: "I'm always trying to disrupt [the painting]. Half my painting activity is disrupting what I can do with ease."[1] Bacon did this by literally throwing paint onto the canvas with his hand, not knowing how it would land and what it will do to the images previously and safely rendered. More important, he viewed risk taking as a form of artistic growth. Without risk his art would have become stale, because he would have repeated "what I can do with ease."

Every great artist experiments with and pushes the artistic medium. Every great artist plays with techniques and searches out new ones. Every great artist does so without knowing the outcome ahead of time. In his later years, in a letter to his daughter, Henri Matisse made a powerful observation about himself and the sculptor Maillol: "What harmed Maillol a good deal as a sculptor is that he so often called a halt as soon as his work reached a *satisfactory stage*. And what has helped me a lot is pushing on beyond that point, in spite of the

---

1. David Sylvester, *Interviews with Francis Bacon* (New York: Thames & Hudson, 1975), p. 91.

high risk."[2] On the canvas, Matisse sought not simply the "satisfactory," but the unique, beyond satisfactory. He always pushed toward masterpiece. This was the Matissean Vow he made to himself, knowing full well he risked not only failure on the canvas, but emotional stress as well.

Many great artists took enormous risks, not just in their creative work, but in other areas of their lives, too. Recall Matisse's decision to abandon the traditional, lucrative style of his early paintings in order to venture into an innovative and sometimes misunderstood approach to his work. Of all the great artists who took great risks in their lives as well as their art, there is perhaps none who more fully embodies the many forms of risk than German artist Käthe Kollwitz (1867–1945).

Until the Last Small Twig . . .

Early in her life Käthe Kollwitz envisioned herself as a painter. But after becoming captivated by the printmaking of Max Klinger, Germany's preeminent printmaker of the day, she began to explore lithography and printmaking as possible artistic mediums. She was especially taken by Klinger's realistic dramatization of contemporary life. Kollwitz saw the great potential for this form of "democratic" art to capture the great social issues of the day, in particular the plight of the underclass and working poor.[3] Kollwitz found herself confronted by an early creative dilemma. Should she continue to pursue her aspirations to become a painter, or should she turn in the direction of printmaking and its potential to chronicle social conditions in Germany? As "democratic" art forms, printmaking and lithography were generally rendered in small pieces rather than the larger sizes of traditional painting canvases so the works would be more affordable for the pub-

---

2. Hilary Spurling, *Matisse the Master* (New York: Alfred A. Knopf, 2005), p. 302.
3. Carl Zigrosser, *Käthe Kollwitz* (New York: George Braziller, 1951), pp. 7–8.

lic to purchase. Kollwitz's commitment to making her art available to a greater number of people led her to limit the prices she charged for her work.

Kollwitz was also aware that the subject she chose for her art risked alienating her from the art establishment. In 1894, she began work on a remarkable series of prints inspired by Gerhart Hauptmann's 1893 play *The Weavers*, which dramatized the 1840 revolt of Silesian weavers. The six-print series, also titled *The Weavers*, was nominated for a gold medal. Kaiser Wilhelm II vetoed the award, however; he feared that art with such provocative social content might lead to unrest. The Kaiser referred to Kollwitz's work as "gutter art."

Kollwitz's art came under attack from an even greater political scourge nearly thirty-three years later. When Hitler and the National Socialists rose to power, they declared her work to be "degenerate art" and barred it from display or sale. But Nazi attempts at intimidation did not deter Kollwitz. She maintained relationships with Jewish students, friends, and colleagues. When the great German Jewish artist Max Liebermann died, she was one of only four non-Jews to attend

Käthe Kollwitz, *The Weavers*, 1897

his funeral. Ironically, Liebermann had sat on the jury that proposed she be awarded the gold medal for her *Weavers* series.

Kollwitz was a voice against war. The Gestapo visited her in her home and threatened deportation to a concentration camp. Toward the end of the war, Germany came under heavy bombardment and Kollwitz's political situation remained tenuous. American friends pleaded with her to come to the United States. But she refused, believing she belonged in Germany. She remained unbowed. As her 1938 self-portrait shows, Kollwitz bore her age and unyielding commitment with quiet determination. In the etching she is not so much exiting to the right as she is stepping toward the unknown future with the same courage she had displayed throughout her life. This etching was

Käthe Kollwitz, *Self-Portrait*, 1938

her last self-portrait. She died on April 22, 1945, just sixteen days before Germany surrendered.

Throughout her life, Kollwitz accepted risk for herself, and she
counseled others about its importance to the creative process. In a letter to one of her master students, she advised: "If you want to swim,
you must jump into the water." And later, she insisted, "Give yourself
free rein! Risk more. Demand always more from yourself."[4]

Embedded in Kollwitz's art and her life story are not only lessons
related to risk, but a core question we must all ask ourselves. It's a
question that precedes risk taking. It is a simple yet powerful question:
Is it worth it? Is the risk I am about to take worth the time, effort, and
potential cost of taking the risk? Kollwitz had answered the question
for herself. In one of her letters, she wrote: "I do not want to die . . .
until I have faithfully made the most of my talent and cultivated the
seed that was placed in me, until the last small twig has grown."

Looking through the rearview mirror at how others took risks may
lead us to think that it was not as hard for them as it would be for us.
"They are different," we may say. "I could never do what they did."
Even those who take significant risks may claim, "I had no choice," after
the fact. But everyone can choose whether or not to risk. That is the
essence of the creative dilemma. The question is not whether we have
a choice about taking a risk. The real question is: How do we manage
the anxieties surrounding the choice in a way that allows us to step into
the risk?

A Komodo Dragon
in Business Clothing

Jenna Fletcher had always been on the achievement track. Earning an
MBA was part of the natural progression of things, as were regular

---

4. Mina C. Klein and H. Arthur Klein, *Käthe Kollwitz; Life in Art* (New York: Holt, Rinehart and
Winston, 1972), p. 145.

corporate promotions and running an annual marathon. Despite this outward success, Jenna couldn't let go of a nagging feeling. It was as though there was an undertow pulling her down. She couldn't quite put her finger on what it was about, but she felt it nonetheless. As she began to pay attention to this sensation, she grew more and more dissatisfied with her current work. It wasn't bad work and she liked the people she worked with, but she felt it simply "wasn't her." It did not represent her passion. Jenna kept thinking about an experience she had had with her grandmother a number of years earlier. They traveled together to Africa and Jenna had been amazed to learn that there were really two kinds of vultures—ones with big beaks for picking at the flesh of dead animals and ones with finer beaks for picking what remained from the bones. This grim reality struck her as a metaphor for "how perfect nature is. What a marvel it is!" Remembering this experience reinforced an interest in nature that she traced all the way back to her childhood love of animals. She began to take biology classes and wondered if she should pursue veterinary medicine. The answers did not come readily, even though she had concluded she would leave the corporate world. That work no longer represented her authentic passion. She had saved enough money to buy some time. So at the age of forty, she "stepped off the cliff." She left her secure corporate job and "reset my identity to zero." "Who am I really?" she asked.

But there was something else at risk besides her identity. Her husband had misgivings. He did not want her to go to veterinary school. As Jenna began to pursue her interests in biology and the environment, marital differences also came to the surface. And once Jenna left her executive position, her relationship with her husband entered deep and unsettling waters. They were no longer economic equals. The imbalance produced other cracks in the relationship. They argued about where to go for vacations. They had different ideas about how to spend their money. They had different ideas about roles within the marriage. As her husband rose within the corporate world, he expected her to "take care of the errands."

In the midst of this turmoil, Jenna's grandmother passed away. The grief tore at her. Her grandmother had been such a meaningful part of Jenna's journey, and her love of nature such an inspiration. After all, it was nature to which Jenna kept returning. In a fateful last act, Jenna's grandmother left Jenna a small amount of money. To honor her grandmother's memory, Jenna used it to participate in a month-long scientific expedition to Indonesia with the Earthwatch Institute. She kept a journal, taking notes and drawing pictures. She became captivated by the Komodo dragon, reaffirming her love of animals. When she met someone on the trip who was a conservation biologist, she sensed a new pathway opening up for her. Could this be who she was meant to be? Could this be her new identity? Was this the under-ground passion that had been tugging at her all these years? She thought so. Yet a whole set of new risks seemed to flood her airwaves. Can I be good at this? Is this who I really am? Do I go into fieldwork or policy work? How do I know which is the right choice?

Upon her return, Jenna enrolled in a master's program in environ-mental studies at the state university and wrote her thesis on urban wetlands. Her first job, with the Minnesota Forest Resources Council, came a week after she graduated. She's excited about the risks she has taken to get to where she is today: "I'm an environmentalist in business clothes! I do policy. Although sometimes I think I'm an impostor. I mean, I'm in my mid-forties and I've only been at it a short time." Despite these occasional unsettling feelings, Jenna knows she has found her calling. When asked how she knows, she simply replies, "I am being authentically me. That's worth an awful lot." And when asked how she had the courage to choose to leave her well-paying corporate job, she responds: "What choice? I had no choice. It was either pursue my passion or live a slow dying." Jenna realized that the price for choosing not to pursue her passion might be higher than the potential cost of pursuing it. Of course, she could not have known that for sure beforehand. That is the essence of risk. But that belief gave her the emotional fortitude to make the choice she made.

Jenna has answered the "Is it worth it?" question. But not without cost. Her marriage did not survive. She draws comfort from her conviction that she has chosen the right path for herself. The upside of risk has been that she got to ask the fundamental questions again: Who am I, really, and what do I want to do? Trying to respond to these questions has been "exhilarating and scary." In fact, her life change has helped ease her through the divorce because it allowed her to get in touch with her authentic self. It allowed her to deal with the "sadness and grief" of a failed marriage and the loss of her grandmother. Her take: "Sometimes you need the dark in order to appreciate the light."

New light has come into Jenna's life. She has remarried and moved to Stillwater, Minnesota, where she takes long walks with her dog along the Mississippi River, just downstream from where the river comes into being.

The Limits of Logic

Taking risks cannot be reduced to a perfectly logical, analytical process—pros on one side, cons on the other. Even if it could, we still would not be spared the emotional stickiness of it all. Our skill at taking risks depends in part on how we answer some important questions about our emotional makeup: How well do I manage my emotions? What is my level of personal confidence? How strong is my conviction that I need to make changes? How dependent am I on other people's opinions? How do I handle uncertainty? What is my level of resilience? How have I handled disappointments in the past? The way we answer these questions provides clues about whether we will be able to forge ahead despite the inevitable twists and hairpin turns in the road. We each bring our own unique emotional filter to the challenge. Developing an awareness of how that filter works is a first step in facing the risks inherent in our creative dilemmas.

Both Jenna's and Kollwitz's ways of confronting risk suggest that emotional factors may outweigh what appear to be practical factors. What value do we place on emotional fulfillment versus financial considerations? How much importance do we place on living with a sense of purpose against being able to wear an important-sounding title? What is our tolerance for possibly looking foolish as we explore new paths to growth? How important is it for us to meet others' expectations of us versus listening to our inner voice singing, "This isn't all there is." As we'll see in Dan Trujillo's story, emotions can freeze us into inaction. They can also free us to move in a new direction when it might seem more logical to stay where we are.

The Choices One Makes

The nightmares persisted longer than Dan would like to remember. *He's down at the end of a dock in Brooklyn. Something is moving toward him. He does not know what it is but it is ominous, threatening. He has nowhere to turn. He's trapped.* Dan didn't think his life would turn out this way. Not when he was a Marine Corps company commander in Vietnam. Back then he was faced with some hard choices in combat and he believes much of his character was formed there. He knows there were times he chose not to fire when others chose otherwise. He also observed quiet and unreported acts of heroism by others that made a deep impression on him. He believes he ultimately drew on the strength of such grit to prevent his own self-destruction.

After the war, Dan entered the tire distribution and trucking business and spent the next two decades climbing the corporate ladder. He made a decent living, had a solid marriage, and raised a girl and two boys. Yet things were not all right inside. He did not believe the way he earned a living provided much opportunity to express the things he wanted to say. He made furtive attempts at writing poetry, but a sense of obligation to provide for his family kept him in the business.

He was not even sure what else he wanted to do, nor was he willing to explore some possibilities. He wasn't ready to risk the stability he had managed to create for his family for an unknown future. That's when the nightmares began. These were followed by a living nightmare. Dan's oldest son was killed in an industrial accident. Dan sank into a deep depression. It was as though the very air had been sucked out of him. He lost his energy. He was surrounded by confusion and nightmares. He quit the tire business without any clear direction. He sought therapy for five years as he wrestled with the sense of guilt over his son's death. In order to make ends meet he delivered newspapers in the early morning and started a tire brokerage business on his own. But when that didn't work out, he was forced to reenter the corporate environment.

Dan now feared that the "ember was dying out completely." Between the death of his son and an unfulfilling job, he wondered whether "there had been things inside that weren't there anymore." Finally, at age fifty-four, Dan decided not to let his son's death rob his own life of meaning. There was still time, Dan thought, to honor his son's short life by creating a new one of his own. He was finally ready to take a risk. For those who did not know Dan, his decision to enter a master's program in English Literature at his age might have appeared odd. But for Dan it made perfect sense. He wanted to develop the courage to express what was inside him, and what could be better suited to that than literature. He needed to reconnect with and release those early longings to express himself. He felt a palpable fear of reentering the classroom after so many years. But he refused to let that stop him. And once he began the program, despite his initial unease, he felt as though a burden had been lifted and he had stepped into the daylight. He loved the world of ideas. He rediscovered that he did have something to say. The fire rekindled.

By chance, Dan's son-in-law told him that a local college was interested in hiring someone to teach a summer adult learning course. Dan felt a great deal of trepidation over the opportunity. He had never taught before. What if he was not a good teacher? Could he take the humiliation? Just because everyone was encouraging him to go for it did not mean he could do it. Something inside, though, was reconnecting him with what he had been through in Vietnam. He knew he had acted courageously in time of war. He had done the right thing then. Wasn't this also about doing the right thing? Having the courage to face down self-doubt? Dan applied for and got the teaching job. In the classroom, his initial anxiety turned into enthusiasm. He was asked to return and he taught English literature part-time for several years.

While teaching, Dan continued to work at the trucking company. But a few years later the company was sold and he was offered the opportunity to stay or to take a severance package. A moment of truth had arrived. By then Dan's finances were marginal. He had no money in the bank. But he knew that despite the substantial risks, even without a job alternative, he had to take the leap. He spoke to his family. He had to do the right thing. They told him to go for it.

The moment he made the decision, Dan's sense of self-worth surged. For so long he had been burdened by the belief that he had made mostly the wrong choices in his life. But this time he knew he wanted to teach. He knew this was what he was called to do. This couldn't be a wrong choice because he would be given the chance to say all those things that had been held inside for so long. The following year he applied to teach and coach football at a local high school. He got the job, and he still teaches there today. Among the classes he teaches is a yearlong course on the Vietnam era. The course is about choices one makes in life. For those who know Dan, there is very little surprise that there's a waiting list to get in.

Dan Trujillo managed to deny his creative dilemma for decades and thereby avoided taking any obvious risks. That denial ended up being the riskiest of all his choices because the price turned out to be steep indeed. Fortunately, Dan eventually summoned the resources to take the first of many risks he would face over the ensuing years. His first steps into an unknown future felt clumsy. But each new risk better prepared him for the following one. His decision to enroll in a master's program exposed him to the fear of looking foolish and out of place in the classroom after so many years away. His decision to take the severance package without having an alternative lined up felt right, but he had no idea how it would work out. And when he applied for the high school teaching position he risked rejection and embarrassment. But having risked before and landed on his feet, he slowly built the confidence to risk again. At a certain point Dan felt firmly on a path. He had direction. Then it was a matter of not turning back. When Dan is in the classroom talking about the choices we face, he has a lot of empathy to spread around. It's likely he's been there.

When Chocolate Calls

Five years ago, Barbra Vogel was on the high road to success in the New York world of children's publishing, when, as she tells it, "I completely ran out of gas." She walked into her boss's office and told him she was leaving. When he asked her about her plans, she said, "I have no clue." She thought that a woman who had just turned fifty should have a better answer. But she didn't. "I just stepped off the cliff," she says. "Not quite the mature thing to do!"

What followed were "euphoric days and terrifying nights." Had she jumped too soon? It's as though the idea came to her, and then suddenly she was in her boss's office saying see you later. Had her self-confidence outstripped her judgment? She had some cash, but she certainly wasn't financially independent. She had to earn money. So she began consulting for small businesses to get her over the hump. This experience reinforced her interest in running her own small business. She liked the idea of being her own boss and setting her own rhythm. She had originally trained as a cartographer many years earlier and had always enjoyed work that combined using both hands and head. She liked the blend of science and creativity, "left and right brain stuff."

What surprised her, though, was the way she came to a decision about her future. When the idea of opening a chocolate shop crystallized, it was "more like a 'duh' than an 'aha!'" Several years earlier she had visited her sister and brother-in-law in Wisconsin and spent a couple of days in their chocolate shop. She was fascinated by how they spent their days, from creating the candies to working with customers. She loved the way they controlled the direction of the business. Now, several years later, she recalled how her father and grandfather had sold livestock at auction for a living. She came to realize that being an entrepreneur was "in my DNA." Chocolate had been under her very nose all along and entrepreneurship pulsing through her very veins.

Barbra's transition from corporate executive to owner of an artisan chocolate shop has not been easy. At the outset she had worried that the financial risk would be her biggest challenge. She is making much less money. But she has also "crossed over to the light." She has simplified her life, the kinds of clothes she buys, the car she drives. She acknowledges she has traveled a kind of emotional U curve. When people used to ask her what she did, she "spoke with a different voice, a different power, a different identity." She was a successful corporate executive and her voice reflected the confidence that went along with the position. During her transition she struggled to find a new voice. "I went from taking the corporate limo to taking out the garbage." But now that she is doing what she loves, she can claim, "I have become who I wanted to be, who I hoped I would be." Now her voice is both strong and knowing.

In many ways Barbra has come home to herself. On one side of her transition journey she saw risks. They could have short-circuited her decision to confront her creative dilemma. The risks could have killed her appetite for stepping into the realm of unknown outcomes. But now that she is on the other side of those risks, she thinks they were more like windows into future possibilities. It's almost as though she could smell the chocolate all along.

The Two Lives of Risk

The stories of Käthe Kollwitz, Jenna Fletcher, Dan Trujillo, and Barbra Vogel suggest that risk plays itself out on two different planes—one above the surface and the other below the surface. Above the surface are the public facts that form a narrative for all to see. We leave a job, we enroll in a class, we get retrained or get certified in a new field, we apply for a new job or start a business. Or we sell our house and move to a different part of the country. Or perhaps we get divorced. Or we join a support group. Events like these make up our public narrative, and all involve risk. But risk has a below-the-surface life as well. It is a life of fear and uncertainty and self-doubt and passion and authenticity and aspiration—all less visible than the public narrative but far more powerful in shaping the choices that can be seen above the surface. "Euphoric days and terrifying nights," Barbra Vogel tells us. Dan Trujillo feared the "ember was dying out completely." And Jenna Fletcher had to "reset my identity to zero." These below-the-surface lives were for them alone to see.

Successful risk taking means being willing to accept those "terrifying nights" while our public and private selves take the time they need to realign with each other. For the life change artist, risk taking is the skill that ultimately enables us to create synergy between our above-the-surface and below-the-surface narratives. It is the ability to weave these two planes together so they are telling the same story. It is the ability to align our public narrative with the best aspirations we hold below the surface. Risk taking is fundamentally about doing whatever is necessary to live our lives in wholeness with our best selves.

In some sense the creative skill of taking risks takes as its mantra the *Matissean Vow*: "I will not settle for 'satisfactory.'" Ironically, risk leads us in a direction we have not been in before while at the same time acknowledging all the reasons we believe we should not go there.

The risk-taking skill includes the ability to hold countervailing impulses without compromising action. Risk taking therefore works hand in hand with embracing uncertainty. Embracing uncertainty speaks to our attitude toward *current* conditions while risk taking launches us into an undetermined *future* reality. The better we become at embracing ambiguity, the easier it will be to step into that unknown future.

Managing Risk

Our first reaction to risk taking is to ask the "Is it worth it?" question. This question raises all those negative possibilities, all those potentially awful outcomes. And so we often close down our inquiry and continue our lives uninterrupted and unfulfilled. Suddenly quitting your job, as Barbra Vogel did, is not for everyone—maybe not for most of us. But there are ways to think about potential risks that make it easier for us to handle our anxiety about stepping into uncharted territory.

A key to managing risk is to find ways to first identify the specific risks and then to make them smaller so they do not seem overwhelming. The nature of risk is such that we will never know for certain the outcome, no matter how concrete and small we make the risks. We can, however, do two things that prepare us for risk taking. First, by converting bigger risks into a series of smaller risks we reduce the potential costs if the risk we take does not work out the way we hope. Second, since risk-taking is a skill, that means we can get better at it by practicing it, and the best way to practice risk taking is to experiment with taking smaller risks.

An example of this can be seen in the situation Donna Singer found herself in. As a member of a business development group facilitated by coauthor Fred, Donna wrestled with a creative dilemma that confronts many sole practitioners. Do I take on clients regardless of which industry they come from or do I focus on a niche market I really enjoy and go deep with it? Donna was no rookie. She had been a management consultant for over twenty years, and if busyness were an indicator of success, then Donna was madly successful. But she was being pulled in too many directions and she could hardly keep her head above water. She was mentally and physically exhausted. Her greatest risk related to the potential loss of income if she turned down clients who did not fit her preferred area of focus. This was too large a leap for Donna to take. So she decided to go smaller and easier before going larger and harder. She conducted interviews with clients in her specialty, asking for their help and perspective on her prospective move. She even asked clients who did not fall into her specialty sweet spot how they would feel about her refocusing her efforts. As a result, she came away with ideas on how to make the transition, including ways in which her clients both inside and outside her specialty could act as sources of help. Today, Donna focuses on clients in her specialty, and because of her growing reputation in that area, she is in the enviable position of turning down work.

As Donna Singer's experiences demonstrate, taking smaller, more manageable risks before taking on larger, harder ones prepares us for the larger leaps. This method for managing risks keeps fear at bay while we evaluate the parameters of the risks associated with a potential life choice. Dan Trujillo, for instance, experimented with teaching before leaving his "day job." Look at the body of work of many of the great artists and you will see evidence of many incremental changes in their style. Often they took small risks by way of getting used to operating in a never-ending climate of risk. Later, they were able to take monumental leaps. Such was the case with Matisse. It was only after he had experimented bit by bit with a lighter, more colorful palette in the late 1890s and early years of the twentieth century that he took the revolutionary leap to the wild colors of Fauvism. Without taking the smaller risks, Matisse might never have developed the boldness to take more substantial and meaningful chances. The artists teach us that taking risks helps us learn to take other risks. Like any other skill, if we practice risk taking we will get better and better at it over time. We may never willingly jump out of a plane, but we *will* experience the exhilaration that comes with taking on the risks of a more rewarding life.

EXERCISES

1. Interview a Risk Taker

Who do you know that you admire for their ability to take risks in their life—and thrive? Set up some time to talk to them regarding their ideas and experiences on taking risks. Here are some questions you could ask:

- What's your attitude toward taking risks?
- Tell me about a big risk you took that had a positive result. What did you learn from that experience?
- Tell me about a big risk you took that had a negative result. What did you learn from that experience?

Exploring Risks

- Create a two-week plan of small risks that you will take, one for each day. Choose risks that will not jeopardize your health, safety, or basic well-being.

  Example:

Day	Risk	Why It's Risky
Monday	Apologize to my significant other for losing my temper the other night.	I'll have to admit I was wrong; he may hold it over me later.
Tuesday	Dress more (or less) casually at work.	Maybe people will think I don't look right.

Wednesday	Go to a tai chi class.	I may feel uncomfortable and won't know what I'm doing.
Thursday	Say hello to the woman I see in the elevator every day.	She may think I'm flirting with her.
Friday	Serve guests a meal that I've never cooked before.	It might not be "perfect" and I might be embarrassed.

- As soon as possible after taking each risk, use your sketchbook to reflect on your experience. What happened? How did you feel? What might you do differently?

- At the end of two weeks, record your thoughts related to all the risks you have taken. What have you discovered about risk taking from these deliberate experiments in risk?

- To what extent did you notice that you were using other creative skills, such as seeing or embracing uncertainty, to help you take a risk?

- How might your experience with these scheduled risks affect the way you deal with the risks you face in any change dimension, such as exploration?

Risk Reflection

- Consider a creative dilemma you are facing at the moment. What is your dilemma?

- Consider how you might tackle it in the most exciting, interesting, and innovative ways you can imagine. Don't censor yourself in any way. Don't let the "shoulds" and "should nots" come into play. Don't allow "practical" to rear its head. Don't worry about "the right" solution. Simply allow yourself to play and imagine! Write and

doodle in your sketchbook all the ideas and images that come
to mind.

- Now identify where you think the risks are, and fully imagine the
  impact of those risks. What do you fear might happen? What is
  your worst-case scenario if you were to move forward with your
  ideas?

- Now decide which of the risks you've identified is the smallest.
  What could you do to manage the smallest risk?

- Now decide which risk is second smallest. What could you do to
  manage this risk?

- Continue until you've thought about strategies for managing all the
  risks you've identified.

- Now that you've thought through options for managing risks,
  record your thoughts and feelings about how and whether to
  proceed with the ideas you have for responding to your creative
  dilemma.

Chapter 10

Collaboration

Braque would look back on cubism and see it as a mountaineering expedition: he and Picasso roped together, establishing precious footholds as they scaled uncharted heights.

—JOHN RICHARDSON,
A Life of Picasso, 1907–1917

Unlike the other creative skills, collaboration *requires* involvement with other people. The contribution of collaboration to any creative process has been vastly underestimated. For instance, many of us imagine the great artists as intense individualists on a lonely quest for creative expression. Their ideas, we imagine, burst forth from a solitary battle with their creative genius. Intense individualists, yes. But solitary and alone? Nothing could be further from the truth. The great artists were consummate collaborators who relied on collaborative relationships, communities, and mentors to feed their thirst for new ideas, techniques, and sources of inspiration. The great artists not only understood and appreciated the exchange of ideas with other artists, but actively sought them out.

Collaboration is not just a creative skill but a precondition for sustainable life change. Collaboration acts as the combustion chamber of creativity. It fires, forges, and tempers creative ideas. Collaboration means *engaging with others to help us make desired change*. When collaborating, we:

- believe we can make better life choices by collaborating with others than we could on our own.
- actively seek out others engaged in their own life change for mutual support.
- are willing to build on others' ideas, even if they don't match our preconceptions of what is right.
- share ideas with others.
- rely on a group of trusted advisors to help us think through strategies for life change.

There are three major forms of creative collaboration: working relationships, collaborative communities, and mentors and coaches. Each of these modes of collaboration offers unique and critical contributions to the creative process and to life change. And each can be transformative—both to the individuals who collaborate and to their shared work.

Working Relationships

Collaborative relationships are intentional working interactions between two or more individuals working on a shared endeavor or project.

In many ways, Pablo Picasso (1881–1973) and Georges Braque (1882–1963) could not have had more different personalities. Picasso was an intense, intuitive, and often unpredictable Andalusian from Spain. Braque, from Le Havre, France, was more deliberate, shy, and contemplative. Over the years, Picasso developed the reputation of a highly egotistical prodigy playing out his creative drama on the world stage. Braque, on the other hand, was an unassuming man who settled in Normandy after World War I and dedicated himself to the quiet pursuit of his art. But when this unlikely pair began working together in 1907, their magical collaboration revolutionized modern art. Not only did they exchange ideas, but they would regularly visit each other's studios. At some point they began putting brushstrokes on each other's paintings. It got to the point where Picasso acknowledged that his work was never done until Braque said it was done, and Braque agreed that his work was not finished until Picasso told him it was complete. Braque claimed that he and Picasso were like two mountain climbers roped together as they ascended the mountain of creative expression.[1]

Which Painting Is by Picasso, and Which Is by Braque?

Working together, Braque and Picasso invented Cubism, which is generally regarded as the beginning of modern art. Cubism is based on the idea of showing a subject from many different viewpoints. In the process of developing this new art form, Picasso and Braque worked so closely together that it is difficult for the untrained eye to tell their paintings apart at this point in their development. The Picasso–Braque collaboration was intentional, and it belies the myth that creativity is primarily an individual process. Several elements characterized their working relationship. First, they were very different in background and temperament, yet they respected each other's thought processes and skills. Braque needed privacy and shied away from public visibility. Picasso was highly verbal and let his opinions be known to whoever would listen. Second, their collaboration focused on both the specific techniques of their craft and the grand ideas that informed their application. Their collaborative innovations emerged through the integration of high-level ideas and detailed technical experimentation. For instance, Braque taught Picasso how to grind pigment. He showed Picasso how to incorporate stenciling into his paintings. Picasso's imagination introduced novel subjects such as brothels and African masks as well as geometric renderings that became the foundation of Cubism. Picasso and Braque did not start out with the intention of

1. John Richardson, *A Life of Picasso* (New York: Random House, 1996), p. 59.

Georges Braque, *Le Portugais*   Pablo Picasso, *The Accordionist*, 1911
(*The Emigrant*), 1911

creating Cubism. They simply played with each other's techniques and perspectives. "We had no intention whatever of inventing Cubism," Picasso claimed. "We simply wanted to express what was in us."[2] Third, each artist was open to improvisation and play, even if the ideas originated from the other. Personal style was less important than substance. What mattered most to Picasso and Braque was the quest for a different kind of art, a new mode of expression. Yet their collaboration did not end there. They also began to explore the possibilities of composing art through the technique of pasting various materials onto pictures or other material. Through this experimentation they invented the art form of "collage," which comes from the French word *coller*, meaning "to paste" or "to stick." Today, collage is a widespread and popular art form. Would collage have been invented had Picasso and Braque not collaborated? Would Cubism? Who came up

---

2. Ibid., p. 105.

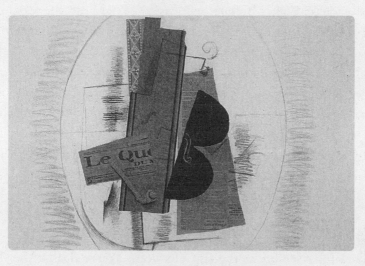

Georges Braque, *Violin and Pipe*, 1913

Pablo Picasso, *Guitar, Sheet Music,*
and Wine Glass, 1912

with the ideas? Was it Braque or Picasso? Where did the ideas come from? How did they each respond to the other's ideas? We really don't know the answers to these questions. What we do know is that as a result of their collaboration, new art forms came into being. For life change artists the lesson is in the nature of the collaborative interaction, where the outcome is greater than the sum of its parts. Just as a new art form can be brought to life through collaboration, so can a new life direction or new life possibilities. And so it was with Jamie Gaviser.

A Caring Presence

Some folks see life as the flip of a coin. You're dealt either heads or tails, and you need to learn to live with it. For Jamie Gaviser, the flip of the coin came up both heads and tails, and through an unexpected collaboration led to a life change drawn from both sides of the coin. Jamie practiced plastic surgery for twenty-seven years. He was also a patient for each of those twenty-seven years. He lived both sides of the coin. While a medical student in his early twenties, Jamie was diagnosed with an abnormal kidney function. Over the years, the condition deteriorated until renal failure required that he undergo a kidney transplant. The procedure itself went smoothly but his body reacted with a string of negative side effects over a period of thirteen years. When the kidney ultimately failed, Jamie's son provided him with a new transplant. The fit went well. But several years later, Jamie had a stroke and went through extensive rehab. It was a time of deep soul searching as he reflected on what would come next for him.

Jamie knew he could not practice surgery any longer. But he cared deeply about the practice of medicine and especially about the experience of the patient in the hospital setting. He had always been an advocate for patient-centered medicine. Having lived both sides of the coin, he believed there was a significant gap in hospital care between the needs of the patient for a meaningful and empathetic relationship and the way medical care was delivered. Physicians no longer had the time to devote to building a relationship with the patient. Technology advances, for all their positives, only further depersonalized the medical care experience. Jamie's idea was to bring together retired physicians to offer a "caring presence" to patients.

That's when Jamie unexpectedly met Sharon Mertz, a former nurse manager at a major hospital. "We were very different," Jamie acknowledged, "but what we eventually came up with would never have been as successful if Sharon and I had not worked together." Jamie and Sharon were different in terms of background, training, and the way they related to patients. "She is more touchy. I'm more talky," Jamie observed. But they "were philosophically aligned" in their intention to provide a different kind of experience for patients. Together they recruited and trained twenty-five retired physicians and nurses. The initiative did not go flawlessly. Practicing physicians and nurses expressed concern that involving retired volunteers would complicate their patient relationships or even potentially undermine them. But when Jamie and Sharon approached the active health care professionals as collaborators, they were able to develop lines of communication that led to greater coordination. "We did a lot of listening," Jamie said. And they adapted. Today, the volunteer nurses and physicians are accepted and appreciated by hospital physicians. Requests for the caring presence of retired health care volunteers come directly from nurses and physicians, as well as from patients and family members. Since Jamie and Sharon began the program, they have noticed that practicing physicians in the hospital are paying closer attention to the patient relationship. As a result of the program, hospital evaluations for responsiveness to patient needs and their comfort have noticeably improved. Jamie has received requests from other hospitals to introduce the program into their settings.

We might ask the same questions of Jamie and Sharon that we asked of Picasso and Braque. What made the collaboration work? Where did the specific ideas come from? How did they respond to each other's ideas? Would the program have worked without the collaboration? Did Jamie begin the project with a fully developed skill set related to collaboration or did he develop it over time? Jamie gives us a few clues. He says the differences between him and his nurse-partner Sharon "melted away" as they worked together. While he acknowledged they were different, he also says with much appreciation that "I have learned much from her." In many ways, Jamie put his finger on the essential dynamics of collaborative relationships: the opportunity to learn from each other and openness to the ideas, experiences, and perspectives of the other. Collaboration is the respectful give-and-take of ideas, experimentation, and flexibility. It is the recognition that "my" idea is only a beginning point, not an ending point. Jamie acknowledged he has gotten better at collaborating through his relationship with Sharon. Jamie notes that collaboration rests on a belief that the best, most creative solutions come from "working together, listening to each other, and suspending what you thought you knew." On the artist's canvas it may lead to Cubism and collage. In the field of medicine it has led to the innovative practice of a caring presence.

Not only did the collaborative relationship between Jamie and Sharon help make their program more successful, it eased Jamie's life change from a practicing surgeon and recently recovered stroke patient to a fully engaged and productive life change artist. The collaboration skill, then, has multiple applications and can serve many intentions. In Jamie's case, learning to collaborate effectively led to an important technical innovation in patient care. But collaboration also was the linchpin that led Jamie into a fulfilling new life.

Collaborative Communities

Collaborative communities are groups of individuals who come together for a shared purpose, with shared values, vision, and mission in support of one another. Members do not necessarily need to work directly with one another as they do in a direct working relationship.

When one is in a direct working relationship with another, ideas can come accidentally as well as methodically, as they did with Picasso and Braque and Gaviser and Mertz. While creating the technique of collage, Braque and Picasso were quite deliberate regarding their trials and errors. So, too, Gaviser and Mertz were deliberate in experimenting with different elements of their hospital care model. Much like collaborative relationships, collaborative communities accelerate the creativity of their members. Sometimes this occurs intentionally, and at other times the existence of the community creates the conditions for unexpected or serendipitous events that foster innovation and change. Such was the case when a group of mischievous boys roamed through a park outside Paris in 1864 and started a scuffle with a twenty-three-year-old aspiring but unknown artist by the name of Auguste Renoir.

A shoving match followed when an older man with a limp and a cane came to his rescue. Renoir was surprised to discover his rescuer was none other than Narcisse Virgilio Díaz de la Peña, a well-known landscape painter. Díaz de la Peña and Renoir befriended each other and spent many days painting side by side that summer. Díaz de la Peña, thirty-four years Renoir's senior, admonished him for using dark, "tobacco juice" colors in his paintings. In response, Renoir lightened his palette and introduced bold color combinations. When Renoir showed his brightened paintings to Alfred Sisley, a member of the emerging Impressionist community, he was greeted with mockery—"Trees blue and the ground purple! Are you crazy?" But then others within the Impressionist group quickly adopted his more colorful palette. And when Renoir later painted side by side with Monet, "the father of Impressionism," he influenced Monet himself to lighten his color palette.

Impressionism, perhaps one of the most notable Western artistic movement, was fueled by encounters such as that between Renoir and Díaz de la Peña. But without the presence of a collaborative community of artists to spread new ideas, Díaz de la Peña's insights about color might never have gone beyond Renoir's canvas. It was not simply the collaborative relationship between Díaz de la Peña and Renoir that helped shift the way several painters of that era used color, but the existence of a collaborative community of painters who were dissatisfied with the current state of painting that led to the Impressionist revolution.[3] This small group of dedicated painters—Claude Monet, Auguste Renoir, Frédéric Bazille, and Alfred Sisley—regularly gathered at the Café Guerbois in Paris to banter about ideas related to art and painting. The conversation often became heated, and disagreements were passionately aired. The group was soon joined by Camille Pissarro, Édouard Manet, and Edgar Degas. Paul Cézanne regularly showed up. Unfortunately, Berthe Morisot, considered a key member of the Impressionist circle, did not attend, because of the less than savory reputation of the café setting of the era. But Morisot's mother was famously social and welcomed these artists to her "friendly and unpretentious Tuesday dinners,"[4] where new ideas and trends were discussed. Together, these artists form a virtual pantheon of Impressionist painting. During the day they would often break up into pairs and paint side by side. Monet painted with Cézanne. Pissarro with Cézanne. Pissarro with Renoir. Morisot with Monet. Cassatt with Degas. In fact, Mary Cassatt worked so closely with Edgar Degas that in her famous *Little Girl in a Blue Armchair* (1878), she painted the girl and the dog, and Degas painted the entire background.

It was during these daytime painting duets that ideas discussed in the café or in the Morisots' drawing room were translated into experiments on canvas. But the collaborative community of the Impressionists had an impact that went far beyond these immediate works on canvas. It revolutionized Western art. The Impressionist community of the nineteenth century facilitated the rapid dissemination of important knowledge—new techniques, new material, new ideas—thereby

---

3. Michael P. Farrell, *Collaborative Circles: Friendship Dynamics & Creative Work* (Chicago: University of Chicago Press, 2001), p. 35.
4. Anne Higonnet, *Berthe Morisot* (New York: Harper & Row, 1990), p. 24.

accelerating the pace of artistic innovation and change. The existence of their community created the conditions by which Renoir and Díaz de la Peña's random encounter and subsequent relationship became transformed into teachable techniques and ideas for the entire Impressionist movement. Had it not been for the Impressionist community, the encounter between Renoir and Díaz de la Peña might have been a quaint but isolated tale. The existence of the Impressionist community assured that ideas learned by one of its members would receive the attention of the many, thereby adding fuel to the prairie fire of change. The Impressionist community also served as a base of influence to introduce change into the broader environment. Impressionism changed art forever, not because of the work of a single artist, but because of the dedication of a community of artists who pooled their resources, talents, and commitment to mount a series of exhibitions as an alternative to the Salons, the official exhibition outlets of the day. The series of eight exhibits between 1873 and 1886 grew in influence until Impressionism had become the dominant art movement of its time. It also made art ownership more accessible to the growing middle class by stimulating rapid growth in the number of galleries where "nontraditional" paintings could be viewed and purchased. Ultimately the vibrant world of the galleries made the insular Salon system obsolete. The Impressionist circle also was influential in opening the elite École des Beaux-Arts to women students in 1897. Impressionist painters such as Berthe Morisot and Mary Cassatt demonstrated that women could and should be taken seriously as artists.

The Impressionist circle also provided what may be the most important role collaborative communities play—emotional support. Creative expression always pushes the envelope. It pushes against the status quo, and invariably the status quo pushes back. But each of the members helped the others. Every artist and every life change artist encounters doubts. Everyone on a creative journey gets thrown off balance or knocked down from time to time. A collaborative community provides encouragement and a sense of connection to something greater

Mary Cassatt, *Little Girl in a Blue Armchair*, 1878

than oneself. Members are surrounded by fellow travelers taking the same risks and encountering the same doubts. Without a collaborative community to support her, Mary Oestereicher Hamill, whom we will meet below, might never have made her improbable career change.

If Crutches and Rubber Gloves Could Scream

How does one make the journey at age fifty-five from an academic with absolutely no formal art training to an internationally recognized installation artist? Not easily, Mary Oestereicher Hamill will tell you. And with a great deal of help. Mary launched her professional life working in the field of mental health policy. But when she bumped up against the entrenched bureaucracy of state and federal government, she decided to pursue a Ph.D. in psychology. She then led an effort that yielded major policy changes for the treatment of mentally disadvantaged students. After that, she taught at Brooklyn College and then went on to shape large-scale curriculum reform as a dean at Babson University. Over the years in academia, Mary had become highly effective at navigating the politics of higher education. But then something strange happened on the way to a faculty forum.

Mary's mother became ill and nearly died because of a misdiagnosis and improper treatment. Her condition required her to remain in the hospital for seven months. Mary found herself overtaken by anger and frustration and for the first time in her life felt powerless. All her academic training and verbal abilities were inadequate to serve her need to express profound feelings of anger and vexation. Words simply could not convey the immediacy of her feelings. She began picking up odds and ends from the hospital. Plastic gloves, wooden throat sticks, gauze pads, crutches, X-rays. She began to create visual images from the material she collected in the hospital. She had no idea where this artistic urge came from. She had had no prior "intimations." Yet she found great power in the images she was creating. "If crutches and rubber gloves could scream, this is what they would express," she told herself. She showed her first visual work, entitled *Constructs of Frailty*, made up entirely of hospital material, at a conference for health care professionals. The response was visceral and powerful. Mary immediately saw the opportunity to create powerful interactive experiences that could act as a platform for social and institutional change. She sensed another path was opening up for her. It all seemed so clear. Except for the uneasiness.

Uneasiness can act as forcefully as gravity in holding us down. There was a great deal that Mary did not know. She did not know how to translate the feelings and ideas roiling inside her into visual experiences for others. She knew nothing about the technical aspects of making art. She wondered whether she was too old to enroll in art classes and be surrounded by "a bunch of nineteen-year-olds." In academia, words act as the coin of the realm, but in art, it's all about the visual experience. Was she too old to learn this new language?

Mary believes two sources helped her step into this uneasiness. First, she came from a large Catholic family. Six brothers and sisters. "We had our own subculture," she observes, "with parents who expected us to do well and to achieve." Mary admits she came out of this subculture with a high level of willfulness. There was an under-current of belief that she could accomplish what she set her mind to. In her own words, she was "mission driven." And up until this mo-ment her history seemed to validate this belief. She had successfully made several transitions—from student to professional, from working woman to Ph.D. candidate, from Ph.D. to policy activist, from policy activist to professor, from tenured professor to academic dean—and each transition followed a kind of template for accomplishment. The template was there. She had used it several times. Yet this transition seemed different. It required more than ideas and words to be success-ful. This new enterprise of making art used an entirely different lan-guage with different sensibilities and skills. Old templates and ancient history weren't enough. She needed practical support in the here and now. And this is where the second source of support came in.

Mary had been one of the original members of the Women's Studies Research Center at Brandeis University, a community of pro-fessionals steeped in the traditions of the arts, activism, and scholar-ship. Her initial association with the center grew out of her academic work. But now everything was shifting. The impulse to create art knocked up against her lack of training; her academic role knocked up against her need to express herself in an entirely new way.

To complicate things further, Mary's personal life seemed to par-allel her inner turmoil. She was caring for her ill mom and at the same time she had the major responsibility for her two sons. And so it was to the members of the center that Mary turned for support and active collaboration. Being part of this collaborative community enabled her to cope with the experience of attending the Museum of Fine Arts advanced certificate program "with all those nineteen-year-olds." When a visiting instructor from New York who reviewed her early work told her to "go back where you came from," she drew on the community to stay focused. The center consisted of other women pursuing individual academic and research interests. Yet they indi-vidually and collectively represented a kind of home for Mary. A safe place she could go to and share her aspirations and her anxieties. She would spend time with members of the center, exchanging ideas, and in return they encouraged her to take the bold step of making a major shift in her work and means of expression.

Members of the center also acted as a powerful network of resources. In one of Mary's early projects she needed someone to collaborate directly with her to create the musical composition that would accompany a major installation project. It was from the ranks of the women at the center that the composer Ruth Lomon stepped forward and wrote the music for *regarddisregard*, an award-winning multimedia installation about the homeless in Cambridge, Massachusetts. "When my world was turning upside down," Mary recalls, "the center gave me the gift of time and space and the people. They nurtured me." Today, she and members of the center continue to collaborate.

Mary's installations have been displayed in museums around the world. In addition to her work *regarddisregard*, she has created collaborative works such as *Constructs of Frailty*—inspired by her hospital experience with her mother—and *Aged in China*, in which she documents the threatened life of *hutong* (traditional Chinese neighborhood) residents of Beijing. Since she now travels a great deal, she has sold her house and moved into an apartment. In fact, she rents places in New York and California. But the collaborative community at the Brandeis Women's Studies Research Center remains her true professional home.

Mentors and Coaches

A mentor is a trusted guide, someone with experience and wisdom who can advise and encourage you along the path. The word "mentor" comes from the name of the person the Greek hero Odysseus entrusted to educate his son Telamachus during his years of absence fighting the Trojan wars.

One of the less known heroes of the Impressionist movement was Camille Pissarro. Pissarro had neither the bold, larger-than-life per-

Camille Pissarro, *Self-Portrait*, 1873

sonality of Claude Monet, nor the cranky single-mindedness of Paul Cézanne. But he was nine years older than Cézanne, ten years older than Monet, eleven years older than Berthe Morisot and Auguste Renoir, and they all considered him an artistic father figure.[5] They came to him for advice and he offered it generously. He always seemed to be there when times got tough. He is credited with transforming Cézanne from an unruly experimenter into a disciplined artist who harnessed his imagination in the service of his painting.[6] He consoled Monet and encouraged him to continue his efforts even during a time when sales of his work were far and few between. Younger artists looked to Pissarro for his disciplined commitment and understanding of their dilemmas. When the Impressionist exhibitions were threat-

---

5. Sue Roe, *The Private Lives of the Impressionists* (New York: Harper Perennial, 2006), p. 261.
6. Ibid, p. 110.

ened, he remained the most steadfast in helping to move the work forward.

What makes the mentor interaction collaborative is the two-way nature of the relationship. Problems are presented, approaches discussed, solutions suggested, and learning incorporated through the open exchange of ideas and experiences. Full disclosure occurs. Ideas and emotions surface. Vulnerabilities are expressed and honored. The mentor is committed to the success of the person being mentored. The person being mentored respects the experience of the mentor. But both understand that the decisions made and the paths taken emerge from the mutual listening and perspectives of both parties.

Without mentors, Jeffrey Carron might still be nestled in a prestigious home in the Hollywood Hills and living the life of a successful Hollywood entertainer—never realizing what he had missed.

Who Would Have Thunk It?

When Jeff Carron moved in his early twenties from Brooklyn to Hollywood, he had no idea he would meet with the kind of success he did. Though he had always loved music and singing, and he would often sing with a group on weekends, he had started his work life teaching elementary school in the tough Bedford Stuyvesant area of Brooklyn. After several years, though, he felt a yearning to try something different. Shortly after arriving in Los Angeles, he started a band and began entertaining at private parties. Over the next twenty years his band's reputation grew to the point that he performed for the likes of Merv Griffin, Michael Douglas, George Burns, Jane Fonda, and the Sultan of Brunei. He had purchased a large home in the Hollywood Hills and adopted a young daughter. Life was good and so was his reputation.

But then everything began to change. A small group planning to start a new synagogue asked Jeff to act as cantor for the Yom Kippur services in their new spiritual home. Jeff barely knew how to read

Hebrew, and he certainly did not know the prayers or melodies. Besides, he was totally ambivalent about the God business. He told the new rabbi he simply wasn't the right person for the job. But when Jeffrey visited his mother back in Brooklyn, she scolded him: "You said no to a rabbi!" As much as he wanted to please his mother, Jeff feared the prospect of getting ready in only a few months to sing melodies he did not know. But the rabbi would not give up so easily. He told Jeff that with his reputation he would draw people to the synagogue, and so would be doing a *mitzvah*, a good deed. The rabbi encouraged Jeff to speak to a couple of other cantors who would teach him the prayers and coach him on how to perform as a cantor. Reluctantly, Jeff came around. He agreed to perform.

For the next few months, under the tutelage of the other cantors, Jeffrey dedicated himself to learning the melodies and prayers, often staying up until two a.m. to practice. When Yom Kippur came and the chosen moment approached for Jeff to step up to the podium and chant the prayers, he was overcome by "something beyond fear." He had to go into the rabbi's study to gather himself. He found himself "telling God I really needed help." But his nerves refused to calm down even as he stepped up to the podium. He white-knuckled his hands tightly on the sides of the lectern, and just before he began to sing, he suddenly felt "an electric shock like I never felt before or since." And then he was singing. "Before I was done I knew this wouldn't be the end of it." Jeff returned as guest cantor once a month. The following year his chanting at the synagogue increased to twice a month.

Jeff began studying the liturgy more seriously and "asking the really big questions." He found great support and encouragement from others in the spiritual community. But the more he studied, the "more petrified" he became. He realized he knew almost nothing, and yet he felt powerfully drawn to the liturgy and the spiritual dimensions of the music. For the next several years he continued to take classes and sing for the congregation. One day the dean of his graduate program asked him, "So tell me why you are not going to rabbinic school?" Jeff burst out, "I'm too old! I'm forty-six! I don't know anything!" To which the dean calmly responded, "I will write the recommendation."

These simple words belied a much more meaningful role the dean had played in Jeff's development. He had guided him academically. He had provided emotional support and reassurance. And when the dean sensed the time was right, he acted as a catalyst. The dean understood from deep and broad experience the challenging journey of becoming a rabbi. He also knew Jeff's family situation. Yet he also saw the great potential in Jeff. When he said, "I will write the recommendation," he was using a kind of shorthand to express his faith in Jeff's potential as a rabbi.

Jeff was thrown into a quandary. His adopted daughter was eleven years old. He had a thriving music entertainment business. He had a four-thousand-square-foot house in the Hollywood Hills. And all he had to do was make a decision that would involve selling his business, his home, and uprooting his daughter in order to move to Israel for several years. Practicality led him in one direction. A sense of calling led him down a different path. He knew he had become a different person since feeling that electric shock the first time he chanted the Yom Kippur melodies five years earlier. He was no longer the person represented by the large house and the high-visibility business. He had begun to ask people to call him Jeffrey instead of Jeff. It was his way of acknowledging the demarcation between his older, more publicly lived self and the emerging spiritual self. Jeffrey also appreciated the paradox of his life. What appeared to be impractical was, in fact, the most practical thing he could do. Choosing to become a rabbi may be inconvenient in the short term, but such a step would put him in a position to touch the lives of others in ways that only his unique gifts and perspective could make possible.

Within a few weeks, Jeffrey sold his house and his entertainment business and put his furnishings in storage. As anguished as this decision had been, he had not realized what he had stepped into. At the Hebrew Union Seminary in Israel, he was surrounded by younger students. Their life references were different. Their approaches to their studies was different. For Jeffrey, time was short. He had a sense of urgency. His emotions had an intensity that was sometimes difficult to fully understand. To his good fortune, he was able to turn to the head of the seminary. He encouraged Jeffrey. "He saw something in me I didn't see in myself. I was focused on how my age put me at a disadvantage. I had this emotional edginess. He looked at my age and experience and saw depth and a reservoir of compassion. He made all the difference. He gave me perspective when I really needed it." After several years at the Hebrew Union Seminary in Israel, he returned to California as an ordained rabbi.

Jeffrey made one final change to his name. Today he is known as Rabbi Yossi Carron. He rents an apartment. He sings at different congregations. His daughter recently graduated from college. But his great work of service is as a chaplain in the prisons. He has found his calling in providing more than spiritual guidance to "the forgotten and abandoned." He has a flock of seventy to eighty inmates and former inmates, petty thieves and addicts with whom he works directly. He gathers them for Friday night services. He provides them with clothes, pocket change, money for books. He gets them into rehab programs and junior colleges. He gives them tough love and compassionate love. He has founded A Place of Hope, a nonprofit dedicated to supporting the reintegration of former inmates into productive roles in society. The prisons have a recidivism rate of eighty-six percent. His flock has a recidivism rate of fourteen percent. Yossi is not only a spiritual resource; he is a mentor to the abandoned.

He has also taken on the role of mentor to rabbinic students. Traditional internships place students in synagogues, hospitals, or schools. But Yossi created a special internship. He brings the students into the prisons and introduces them to a different kind of population. He brings the students with him when he holds Friday-night Shabbat dinners for former inmates. He brings them with him when he gets a distress call from a former prisoner who needs help. Yossi is mentor and guide to both the abandoned and the future spiritual leaders of the Jewish community. "What goes around comes around" is a common phrase he hears on the street. Usually what goes around is bad stuff. But Yossi is giving new meaning to the phrase. His old dean mentored him, provided him with practical and emotional support. And when the time came, the dean stepped up for him and let him know he had faith in him. Now it's coming around. Yossi is doing the same not just for his current and former inmates; he is stepping up to the plate for a new generation of rabbinic students. He is expanding their understanding of service and religious community. He is modeling how to bring together courage and commitment and service of the heart to "the abandoned and the forgotten." Just as Pissarro helped Monet and Cézanne expand into a new kind of art, so Rabbi Yossi is mentoring others to realize new possibilities in their lives. "Who would have thunk it?" Yossi says. "This kid from Brooklyn, this entertainer to the stars. But here I am."

An Advisory Group

> *We haven't had oracles since the ancient Greeks, and I certainly couldn't divine the future. I needed help.*
>
> —NANCY IMHOLTE, *life change artist*

An advisory group is a group of individuals that can offer perspective, feedback, support, and accountability as you move through the dimensions of life change. An advisory group can play a vital collaborative role in facilitating your transition.

Aim to create a group of advisors who will take on complementary roles in supporting you. The great artists offer examples of the different ways that your advisors can provide guidance and help. Here are roles to consider:

    °   **Rembrandt, the Empathic Listener**. Perhaps you recall that Rembrandt was considered to be one of the most humane painters in the history of art. It is no accident that he is perhaps the greatest portrait painter of all time. He had a gift for understanding and conveying the full range of human emotions in a highly sensitive and respectful manner. He possessed keen observational abilities. For your advisory group, you will want someone who is a keen and empathic observer of you, and who is able to communicate to you what he or she observes.

°   **Pissarro, the Mentor**. Camille Pissarro mentored an entire generation of Impressionist painters. These included Monet, Cézanne, Renoir, and Morisot. Pissarro happened to be a decade older than the artists he mentored. He had more experience than they did and understood "the ropes" of the French art world. He could reflect on his experience in ways that helped younger painters avoid his mistakes and feel supported in the arduous challenge of becoming successful artists. For your advisory group, try to include a mentor who can draw on his or her professional and life experiences to direct you toward resources, networks, and experiences that will enhance your success.

°   **Picasso, the Catalyst**. Pablo Picasso was brilliant at translating ideas and concepts into actual art. In the collaborative relationship he developed with Georges Braque (which led to the revolution called Cubism), it was generally acknowledged that Braque was the more intellectual, but it was Picasso who pushed the pair to commit their experimental techniques to the canvas. Life change requires that we be reflective and self-aware. Life change also means we must actually begin to act on that self-awareness. For your advisory group, look for a catalyst, an action-oriented person who can encourage you to take concrete steps to make your aspirations a reality.

°   **Leonardo, the Strategic Thinker**. Leonardo was brilliantly versatile. He was not just an artist but an inventor, a musician (he sang for the king of France), a scientist, an architect, and a military strategist. In other words, not only did he know a lot about many things, he demonstrated the ability to see the big picture. For your advisory group, try to include a big-picture thinker, a strategist who can take in all the little stuff, step back and identify the big themes in your life, and then help you translate them into a larger vision for yourself.

By including each of these roles in your advisory group, you will have the benefit of a diverse set of perspectives that you could probably never achieve on your own. Finally, when choosing members of your advisory group, look for people who have a track record of extending themselves to help others. It does little good to identify a strategic thinker who turns out to be too busy to spend any time with you. American Impressionist Mary Cassatt is a wonderful example of someone who reached out to help other painters. She devoted much of her time to promoting the work of her fellow artists. She even felt responsible for buying paintings of artists who were poor and needed money.

One of the benefits of forming such a group is that it pushes you to declare your intention about your future. When you ask someone to be your life change advisor, you have to be clear about why. Clarifying the purpose of your advisory group for others helps you commit to doing the creative work of change. Keep in mind you are not expected to have all the answers. In fact, you are expected to have virtually none of the answers. Your group will help you explore, discover, and integrate them.

You will want to think about some of the mechanics related to convening your advisory group. Even though we are referring to the advisory group as a group, you do not need to physically bring them together. We suggest that you initially meet with your advisory members individually and discuss what you have in mind and why you believe they can play the role you envision for them. You should be prepared to let members know how often you would like to meet with them. There is no reason you need to meet with each member according to the same schedule or at the same intervals. For instance, you may wish to initially meet with your Rembrandt, the sympathetic listener, once a month for a period of time and with your Leonardo, the strategic thinker, once every four months. How often you meet will depend on their role and your need to access that role as you move through your journey. Whenever you meet with members of your advisory group, set aside time afterward to reflect on your conversations and record those ideas in your sketchbook.

A Life Coach

> *My coach asked me hard questions. She helped me discover things about myself. She made me think deeply. I had to come up with some hard answers.*
>
> —RICHARD CLARKE, *life change artist*

Many of the life change artists highlighted in these chapters used professional coaches to help them make important changes in their lives. Professional life coaches are relatively new on the scene, but their potential value cannot be overstated. They serve a function that complements your advisory group but is quite distinct. While your informal advisors are there to support you with their perspectives and experience, a professional life coach is a paid resource who understands the full process of life change, assists you in developing critical life change skills, and holds you accountable for accomplishing what you set out to do at each phase of your transition. Coaches facilitate the exploration of your needs, motivations, skills, and thought processes to assist you in making genuine, lasting change. They often ask questions, listen, and observe as ways to facilitate your own thought processes in order to identify solutions and actions. Coaches encourage you to commit to action.

Life coaches are especially helpful if you know that you're dissatisfied with your current life, but have no idea *what* to do, or if you know *what* you'd like to do but don't know *how* to go about it. Life coaches are especially helpful for those who find themselves knowing what they want but are surrounded by people who do not support the direction of their desired change.

Coaches do not claim to have the answers, but they work closely with you to identify a path based on your passions, gifts, and values. A life coach can make the difference between floundering and true self-discovery, between lack of direction and purposeful structure, between feeling lonely and feeling connected.

Coauthor Kathy, herself a life coach, also has her own life coach, Donna Krone, whom we met in Chapter 2. Kathy doesn't hesitate to admit that discipline is one of her creative challenges. Meeting regularly with her life coach has provided a structure for exploring new options and actually taking steps to turn her vision for her future into reality.

Not all coaches are created equal. Ask people you know for rec-ommendations, or contact an accrediting organization such as the International Coach Federation for a list of coaches who have been trained to their standards. The cost of coaching may seem prohibitive. Many coaches charge between $100 and $200 per hour. So be cre-ative. Offer to barter a skill you have for some coaching sessions. Or take a hard look at what you are spending your money on and find ways to reallocate your expenses. One coaching client we know can-celed her TV cable service in order to afford a coaching program. She found that she doesn't miss TV a bit. In fact, she has rediscovered read-ing fiction. Plus, she is headed toward an exciting new career, thanks to the work she did with the support of her coach. You can find more information about life coaching in Appendix E.

What Does Collaboration Do for Life Change?

Collaboration gives us access to a broader network of people who can link us to new ideas and opportunities. It helps us make better decisions, informed by ideas and experiences we would not encounter on our own. Collaboration is a powerful source of emotional support. Collaboration also ensures that we stay on course with desired changes, since we are surrounded by people who care about our progress.

Bridge to new networks. As we have seen throughout this book, personal change often involves developing new social and professional networks. Collaborating with others helps bridge us into new networks that facilitate change. For Berthe Morisot, Édouard Manet acted as her entry point into the Impressionist circle. For Mary O. Hamill, her association with the Women's Studies Research Center at Brandeis acted as an accelerant to her installation art and to new collaborative resources.

Better decisions. As powerful and inventive as our minds are, they work within the boundaries of our own backyards, but when we collaborate with others we extend our boundaries. We see how others have arranged their gardens. We benefit from their perspective and creativity. Collaboration is a source of fresh ideas that in turn get us to better solutions. As brilliant as Picasso was, by his own admission it is unlikely he would have invented Cubism by himself. Nor would Jamie Gaviser have been as successful in establishing a new form of patient care.

Emotional support. Life change has its good days and bad days. Change even has its very painful days. Sometimes we have the sense that time is moving much too slowly, and other times we feel that events are getting the better of us. Collaborating with others provides not only practical support in figuring out how to navigate change but the emotional support to remain afloat during the tough times. When Jeffrey Carron felt out of place among all the young students at Hebrew Union, his seminary head helped him see how his age was an asset.

Accountability. Sometimes support for personal change comes in the form of being accountable to others for things we say we will do but let slip. Change never follows a straight line, but true collaborative partners will call us on those slips. When the aspiring Impressionists met at the Café Guerbois to argue their ideas about painting, they were then expected to demonstrate those ideas on canvas when they went out to paint together.

Making Collaboration Work

As we have seen, collaboration takes many forms. But it always begins with a sense of humility. We acknowledge we do not have all the answers. In fact, we may not have any of them, even though we work under the illusion that we do. There are always other perspectives that can help modify, refine, enrich, or change the answer we begin with on our own. Even in an endeavor as uniquely individual and personal as life change, the active engagement of others will enhance our ability to deploy all our other creative skills. And when we discover how much our collaborators have contributed to our journey, we can only be overcome by gratitude.

EXERCISES

1. What's Your Collaboration Mind-set?

Place a check mark next to any statement below with which you agree:

- I generally believe I can get things done faster and better when I do them myself.
- I generally do not like acknowledging I don't know something even if others do acknowledge it.
- I am fully aware of my blind spots.
- I generally don't like feeling vulnerable.
- I don't like dealing with others' personal quirks.

If you checked one or more of these questions, you may be placing constraints on your ability to fully collaborate with others. Reflect on what attitudes could help you develop your collaboration skills.

2. Study an Improvisational Performance

Improvisational theater (usually called improv) is a form of theater in which the actors perform without a script. Actors use audience suggestions to guide the performance as they create dialogue, setting, and plot spontaneously. Improv groups perform in most metropolitan areas. Check out the Applied Improvisation Network, http://appliedimprov.ning.com, which has many resources related to improvisation. If you don't have access to live improv performances, consider getting the DVD of the former improv comedy game show *Whose Line Is It Anyway?*

When you view an improv performance, pay particular attention to:

- how performers build off of one another's statements or movements.
- how they don't introduce constraints or obstacles that would lead to narrower plot options for other performers.
- performers' playful attitude—any topic chosen as the subject of the skit becomes the raw material for play.

Once you've observed the improv performers' approach, reflect on what aspects of improv you could incorporate into your collaborations at work and in your personal life. For example, *don't prejudge another person's comments, observations, and ideas. Rather, build on them. Explore their possibilities.* Try this in casual conversations first. See where improv techniques take you. Notice the energy that is created for you and others.

3. Interview a Master Collaborator

In addition to watching a talented collaborator in action, consider interviewing him or her about their collaboration experiences. This will help you identify ways to further develop your own collaboration skills.

Tell your interview subject why you are interested in this topic. Here are some questions you may ask in order to get the conversation rolling:

- What role has collaboration played in your success?
- What skills does one need in order to make collaboration work?
- What have you done to develop your own collaboration abilities?
- What have you learned about being an effective collaborator?
- What are the biggest challenges you've faced in making collaboration work?
- What might be some of the reasons collaboration stalls or breaks down?
- What can be done about them?

4. Helping Others

- Collaboration is by definition a two-way street. But when we are involved in our own life change, it's easy to think of collaboration only in terms of who can help us. For this exercise, reflect on someone, perhaps a friend or family member, who is going through an important life transition.
- Ask yourself: What skills or assets do I have that might be useful to them?
- Make contact and offer to help in some specific way. Let that person know, for instance, that you would be happy to be a sounding board, or introduce them to people in your networks, or help them learn to do something you're skilled in.
- Even if you don't get an immediate response, make a point of getting in touch with that person within a month to offer to support them. Next time, that person might realize you are serious about wanting to help.

- Once you've had an opportunity to collaborate with someone else on their life transition, take time to reflect on what you are learning from your interaction with the person you are "helping." You will probably discover that you are getting as much help with your life change as the person you are supporting!

Chapter 11

Discipline

Talent! What they call talent is nothing but the
capacity for doing continuous work in the right way.

—WINSLOW HOMER

Life change can be many things at different times: it can be
thrilling, exciting, fun, scary, or confusing. But one thing it
is at all times is work. Life change, like any creative process,
requires sustained effort. If we imagine a new life, but don't
take active steps to make it happen, we'll stay the same as always.
Discipline is a key to successful life change. As much as we may want
to change, our life change process coexists with our "day job" of life
as usual. And our current life is full of distractions. Discipline is what
keeps us focused on the myriad tasks we take on when we commit to
change.

At its simplest, discipline requires *acting consistently whether or not we*
feel motivated. When we are being disciplined, we:

- are able to quickly return ourselves to the task at hand if distracted.
- recover quickly from disappointment and failure.
- adopt habits that help us work consistently and effectively.
- stay engaged in the task at hand for as long as we need to.
- hold ourselves accountable for following through on actions to
  which we have committed.

In order to be disciplined when we really need to be, we must develop habits that facilitate consistent behavior over time. Some of these habits are familiar tools of discipline, such as writing down goals and keeping track of our progress toward those goals. Other elements of the discipline skill are less obvious, such as adopting practices that promote regular self-renewal. Self-renewal routines such as daily exercise, yoga, prayer, bird-watching—whatever is restorative for *you*— are essential to discipline. Without ongoing self-renewal, we may run out of the personal energy that sustains our willpower. And we need willpower to move successfully through each of the dimensions of life change. For instance, we need discipline to confront our creative dilemma. If we ignore our creative dilemma, it's often because we don't trust ourselves to have the stamina to work through the changes we know will be required. Once we've decided to move in a new direction, we discover that exploration and discovery don't happen magically on their own. Exploration requires effort, and effort requires discipline.

When the tasks that must be done are not easy, we can be quite inventive in coming up with reasons not to engage. Passion and commitment can falter. We may not be "in the mood." When we find our motivation taking a vacation, it is the role of the discipline skill to step in and keep us going.

Creativity and Discipline

For many, the notion of pairing discipline and creativity does not make sense. Many of us hold a stereotype of artists as undisciplined, putting brush to canvas only when moved by inspiration or when the creative muse shows up on the artist's shoulder and awakens her spirit with flashes of creative magic. The truth is, as Picasso once observed, "Inspiration exists, but it must find us working." Discipline is the skill of putting forth effort even when we don't feel like it. So it is important that we distinguish effort that flows out of motivation and passion from effort put forth in their absence. It is the latter that signals the presence of discipline.

The great artists were all, without exception, driven individuals. They were committed, passionate, and motivated to create, to express their unique way of seeing. But equally without exception they each encountered obstacles, defeats, disappointments, and powerful doubts—any one of which could have discouraged them and led them down a different path. Early in his artistic career, one of Matisse's teachers told him that one of his drawings was "so bad I hardly dare tell you how bad it is."[1] He could easily have packed up his easel and gone home. At the pinnacle of his career, Rembrandt was thrown into a devastating bankruptcy and had to sell his home and his entire art collection. For almost her entire artistic career, the great Mexican artist Frida Kahlo was racked by intense physical pain caused by an almost fatal trolley accident. Francisco Goya went stone deaf in mid-career. Monet went nearly blind in his later years. Renoir was stricken by debilitating arthritis. *But they all kept working at their art.* They all had their doubts and lapses and physical tribulations. Yet they all called upon the power of discipline to keep creating, often under extremely trying circumstances.

Doubt and Discipline

When we think of the nineteenth-century Dutch artist Vincent van Gogh, the stories of his mental illness quickly come to mind. Most of us don't realize that despite his profound emotional instability, his artistic career was a model of discipline. Van Gogh did not begin painting until he was twenty-eight years old. By the time he died eight years later, only one of his eight hundred paintings had been sold, and

---

1. Hilary Spurling, *The Unknown Matisse* (New York: Alfred A. Knopf, 1998), p. 68.

Vincent van Gogh, *The Digger,* 1889

that to his brother Theo. Van Gogh's letters to his brother are a revelation of his doubts, aspirations, and practices. They reveal a man of striking intellectual depth, breadth, and insight, great generosity, selflessness, and commitment to his art. Yet he is haunted by doubts about his ability. He knows he is trying to use color in painting in ways that no one has ever tried before. He fears being lost in the mist of failure. What kept him creating throughout this intense life of emotional ups, downs, twists, and turns? Having started his pursuit of painting rather late, he always felt he had to make up lost ground. From the outset, van Gogh realized he would need to dedicate himself to improving his painting skills every day. His drawing took on the character of a daily religious ritual, and slowly he began to notice improvements. He found the work hard, even discouraging. On some days he felt like chucking it all, but he knew that discipline was essential to his creative aspirations. In one of his letters to Theo, van Gogh describes his persistence:

> Careful study and the constant and repeated copying of [Charles] Bargue's *Exercises au Fusain* have given me a better insight into figure-drawing. I have learned to measure and to see and to look for the broad outlines, so that, thank God, what seemed utterly impossible to me before is slowly becoming possible now. I have drawn a man with a spade five times over, a girl with a broom twice, then a woman in a white cap peeling potatoes and a shepherd leaning on his crock, and finally an old sick peasant sitting on a chair by the hearth with his head in his hands and his elbows on his knees.[2]

Vincent religiously keeps his brother informed of his progress, of his trials, tribulations, and doubts. When they show up, he writes:

> But I must continue on the path I have taken now. If I don't do anything, if I don't study, if I don't go on seeking any longer, I am lost. Then woe is me. That is how I look at it: to continue, to continue, that is what is necessary. But you will ask, what is your definite aim? That aim becomes more definite, will stand out slowly and surely, as the rough draft becomes a sketch, and the sketch becomes a picture—little by little, *by working seriously* on it, by pondering over the idea, vague at first, over the thought that was fleeting and passing, till it gets fixed.[3]

One of the remarkable things about van Gogh's outlook is that he did not know the outcome. He acknowledged it was all vague in the beginning. Yet he plowed ahead. "By working seriously," he believed, he would triumph. Even though he sold none of his paintings, he remained disciplined. Even during his stay in the mental asylum at St. Remy de Provence in southern France, he had his brother Theo send

2. W. H. Auden, *Van Gogh: A Self-Portrait* (New York: E. P. Dutton, 1963), p. 75.
3. Ibid. (emphasis added).

him paint, brush, and canvas. And he wrote regularly to his brother. The letters not only kept his brother Theo current, but provided van Gogh with perspective. Writing them was a discipline that made it possible for him "to continue, to continue" his painting. Revealing his deepest thoughts, yearnings, and anxieties in his letters was a source of renewal and gave van Gogh the strength to continue the battle the next day. The letters helped him manage the doubts and fear of failure and uncertainty about his success. They helped him process his creative struggles. When motivation and inspiration seemed to flee the fields at Arles, he found strength and renewal in the act of writing his letters.

The Discipline Within

Centuries before van Gogh, Michelangelo (1475–1564) dedicated himself to a form of discipline that is especially relevant to life change artists. He believed that the form of his famous *David* sculpture was already in the block of marble. He simply needed to bring it out. As Michelangelo put it: "Carving is easy, you just go down to the skin and stop." This is a very different concept from the modern notion that we create from nothing. Life change artists today have the opportunity to reconnect with the spirit by which Michelangelo pursued his sculpture. Such is the case when we consider that the life we want to bring forth is already within us. It's a matter of creating our new lives out of the rough marble of our existing lives. Discipline is the consistent effort to access, develop, and shape what is already within our potential.

Discipline and Pursuing the Dream

In Chapter 6, "Seeing," we met twenty-eight-year-old Randi Carney, who had an encounter with a university president who helped turn her view of her life upside down. Randi was living on the edge of poverty. She relied on food stamps and waitressing to scrape by. She was divorced and had two young children. When she looked back, she didn't think she had much to build on, having graduated from high school with barely a C average. But on that particular day, as she waited on the president's table, he saw something in her sense of humor and natural intelligence that led him to believe she had more potential than she thought she had. So when he asked her what she wanted to do with the rest of her life, she told him she wanted to go to medical school. The president said he believed she had it in her, and he gave her a referral to the dean of the college.

Of course, it's one thing to have a dream. It's an entirely different thing to turn that into a reality—especially given the deficits Randi had to work with. She had no financial means. She was the primary caretaker for her two young children. She had an abysmal academic record.

A new sense of purpose took hold of Randi. She talked her way into a baccalaureate program at the university. She graduated Phi Beta Kappa, and in retrospect she says she does not know how she managed to attend classes, work, and raise her kids. Barely stopping to take a breath, she earned a master's degree in medical anthropology. By this time she was, she says, "wracked with guilt." Her apartment was a mess. She left her kids with neighbors for long stretches of time. She lived in a poor section of the city. Torn between the impulse to say, "Hey, this is too much," and the desire to finish the job, between the chaos of the present and the possibilities for the future, Randi called on "the Irish in me. No one was going to tell me I couldn't do it. Not even myself." There were times she felt mentally exhausted and depleted of any emotional reserves. Under the weight of too much to do and too few resources to do it with, she felt her motivation leak from her very bones. Those were the moments she called on the Irish in her. She used it as a mantra, she used it to focus, she used it to renew her commitment. "People tell me I have incredible discipline, but it felt more like I just focused on what was really, really important. Then I knew what I needed to do. It wasn't a matter of whether or not I got up and kept going. The Irish in me didn't give me a choice."

This commitment not only carried her through medical school but also pulled her toward the practice of community service medicine. Randi used her own experiences to establish innovative health care programs in clinics in underserved areas. She has created programs in urban areas in the Midwest and on Native American reservations in the West. She has developed an unusual emotional portfolio that combines hard-edged activism with deep empathy for her patients, a calculated realism about the politics of medicine with a powerful sense of optimism, and tough-mindedness with humility. She realizes that many of the people she serves may not have the benefit of a chance meeting with the president of a university who expresses belief in their potential. And she realizes that not all people have the equivalent of the Irish in them to overcome the odds. She understands that she might be her patients' chance for change, and in order for that chance to take root, she must see her patients and their families not for the circumstances they are in, but for who they may become. Today, Randi says all she wants to do is "teach, write, see my patients, and change the world." We can count on her Irish to get her there.

Building Blocks of Discipline

There are many ways of cultivating discipline, but the great artists and life change artists alike tend to rely on one or more of the following activities:

- Personal accountability
- Self-renewal and resilience-building practices
- Goal-setting
- Positive self-talk and self-awareness

Personal Accountability

Personal accountability acts as our conscientious auditor. It keeps the books on what we have or have not delivered. Have we accomplished what we signed up for, what we committed to? We cannot escape the results of our accountant's audit. We alone are the source of disciplined behavior. As Leonardo da Vinci said, "You can have no dominion greater or less than that over yourself." We alone have the power to act consistently, regardless of all the other things going on in our lives. We are vulnerable and imperfect creatures. But despite our imperfections, we are ultimately accountable to ourselves. Our intentions may be pure, but our behaviors often falter. The tough part about discipline is converting our intentions into actual, consistent behaviors.

Fortunately, several tools are available to assure we honor our commitments.

Creative Mantra

What is it that animates us? What gives us energy? When are we most alive? What's our purpose? What if we could crystallize the answers to these questions into a mantra that we chanted to ourselves several times a day? That is exactly what a creative mantra does. Co-author Fred has used a creative mantra to guide his ever-evolving change journey from business executive to writer, artist, and personal change catalyst. "Create, Integrate, Make a Difference." This is his mantra. It is an expression of what he cares about. It identifies in crystallized form those things that give him energy and purpose. He has placed it on his business cards. He has written it on his easel. He shares his mantra with others and tells them that this mantra guides his decisions in relation to how he will spend his time. The mantra is a clarifying call. Each morning he asks himself, "How will I live my mantra today?" How will I "create, integrate, and make a difference" today?

He expects to align his time and efforts with his mantra. And every evening he asks himself, "Specifically, how have I created, integrated, made a difference today?" These are self-accountability questions, but they are also more. These questions connect him to his source of energy. When he has a sense that things are drifting or he is faced with some choice for which there is no immediate answer, he takes a time-out and writes down his mantra and uses it as a reference point in making his decision or renewing his commitment. His creative mantra keeps him on track and keeps him accountable to his values.

Write Them Down, Take Them Out, Start All Over Again

The first line of defense in holding true to our life change commitments is us. While we may often declare noble commitments to change, we, in truth, may be more influenced by less noble but more powerful countervailing commitments. We declare to ourselves an intention to start a small entrepreneurial business, but we may not take the steps because our less noble fear of uncertainty holds us back. We may want to move to Santa Fe, but our countervailing reluctance to building a brand-new network of friends overpowers our initial commitment. One way to neutralize this effect is to be clear with ourselves regarding our less noble and potentially limiting fears that lurk beneath the surface and are ready to derail our more public intentions. Once we have made that decision, we can take the simple step of writing down our declared commitment and reviewing it regularly. The act of taking out the piece of paper and reading aloud what we wrote down serves as a kind of self-auditing check-in.

Turn Your Commitments into a Public Offering

Declaring our intentions to others can be a powerful tool in holding ourselves accountable. By doing so we turn friends and family into enablers of our intentions. This is exactly what helped Margaret Madsen develop new habits. Being gregarious was lots of fun, but it was also time-consuming. She spent huge chunks of time on the telephone "catching up" with her friends. Then Margaret took a workshop on personal change. She was interested in creating more balance in her life and reflecting on her experiences in a deeper and more structured way. Coming out of the workshop she decided to begin journaling in a serious way. Margaret had tried journaling in the past but succumbed to her own gregarious nature. She "just couldn't find the time" to journal because spending time with her friends on the phone "just came so naturally." Then Margaret decided to go public. She told her five closest friends about her intention to journal regularly but that she was having difficulty sticking to it. She asked each one to help her out. "Whenever I call you or you call me you must begin the conversation with the following question: Have you written in your journal today? If I have, then we can talk. But if I haven't, then we need to reschedule our talk." By going public, Margaret was turning her time demanders (her friends) into time enhancers. They helped her develop new habits that moved her toward her commitment of greater balance and personal reflection.

Resilience and Self-Renewal

Resilience is our emotional bounce-ability power. It is highly elastic. It stretches but does not break. It wants us to get back on the horse right away. When van Gogh can't sell any of his paintings, resilience rallies his discipline to continue his work. When Matisse is told his drawing is "bad, so bad," resilience helps him show up in the class-room the next day. Resilience clears the emotional underbrush so discipline can support the actions we need in order to move ahead. Randi's story demonstrates the interdependency between discipline and resilience: discipline supports our resilience and resilience renews our discipline.

Kira McGovern is a life coach. Over the years she has learned to help her clients "normalize screwups." We all have them, she says. It's not a matter of if we screw up or if we run into a pothole. It's a matter of when. Kira also recognizes that these screwups come in both the small and large variety. So she encourages her clients to build in a "recovery plan." Kira encourages not just her clients but all of us to be prepared ahead of time so when situations get the better of us or we get knocked down, we know how to renew our commitment and motivation.

Recovery plans vary from person to person. We each get recharged in different ways. The important thing is to know what recharges us and then to tap into it. Even better, we can be proactive by regularly engaging in those activities that recharge us. We can strengthen our emotional durability.

Jane Heifetz has taken this to another level. She has built in a "preemptive" recovery plan. She runs. As Jane reflects on her many transitions and the uncertainties and trials they have each presented, she says running has been her salvation. And an unlikely one, for sure. Growing up she had never been athletic. Initially her running was more a matter of "will than skill." But it has gotten her through good times and rough times, through her journey from special education teacher to financial analyst, business manager and program editor at WGBH television to an executive editor at Harvard Business School Publishing. "It hasn't been all clear sailing. I had to pick myself up a lot. Sometimes it was terrifying. Sometimes I had no idea what would come next. I've been through career change, job change, organizational change, family change, change change. But running has been the constant." So every morning five days a week, Jane gets up at four-thirty and runs from five to five forty-five. "Sometimes it helps me recover before I even know I need to recover."

Of course, running at five a.m. may not be everyone's cup of tea. Self-renewal activities can be as simple as having dinner with a good friend. Or reading a good book. Or going for long walks. Self-renewal can also take more dramatic forms, such as going on a trip to a place you've never been or a place you have already been and really love. You can take a painting class or listen to Mozart or the Grateful Dead. The key is not the particular form of renewal but rather knowing what form of self-renewal will work for you when the need arises.

Goal Setting

A remarkable quality of the great artists is that even if their personal lives were chaotic, when it came to their art they demonstrated fanatical integrity. They did not allow themselves shortcuts. They drew on discipline to align their actions with their vision. They set high goals for themselves, as van Gogh did in pushing himself to do mountains of sketches each day when he was learning to draw.

Goals give us something to work toward every day. We may question our ability to do what is necessary to realize our goals. We may resist setting goals for life change because we fear that we will fail. We may hold back from stepping through our creative dilemma into exploration. Sometimes we resist setting goals because we fear what will happen if we actually succeed. A Chinese fortune cookie captures this fear: *Beware of what you want. You may get it.* What will we have to give up when we succeed in forging a different life? Will our expectations be even higher than before? Will we expect ourselves to continue to grow in new and different ways? So before we are able to commit to goals, we may need to explore our feelings about the prospect of actually accomplishing them, or failing to achieve them. Being aware of the ways in which our emotions enable or hinder goal-setting is as important as establishing tangible goals.

Jim Hime has always had goals. He graduated at the top of his law school class at the University of Texas. He became the youngest partner at a prestigious Houston law firm. He ardently pursued the woman who would become his wife until he won her heart. But on September 11, 2001, Jim's only goal was to get from the sixty-sixth floor of

One World Trade Center to safety. And it would be his intense commitment to setting and working toward goals that would help him cope with the aftermath of the terrorist attack.

In the years before 9/11, while pursuing his legal career, Jim had started two or three novels but never finished them. During the Thanksgiving holiday of 1998, he wrote a short story about an old rancher whose daughter was dying of cancer. He put it in a drawer and forgot about it until he enrolled in a crime fiction writing course at Rice University some time later. He used his short story as a basis for his weekly homework assignments. By the time he finished the full draft, it ran to 25,000 words. He eagerly shared the early version with his class, who told him it "read like a legal brief." So he stopped writing and set a goal to read his favorite western writers—Larry McMurtry, Cormac McCarthy, Elmore Leonard, and James Ellroy—to get a better feel for writing in a distinctive voice. He began rewriting his novel in a much looser style. It was a draft of this novel that he carried to New York on September 10, expecting to show it to an agent the next day. Before meeting with the agent, however, he had a business meeting in the World Trade Center. Jim got out of the building physically unscathed. Outwardly not much had changed. But in his inner life, big changes were brewing.

Jim had difficulty sleeping. He began to work out more in the event that some other unexpected event would require him to be fit. He hugged his two sons and wife more. But Jim's goals remained the same. He still wanted to write. He wanted to become a good writer. He wanted at some point to transition to writing full-time. But he realized that wanting something is not the same thing as behaving consistently with your wanting it. So every morning he would wake up early and get in a couple of hours of writing before heading to the office. Jim acknowledges that having the goal was only the beginning. It acted as a reference point to measure whether his discipline was adding up to something meaningful. And he continued his legal career. In 2003, he published *Night of the Dance* and received a nomination for the prestigious Edgar Award as best first mystery novel. Jim reflects that having goals helped create "a rhythm for me. It organized me. I had something to measure myself against. Without goals, I might have easily been swallowed up by all those awful events."

Self-Talk and Self-Awareness

It's rare to find someone who has accomplished all her goals without a hitch. After all, there are strong headwinds at work in our lives that can waylay the innocent goal-seeker. Fortunately, when things get tough or, most painfully, when we disappoint ourselves, there is a powerful approach we can use to return us to a more productive, creative frame of mind: positive self-talk, or what psychologists call reframing. Reframing involves taking a negative interpretation of an experience and turning it into a more proactive frame of reference.

As a young adult, Michelle Conti was struck by an intense case of rheumatoid arthritis, and her life seemed to evaporate before her very eyes. She had been an avid swimmer and had planned on beginning a joint M.D./Ph.D. program. She was impatient to achieve and make her mark. But now everything changed. The acute pain led to further complications and a variety of treatments that included chemotherapy and at least thirty different medications. She found herself putting on a hundred pounds and living on Social Security. The dream of medical school faded. She had wanted to get married and have children, but one effect of chemotherapy was infertility. For ten years she would not look at herself from the neck down. She defined herself by "who and what I used to be." Her original goals seemed out of reach. Suicide seemed a viable option. But "my impatience saved me. I simply lost patience with being a patient. That patient mentality colors your whole outlook. Patient as victim. Patient as not responsible. So I began to talk differently to myself. I used different language."

Michelle says she did not like being defined by her illness. While she could not control her condition, she could take responsibility for her life. "I had to give up grieving and start using words like 'possibility' and 'responsibility.' I started to shift my anger from myself to others who failed to hold me responsible. Responsibility began to make me whole again. I've learned to live with the pain, but I won't live with not being responsible for my life." Michelle accepted the help of others. She enrolled in a program to become a physician's assistant. She's no longer on disability. She rarely misses a day of work. She looks back on the days when she whined a great deal. She doesn't like whining. "I don't like that kind of talk."

Michelle faced a major life crisis and used positive self-talk to turn her life around. For most of us, though, negative chatter has the knack of invading our mental space daily. In some ways, negative chatter offers an easy escape from personal accountability. Negative chatter can leave us with the impression that we do not do things because of forces outside ourselves. "I just don't have the time," we may say. "No one has ever shown me how." "I'm not very good at that." "I don't have enough money." "I've got other commitments." But this negative chatter is really designed to maintain the status quo, because we somehow believe that the status quo, as painful as it may be, is less painful than the alternative.

Negative chatter can be discouraging enough. But what makes it potentially lethal for life change is that it can also throw a thick blanket over our self-awareness. And self-awareness is a requirement for understanding when we most need to call on our discipline skill to help us make the changes we seek.

Everyone has a talent for making up excuses for not doing things that are required for making a successful life change. The danger is not in succumbing to occasional lapses in motivation, but in being unaware of when we are playing the game. "Oh, I had to take care of this task or that task." "Oh, I had to shop for dinner." "Oh, I had this appointment or that appointment." "Oh, I just wasn't up to it today." "Oh my, where did the week go?"

These excuses may be garden-variety ways to dull our self-awareness, but they can be effective. They become the language of procrastination we speak to ourselves. How, then, can we prevent this language from playing tricks on our self-awareness? How do we develop the ability to recognize these games of self-foolery?

These questions offer an opportunity to emphasize the interdependencies between the creative skills. For instance, by applying the seeing strategies that are part of the seeing skill, we can heighten our self-awareness and enhance our discipline skill. For instance, by stepping back from the canvas of our life we can ask ourselves: What's really going on here? What patterns of thought and behavior are emerging in my life, and are they aligned with my intentions? These simple but powerful questions help us identify where we are out of alignment.

We can also use the strategy of paying attention to negative space as a way to identify thoughts and feelings that lurk in the shadows of our life and that may be getting in the way of our making the changes we say we want to make. What am I afraid of? What feelings am I tamping down, and why? Are these real obstacles or excuses?

We can call on the turning-the-subject-upside-down strategy to reframe our excuses into positive opportunities. "Oh, I had to take care of this task or that task" becomes "If this task had to take care of me, what would the task be?" "Oh, I had this appointment or that appointment" becomes "If I had an appointment with my intentions, what would I be doing?" "Oh, I just wasn't up to it today" becomes "What would my ideal day be up to if I was up to it?" And "Oh my, where did the week go?" becomes "A new week is beginning [regardless of what day of the week it is], so what do I want to be able to say at the end of it?" Turning things upside down does not guarantee that we will become more disciplined. But this approach makes us aware of an alternative way of looking at our situation and reshapes our awareness, and it may lead to a stronger alignment between behaviors and intentions.

The Illusion of Hunky-Dory

Sometimes, a lack of self-awareness represents a deeper pattern of thought that we developed earlier in life. Sharon Sokoloff, who is the director of a lifelong learning organization, learned to construct a "Plexiglas bubble" around herself when she was a child. Her mother had a breakdown in response to the unexpected death of *her* mother. Sharon's parents separated, and for a number of years she was raised by other family members. Survival for Sharon meant "not moving, not speaking, and not rocking the boat." Over the years, she carried this pattern into other aspects of her life, and as a result she always had a "delayed response" to difficult situations. For a long time she was not even aware of this pattern. As a result, she held herself back from making the changes she needed to make, one of which was her own healing. "I don't see how people make changes or make a life without self-awareness," she noted. "Whenever I allowed the old pattern to take root, I became a victim, including not confronting sexual harassment. It's like having a disability. The thing is, the more you work at it, the quicker you recognize when you're falling into the old pattern of not recognizing the pattern in the first place."

Sharon has taken advantage of psychotherapy to help her break the pattern. During a recent weekend she and her sister moved their mother from another city to be closer to where they live. Decades of unspoken pain and neglect "were in the air." Sharon acknowledges that her old pattern would have tricked her into "believing things were hunky-dory." The old Plexiglas bubble hung over her head. But she wouldn't let it "keep me quiet anymore." She has trained herself to become a lot quicker at recognizing the pattern. She knows she has to be constantly vigilant. This awareness is the precondition for giving herself the opportunity to make healthier choices. Sometimes they are painful, but she can confidently say that at age fifty-nine, "the healing is a lifelong work in progress. My mom and I are getting there. And for me that's a lot better than hunky-dory." A hard-earned self-awareness has made it more difficult for her to play tricks on herself and has made it easier for her to live a life of meaning and integrity.

Heavy Lifting

As you can see, the discipline skill has a number of building blocks: personal accountability, self-renewal and resilience, goal setting, self-talk and self-awareness. All represent the sinews of the discipline muscle. When these sinews are not actively exercised, our discipline loosens up and stands at risk.

The discipline skill is pivotal to becoming a life change artist because the very consistency inherent in discipline also helps us to develop our other creative skills. Discipline brings us to our preparation practices. Discipline helps us manage risk taking. Discipline provides structure during times of uncertainty. Discipline is not one of the more glamorous skills. Discipline is the heavy lifter of the crew of creative skills. And that is why it is so critical to the arduous journey of life change.

EXERCISES

1. Goal Setting

- People who write down their goals are more likely to accomplish them than people who do not. Write down the goals you want to accomplish this month, and put your goals in some place where you easily see them during the day.
- Give this list of goals to three other people you can trust to check in with you on your progress.

2. Self-Renewal

- If you have adopted a certain practice, say a walk, as a preparation activity, take this opportunity to commit to regular practice. Decide on the number of times each week that you will engage in this practice. Then schedule the practice in your calendar.

- Record in your calendar each time you engage in that self-renewal practice.

- At the end of each week, note what percentage of the time you have engaged in your practice relative to your commitment. If your percentage is over zero, express appreciation to yourself for having done what you have done.

- If your percentage is under 100, reflect on what may be keeping you from engaging in your practice more consistently. Also ask yourself what you could do that would make it easier to be more consistent.

- At the end of the first month, note your percentage of engagement in your renewal practice. If the percentage is low, consider whether the practice you chose is one that really suits you. Consider experimenting with another practice that you may find more satisfying.

3. Rewards

- Establishing new habits can be difficult, no matter how useful in the long run. To build motivation for accomplishing tasks related to your life change, establish some rewards for accomplishing them. For instance, your goal for the week may be to call three people you know who are good at taking risks. Reward yourself for meeting that target by doing something highly enjoyable for yourself; say a trip to an art gallery, a massage, or a piece of yummy dark chocolate.

Part Three

. . . .

LIVING CREATIVELY

Chapter 12

The Way of the
Life Change Artist

*The greatest danger for most of us is not that our
aim is too high and we miss it, but it is too low and
we reach it.*

—MICHELANGELO

B y looking closely at the creative process and skills of the
great masters of art, we have learned a great deal about how
to create a vibrant and meaningful life. Some great artists
also offer additional inspiration for life change artists—by
the way they responded to painful or difficult personal circumstances.
Many made great sacrifices to support their creative labors and protect
the integrity of their work. Of course, there are a substantial number
of great artists whose lives were dysfunctional despite the grandeur of
their work. But other artists, and in particular many of the great
women masters, have much to teach us about the challenges and opportunities of living as a life change artist.

Not for the Fainthearted

Artemisia Gentileschi was born in Rome in 1593. She was trained as
an artist by her father, the well-known Renaissance painter Orazio

Artemisia Gentileschi,
Judith Slaying Holofernes, 1613

Gentileschi, and at a young age became known as a brilliant painter whose work surpassed that of many mature male painters of her time. She is best known for her depictions of strong, non-stereotyped female characters, such as is shown in her painting *Judith Slaying Holofernes.*

At seventeen, Artemisia was raped by a friend and colleague of her father, who filed suit against her molester. A sensationalized trial ensued, during which Artemisia was tortured to ensure that she was telling the truth about her rapist. Shortly after the trial, in order to salvage her reputation (and his), Artemisia's father married her off to a minor artist, with whom she moved to his home city of Florence. There she became an overnight sensation and was accepted by the Florentine art establishment. She was even admitted to the city's premier art society academy, Accademia del Disegno, which had never before permitted female members. Artemisia did not accomplish this solely on her artistic merits. She became a protégé of her godfather, Michelangelo Buonarroti the Younger, a prominent Florentine and great-nephew of *the* Michelangelo. Buonarroti introduced Gentileschi to the Medici family, the ruling nobility of the city, who were avid patrons of the arts. She made the most of their patronage, producing bold and original paintings for churches and palaces—while also raising a family of four children. After thirteen years of marriage, she separated from her husband, thus becoming perhaps the most famous single mother of the Renaissance era. Despite her artistic renown, it must have been hard for her to support her family on her own. Several of her letters provide insight into the challenges she faced in juggling her art career, her family, and her personal well-being:

From a letter to one of her patrons,
the Grand Duke Cosimo II de' Medici, in 1619:

The many minor illnesses I have suffered, as well as the not inconsequential worries I have had with my home and family, have prompted me to [go home to Rome for a rest]. I shall spend a few months there with my friends. During that time and within two months at the most, I assure your most Serene Highness that you shall have what you ordered, for which I received an advance of 50 *scudi*.[1]

And to another patron in 1635:

The confidence that I have always had in Your Lordship's kindness, and the now-urgent matter of placing my daughter in marriage, impel me to appeal to your generosity. . . . My Lord, to bring this marriage to conclusion, I need a small amount of money. I have kept for this purpose, since I do not have any wealth or income, some paintings measuring eleven and twelve *palmi* each. It is my intention to offer them to

---

1. Mary D. Garrard, *Artemisia Gentileschi* (Princeton, NJ: Princeton University Press, 1989), p. 377.

Cardinals Francesco and Don Antonio. However, I do not want to carry out this plan without your Lordship's advice, as I wish to act under your auspices and not otherwise. . . . I assure you that as soon as I have freed myself from the burdens of this daughter, I hope to come there immediately to enjoy my native city and to serve my friends and patrons.

Gentileschi's life dramatically demonstrates how an artist stayed true to her creative commitment despite obstacles and barriers. But she is only one of a number of women masters who broke through personal and professional barriers to live a life of their choosing. French Impressionist Berthe Morisot worked steadfastly on her painting throughout her adult life even as she fulfilled her role as wife and mother. Morisot was devoted to her husband and daughter Julie, and Morisot's paintings include many depictions of her family life. When her husband, Eugène Manet (brother of the painter Édouard), became too ill to go out in society, Morisot brought the artistic community to her home by reinstituting the weekly dinners for which her mother had been so famous. There were many forces that conspired against Morisot's painting—self-doubt and frail health. Yet she forged on. While her husband was dying in the winter of 1891–1892, she spent half her time keeping him company in his room, and the other half working in her studio. After his death she plunged into a deep depression, even briefly contemplating suicide. But Morisot had the insight to recognize that her anguish was actually a sign of her will to live. In her notebook she wrote: "Never does one feel one's being as much as in the exaltation of deep suffering." Finally it was her commitment to her work that made life worthwhile once again. In the six weeks after her husband's death, she managed to complete the preparations for her first solo exhibition. Within the year, Morisot was mending. As biographer Anne Higonnet describes her recovery from grief: "Work, concerts, theater, dinners, visits to and from old friends—the rhythm of the year before resumed. Morisot was producing more pictures than

Berthe Morisot, *Eugène Manet and His Daughter at Bougival,* 1881

ever. She painted every day, concentrating, never satisfied with what she had done, always striving toward an ideal."[2]

The life stories of Artemisia Gentileschi and Berthe Morisot illustrate that the way of the life change artist is not for the fainthearted. These stories provide glimpses into the soul of the creative process—an artist's commitment to accomplishing the work she was meant to do. It is this commitment that animates us as life change artists to consistently use our creative skills throughout our lives—lives that will inevitably include both happy distractions and difficult struggles. All the skills in the world will not help us if we do not use them. Consider, for example, how two seventeenth-century Dutch masters responded to the life transition of marriage. Judith Leyster (1609–1660) left us with far too few of her luminous masterpieces because she abandoned painting after her marriage in 1636, instead choosing to manage the workshop of her husband, the artist Jan Miense Molenaer.

---

2. Anne Higonnet, *Berthe Morisot* (New York: Rizzoli International, 1993), p. 217.

In contrast, Rachel Ruysch (1664–1750), the celebrated flower painter, juggled a husband and ten children while pursuing an active career as a member of the Hague painters' guild and as court painter to a German prince. We cannot reach back four hundred years to know what led these two artists to deal with their respective creative dilemmas as they did. But Leyster's and Ruysch's differing paths demonstrate that it is not so much our external circumstances (such as getting married) but how our hearts and minds respond to our creative dilemma that determines the paths we choose. Today, having ten children (or fewer) may qualify us as the subject of a reality TV show. Four hundred years ago, juggling a supersized family apparently did not rule out a demanding artistic career. No matter what our external circumstances, we must each decide how we will respond to our creative dilemma no matter in what form it presents itself to us. Whatever our age, gender, marital status, income, job, or location, we have a choice—to listen to the call of our creative dilemmas, and to use our creative skills to enter the journey we call the dimensions of life change, or not. What we choose does make a difference. And the sum of our choices defines our life.

Some of us are entering the "third age" of our lives. We are neither young nor ready to call ourselves old. We have learned a lot in these last decades, and we have worked hard. As we grow older, we may have regrets. After her husband's death, Morisot tortured herself for a time, thinking that she could have been a better wife. The past cannot be relived. But the work of life, and the work of life change, can be a source of vitality and purpose for as long as we *are* alive.

In his later years, Auguste Renoir suffered from acute arthritis. He had come a long way since being accosted by a group of rowdy teenagers in a Paris park in the summer of 1864. His reputation as one of the preeminent artists of his day was secure. He had moved in 1903 to southern France, where he discovered an old farmhouse set in an olive grove. He spent his days painting in the warm southern light in a studio in the garden. In his final years, Renoir had to be lifted by servants and his sons into his wheelchair, his arthritic hands bandaged

Judith Leyster, *Self-Portrait,* ca. 1630

Rachel Ruysch, *Still Life with Bouquet of Flowers
and Plums,* date unknown

to prevent sores. Caretakers inserted his paintbrushes between his bandaged fingers. He died in 1919, nearly paralyzed by arthritis. On the day he died he was still painting. He gave up his paintbrush saying, "I think I am beginning to understand something about it."[3]

In Renoir's last statement, art and life are joined. He had spent a lifetime trying to master painting, yet only in the end could he say, "I think I am beginning to understand something about it." The rest had been journey. Even a great master had not arrived at *the* answer. After a lifetime of dedication, even a great master admitted he was still trying to understand. But *what* specifically was Renoir beginning to understand? Was he referring to the craft of painting or something different, something bigger? We do not know because he said no more. But we would like to believe that it had something to do with the connection between art and life. Art is not a discrete, isolated activity. It grows out of the very creativity that energizes and shapes the rest of our lives, and therefore art is a fundamental expression of who we are, who we aspire to be, how we see the world, and what our possibilities are in the world. And life, like art, is about creating new possibilities—regardless of age or circumstances.

But there is another aspect to Renoir's comment. Maybe he was beginning to understand something about "it" only at the end because "it" was always changing. Art, like life, is always changing. Life is not unchanging sameness. Rather, it is movement, flux, and complexity and maybe that's what Renoir was beginning to understand. And because life never stops changing, we, like Renoir, have the opportunity to be creative to the end, even to the last day.

Finding Your Way

Ultimately, the great masters and the life change artists who inhabit these pages are not only artists—they are consummate teachers. From

---

3. Sue Roe, *The Private Lives of the Impressionists* (New York: Harper Perennial, 2006), p. 269.

them we have learned that the basic questions never go away: Why am I here? How can I be authentic? How do I live my passion? How do I best express what is inside me? The urgency of these questions may recede for certain periods in our lives, but they never lose their relevance. And they always resurface. Whether we are standing before a fresh canvas or an open future, these remain the fundamental questions. And it is our life's purpose to answer these questions over and over, each in our own unique way, as a form of self-renewal, self-affirmation, and reinvention. That is the way of the life change artist.

The artists also teach us that there is no shore—no permanent, long-term resting place—only small islands along the way. They help us accept that change, not stability or stasis, is the natural order of things.

Finally, the artists teach us that the way of the life change artist begins with the commitment that is captured in the Matissean Vow. As Matisse told his daughter, while some other artists settled for *good*

Francisco Goya, *I Am Still Learning,* 1828

enough, he refused to do so. He pushed on, even though he knew there would be risks and potential failure. Like Matisse, life change artists are not satisfied with *good enough*. They push beyond their creative dilemmas to powerful new possibilities. Doubt, frustration, and fear are part of the way of the life change artist, but they are not as powerful as passion, commitment, and purpose. As a life change artist, you, too, will experience doubt and frustration, but by staying true to your purpose, you can overcome what may seem like insurmountable obstacles. And you will move toward greater wholeness.

The great Spanish artist Francisco Goya (1746–1828) demonstrated this in one of his very last works. Illness brought him close to death twice in his life, and one illness at age forty-six left him stone-deaf. He made the charcoal drawing reproduced on the previous page not long before his death at age eighty-two. He titled it *I Am Still Learning*. And that is the ultimate gift that the great artists bring to you—the gift of the Seven Creative Skills, which you can use to be always learning, always creating, and always aspiring to live the best life for you. It takes courage to begin. But the way is open to all of us. And the journey is yours to take.

Appendix A

The Creativity Calculator

BEFORE YOU BEGIN . . .

Research proves that *everyone* is creative. You were born with creative ability and you can develop your creativity even further. The great masters of art produced their legendary works not just from talent but by regular practice of a set of the Seven Creative Skills. Recent brain research has confirmed the importance of those core creative skills to personal and professional success.

Assessing your current level of creative skills will help you understand the role of creativity in your life. And it will allow you to use that knowledge to enhance your personal life and career.

Turn to the next page to use the Creativity Calculator. Then use the worksheets that follow to score and interpret your results.

CREATIVITY CALCULATOR™

This survey will help you understand and assess your creative skills. Creative skills are essential to successful life change and overall life satisfaction. Please answer the following questions as candidly as possible.

Please rate the extent to which the following statements apply to you by circling the number appearing to the right of your rating.		
Item	**Rating**	
1. When faced with a problem, I prefer to come up with a solution as quickly as possible.	Strongly Disagree Disagree Neither Agree nor Disagree Agree Strongly Agree	5 4 3 2 1
2. I notice aspects of situations that other people don't seem to see.	Strongly Disagree Disagree Neither Agree nor Disagree Agree Strongly Agree	1 2 3 4 5
3. I pay attention to trends taking place in my areas of interest.	Strongly Disagree Disagree Neither Agree nor Disagree Agree Strongly Agree	1 2 3 4 5
4. I am able to move forward even when my roles in life are changing.	Strongly Disagree Disagree Neither Agree nor Disagree Agree Strongly Agree	1 2 3 4 5
5. I take actions to achieve important goals even when the odds of success might be low.	Strongly Disagree Disagree Neither Agree nor Disagree Agree Strongly Agree	1 2 3 4 5
6. I actively seek out others for mutual support.	Strongly Disagree Disagree Neither Agree nor Disagree Agree Strongly Agree	1 2 3 4 5

Item	Rating	
7. When I am distracted, it's hard to bring myself back to the task at hand.	Strongly Disagree Disagree Neither Agree nor Disagree Agree Strongly Agree	5 4 3 2 1
8. I believe that I can be more successful in my life if I engage in activities that stimulate creative insights.	Strongly Disagree Disagree Neither Agree nor Disagree Agree Strongly Agree	1 2 3 4 5
9. I don't make assumptions until I take time to get the full picture of a situation.	Strongly Disagree Disagree Neither Agree nor Disagree Agree Strongly Agree	1 2 3 4 5
10. I try to understand what's going on in society and the larger world.	Strongly Disagree Disagree Neither Agree nor Disagree Agree Strongly Agree	1 2 3 4 5
11. I am uncomfortable moving ahead on changes in my life when I lack complete information about how to proceed.	Strongly Disagree Disagree Neither Agree nor Disagree Agree Strongly Agree	5 4 3 2 1
12. I take actions that support important goals even when others doubt the wisdom of my approach.	Strongly Disagree Disagree Neither Agree nor Disagree Agree Strongly Agree	1 2 3 4 5
13. I share ideas with others.	Strongly Disagree Disagree Neither Agree nor Disagree Agree Strongly Agree	1 2 3 4 5
14. I recover quickly from disappointment or failure.	Strongly Disagree Disagree Neither Agree nor Disagree Agree Strongly Agree	1 2 3 4 5

Item	Rating	
15. Before I work on a problem, I engage in some activity I believe will boost my creativity.	Strongly Disagree Disagree Neither Agree nor Disagree Agree Strongly Agree	1 2 3 4 5
16. When faced with a challenge, I am aware of at least several ways of interpreting the situation.	Strongly Disagree Disagree Neither Agree nor Disagree Agree Strongly Agree	1 2 3 4 5
17. Social trends don't affect my personal decisions.	Strongly Disagree Disagree Neither Agree nor Disagree Agree Strongly Agree	5 4 3 2 1
18. I appreciate that there are opportunities in confusing or chaotic situations.	Strongly Disagree Disagree Neither Agree nor Disagree Agree Strongly Agree	1 2 3 4 5
19. I do what I believe is right, even when I know I may suffer negative consequences.	Strongly Disagree Disagree Neither Agree nor Disagree Agree Strongly Agree	1 2 3 4 5
20. I experiment with ideas that come from others.	Strongly Disagree Disagree Neither Agree nor Disagree Agree Strongly Agree	1 2 3 4 5
21. I adopt habits that help me work consistently and effectively.	Strongly Disagree Disagree Neither Agree nor Disagree Agree Strongly Agree	1 2 3 4 5

Item	Rating	
22. I engage in a creativity-boosting activity (e.g., exercise, being in nature, listening to music) on a regular basis.	Strongly Disagree Disagree Neither Agree nor Disagree Agree Strongly Agree	1 2 3 4 5
23. When faced with a challenge, I pay attention to what is missing or not obvious about the situation.	Strongly Disagree Disagree Neither Agree nor Disagree Agree Strongly Agree	1 2 3 4 5
24. When considering a new direction, I assess what's working and what's not working in my areas of interest.	Strongly Disagree Disagree Neither Agree nor Disagree Agree Strongly Agree	1 2 3 4 5
25. I take advantage of opportunities presented by confusing or chaotic situations.	Strongly Disagree Disagree Neither Agree nor Disagree Agree Strongly Agree	1 2 3 4 5
26. I make decisions to move in new directions even when I am not sure of the ultimate outcome.	Strongly Disagree Disagree Neither Agree nor Disagree Agree Strongly Agree	1 2 3 4 5
27. I am able to build on others' ideas whether or not I agree with them.	Strongly Disagree Disagree Neither Agree nor Disagree Agree Strongly Agree	1 2 3 4 5
28. I stay engaged in the task at hand for as long as I need to.	Strongly Disagree Disagree Neither Agree nor Disagree Agree Strongly Agree	1 2 3 4 5

Item	Rating	
29. I engage in a variety of creativity-triggering activities (e.g., exercise, being in nature, listening to music) on a regular basis.	Strongly Disagree Disagree Neither Agree nor Disagree Agree Strongly Agree	1 2 3 4 5
30. I see connections between seemingly unrelated things or ideas.	Strongly Disagree Disagree Neither Agree nor Disagree Agree Strongly Agree	1 2 3 4 5
31. I engage others in helping me understand trends taking place in society and in my fields of interest.	Strongly Disagree Disagree Neither Agree nor Disagree Agree Strongly Agree	1 2 3 4 5
32. I am flexible about changing my approach in order to accomplish a desired goal.	Strongly Disagree Disagree Neither Agree nor Disagree Agree Strongly Agree	1 2 3 4 5
33. I don't let uncomfortable emotions such as fear or anxiety interfere with taking high-risk actions.	Strongly Disagree Disagree Neither Agree nor Disagree Agree Strongly Agree	1 2 3 4 5
34. I am comfortable presenting my ideas in group settings, even if I think others may not agree with me.	Strongly Disagree Disagree Neither Agree nor Disagree Agree Strongly Agree	1 2 3 4 5
35. I take regular breaks from the task at hand in order to renew my energy or attend to other parts of my life.	Strongly Disagree Disagree Neither Agree nor Disagree Agree Strongly Agree	1 2 3 4 5

SCORING THE CREATIVITY CALCULATOR™

Please place ratings for each item in the corresponding box to the right.

Item	A	Item	B	Item	C	Item	D	Item	E	Item	F	Item	G
1		2		3		4		5		6		7	
8		9		10		11		12		13		14	
15		16		17		18		19		20		21	
22		23		24		25		26		27		28	
29		30		31		32		33		34		35	
Add Col A		Add Col B		Add Col C		Add Col D		Add Col E		Add Col F		Add Col G	

INSTRUCTIONS

Add scores for each item in column A, then record in the box at the bottom of the column.

Repeat for columns B through G.

Transfer the total scores for each column to the boxes shown on the Results Worksheet (next page).

RESULTS WORKSHEET

Column	Score	Competency
A Items 1, 8, 15, 22, 29		**Preparation** Deliberately engaging in activities that prepare the brain to undertake creative work.
B Items 2, 9, 16, 23, 30		**Seeing** The ability to discern new connections, gain fresh perspectives and stay alive to new possibilities.
C Items 3, 10, 17, 24, 31		**Using Context** Understanding the environments in which one works and lives and using that knowledge to make life changes.
D Items 4, 11, 18, 25, 32		**Embracing Ambiguity** Acting on the opportunities, sometimes hidden, presented by change and uncertainty.
E Items 5, 12, 19, 26, 33		**Risk-Taking** Acting without certainty of outcome.
F Items 6, 13, 20, 27, 34		**Collaboration** Engaging with others to help one make desired changes.
G Items 7, 14, 21, 28, 35		**Discipline** Acting consistently whether or not one feels motivated.
Add A through G ▶		**◀Total Creative Skills Score**

SCORE RANGES

Total Creative Skills Score: 35–175

Individual Skill Scores: 5–25

Low: 5–10

Medium: 11–19

High: 20–25

Highest Skill Scores _____

Lowest Skill Scores _____

Individual items scored a 3 or lower:

_____

_____

INTERPRETING YOUR CREATIVITY CALCULATOR RESULTS

Your total Creativity Calculator score gives you some idea of your general creative abilities.

Scores above 120 indicate that you have strength in most or all of the key Seven Creative Skills.

Scores below 100 indicate that you probably have some significant weaknesses in a number of creative skills.

It's most useful to look at your scores for each skill, noting which ones are your highest and which are your lowest.

REVIEWING YOUR SCORES FOR EACH CREATIVE SKILL

The higher the score for any creative skill, the more likely it is that you demonstrate the attitudes and behaviors associated with that skill. The lower your score, the more it may help you to develop greater strength in that skill.

A low score on any skill indicates that you had an average of 2 or lower on items related to that skill.

A medium score on any skill indicates that you had an average of greater than 2 but less than 4 on items related to that skill.

A high score on any skill indicates that you had an average score of at least 4 on items related to that skill.

REVIEWING SCORES FOR INDIVIDUAL ITEMS

Go back through your Creativity Calculator ratings and look for items that you rated a 3 or lower. Each item represents an important aspect of a creative skill. As you look at those low scores, reflect on what they may mean to your life direction. What impact might that item have on your personal effectiveness or ability to make desired life changes? For example, is there one aspect of the seeing skill that could make it hard for you to discover new life interests? To see which items belong to which creative skill, look at your Creativity Calculator Results Worksheet. Items related to each skill are listed to the left of your score for that skill.

You may also want to look at the consistency of your individual item scores within each skill area. Do your item scores fall close together (for instance, are most of them 4s)? That would indicate that you are consistently strong—or weak—in that skill. Or did you have a single low score in a skill area in which your other scores were relatively high? In that case you might be able to easily enhance that skill by concentrating on a single habit change. If you rated most items in a skill area at 3 or lower, then you probably need to make a number of changes to build your skill in that area.

IDENTIFYING OPPORTUNITIES TO ENHANCE YOUR CREATIVE SKILLS

After reviewing your Creativity Calculator scores, take a few minutes to summarize what your results might mean to you. Answer the questions below:

Where do you think you have an opportunity to be more creative?

_____

_____

_____

_____

_____

_____

What changes might you make that would enhance your skills?

_____

_____

_____

_____

_____

Throughout the book, there are activities and exercises designed to help you boost your creative skills. You may want to go back to the chapters that discuss skills you'd like to improve to find ideas for enhancing those skills.

Appendix B

The Life Change Viewfinder

LIFE CHANGE VIEWFINDER™

Dimension	Characteristics	Feelings	Questions
CREATIVE DILEMMA Articulating the source of tension in our lives. *Purpose:* "To Disturb"	Arises from tension between status of current life and sense that things can be different or better Accompanied by unsettling emotions Often throws us into state of confusion and uncertainty Confronts us with choice related to whether to act or not act on the dilemma Can be short in duration or last a very long time	Uneasy Drained Helpless Empty Demoralized Disheartened Isolated Irritable Confused Stressed	What's going on here? Why am I feeling this way? What's the source of my tension? How did it come to this? Do I really have to do this? Should I talk to someone about it? Do I need to ask permission?

Dimension	Characteristics	Feelings	Questions
EXPLORATION Searching for and experimenting with new directions and possibilities. *Purpose:* "To Learn"	Reconnects us with an earlier interest or passion Expands our sense of what is possible for us Open-ended Becoming aware of old emotions and experiencing new ones	Energized Expansive Elated Curious Alive Introspective Anxious Sad Absorbed Uncertain/puzzled Doubtful Impatient/restless	Why do I feel uncertain and confused? Who am I really? What are my core values? What do I care most about? What are my gifts, talents, passions? What is my purpose? What have been my sources of joy in the past? What is my vision of the future? Where can I get support in figuring this out?

Dimension	Characteristics	Feelings	Questions
DISCOVERY Using the raw material of our exploration to discern what is meaningful to us. *Purpose:* "To Discern"	Focused and evaluative Often sets off a new cycle of exploring and discovering Identifies new pathways Triggers heightened self-awareness	Excited Exhilarated Enthusiastic Optimistic Vulnerable Overwhelmed Tentative Insecure Determined Reconciled	What information do I need to know if this new direction is aligned with what matters most to me? What (if anything) is holding me back? How good do I have to be, and what does "good" mean? What are the implications for me—financial, social, personal? How do I connect with like-minded people?

Dimension	Characteristics	Feelings	Questions
INTEGRATION Combining elements of our past experiences with what we have discovered about ourselves into a new way of living our lives. *Purpose:* "To Fulfill"	New capabilities Expanded emotional range New forms of personal expression New public and personal identity A sense that we are becoming more whole Our new self is the perch from which we view our next creative dilemma	Relaxed Optimistic Growing Learning Grateful Amazed Empowered Purified Overwhelmed Terrified Persevering Satisfied	Who am I really? What is my purpose? What do I care most about (values)? What uncertainties remain for me? What are my gifts, talents, passions? What is my vision of the future? Where can I get support in solidifying my new identity?

Appendix C

Artists' Chronology

Artists discussed in the book are listed here in order of their time period:

Leonardo da Vinci (1452–1519)

Michelangelo Buonarroti (1475–1564)

Artemisia Gentileschi (1593–1651)

Rembrandt van Rijn (1606–1669)

Judith Leyster (1609–1660)

Rachel Ruysch (1664–1750)

Francisco Goya (1746–1828)

Camille Pissarro (1830–1903)

Édouard Manet (1832–1883)

Edgar Degas (1834–1917)

Paul Cézanne (1839–1906)

Claude Monet (1840–1926)

Berthe Morisot (1841–1895)

Auguste Renoir (1841–1919)

Mary Cassatt (1844–1926)

Paul Gauguin (1848–1903)

Vincent van Gogh (1853–1890)

Käthe Kollwitz (1867–1945)

Henri Matisse (1869–1954)

Pablo Picasso (1881–1973)

Georgia O'Keeffe (1887–1986)

Alberto Giacometti (1901–1966)

Willem de Kooning (1904–1997)

Frida Kahlo (1907–1954)

Francis Bacon (1909–1992)

Appendix D

Preparation Activities

Herbert Benson, M.D., founding president of the Mind/Body Medical Institute in Boston, and William Proctor have documented myriad preparation activities in *The Break-Out Principle* (New York: Scribner, 2003). Below is a list of preparation activities, which Benson identifies in his book as "triggering" activities. As you'll see, there is a wide variety of activities from which you can choose to cultivate your preparation skill. What they all have in common is their ability to make us physiologically receptive to creative insights.

SPIRITUAL TRIGGERS
- Prayer, as defined by your religious tradition
- Meditation, as understood by your tradition
- Contemplation, as understood by your tradition
- "Eastern" triggers, such as tai chi, chi gong, or yoga
- Repeating for several minutes any positive or meaningful word or phrase
- Sitting quietly by yourself or with a group in a chapel or house of worship

MUSICAL TRIGGERS

- Listening to your favorite music
- Listening to Mozart or Bach, even if you're not used to the experience
- Playing or singing music with which you are familiar

CULTURAL TRIGGERS

- Viewing a work of art, such as a painting or sculpture
- Reading or listening to poetry or a particularly stirring speech or prose passage
- Sitting quietly in a tranquil building or other architectural space

WATER-RELATED TRIGGERS

- Taking a long shower
- Soaking in a bathtub or hot tub
- Sitting or floating in a quiet swimming pool or other water

RESTROOM TRIGGERS

- Shaving
- Putting on makeup
- Grooming with a repetitive routine

ATHLETIC TRIGGERS

- Walking, jogging, bicycling, or performing any other repetitive exercise for at least fifteen minutes
- Becoming absorbed *visually* in a sport—such as by focusing intently on a tennis ball or a basketball or watching closely the players' movements on the court or field without thinking analytically about it
- Combining repetitive mental exercises, such as prayer or meditation, with sports characterized by irregular movements, such as tennis (e.g., counting strings on a tennis racket or meditating silently between points)
- Golfing alone
- Repetitive practice (e.g., golf range, batting cage)

REPETITIVE-MOVEMENT TRIGGERS
- Needlepoint
- Regular, conscious breathing
- Slowly beating a drum

NATURE TRIGGERS
- Sitting quietly in a garden
- Gazing over a seascape or a mountain range
- Strolling silently through the woods
- Fishing

HOUSEWORK/YARDWORK TRIGGERS
- Doing the dishes
- Gardening
- Doing repairs around the house or apartment
- Cooking
- Folding laundry

SURRENDER TRIGGERS
- Relinquishing control over a personal or a job problem
- Imagining and accepting a "worst-case scenario"—or the worst possible thing that could happen to you in the circumstances

RESTAURANT TRIGGERS
- Eating at a quiet restaurant, either alone or with one other person with whom you feel entirely comfortable

ANIMAL/PET TRIGGERS
- Sitting quietly with your pet
- Humming to, speaking quietly to, or otherwise communicating with or rubbing a calm animal
- Observing fish in an aquarium

ALTRUISTIC TRIGGERS

- Becoming involved in some significant way in helping others
- Turning from a focus on yourself and your problem to the responses and needs of your companions or coworkers

BRAINSTORMING TRIGGERS

- Sharing ideas with an occupational or volunteer group about a common problem
- Free-associating with one or more family members or friends about a common concern

Appendix E

Finding a Creative Life Coach

Because life coaching is a relatively new profession, there are no broadly accepted standards of practice, such as exist for physicians or psychologists. Therefore, it is important to look for a life coach who belongs to a professional organization whose members pledge to operate under a code of ethics and high professional standards. The professional coaching organizations listed below are a good starting point for locating a competent professional coach.

Before choosing to work with a life coach:

- interview more than one coach.
- establish that they have had training in specialized coaching skills.
- establish that they belong to a professional organization that adheres to a code of ethics and professional standards of practice.
- establish that they carry professional liability insurance.

PROFESSIONAL LIFE COACHING ORGANIZATIONS

International Coach Federation: http://www.coachfederation.org

ICF Member Directory: http://www.coachfederation.org/find-a-coach/ find-a-coach-now/member-directory

Life Planning Network: http://www.lifeplanningnetwork.org

LPN Member Directory: http://www.lifeplanningnetwork.org/find consultant.htm

REFERENCES

About the Artists

Abrams, Harry N. *Monet's Years at Giverny*. New York: The Metropolitan Museum of Art, 1978.

Ackley, Clifford S. *Rembrandt's Journey*. Boston: MFA Publications, 2004.

Adler, Kathleen, and Tamar Garb. *Berthe Morisot*. London: Phaidon, 1995.

Biesboer, Pieter, and James A. Welu, eds. *Judith Leyster: A Dutch Master and Her World*. Zwolle: Waanders, and Worcester, MA: Worcester Art Museum, 1993.

Boorstin, Daniel J. *The Creators: A History of Heroes of the Imagination*. New York: Vintage Books, 1992.

Borzello, Frances. *A World of Our Own: Women as Artists Since the Renaissance*. New York: Watson-Guptill, 2000.

Carpenter, Elizabeth, ed. *Frida Kahlo*. Minneapolis: Walker Art Center, 2007.

Castro, Jan Garden. *The Life & Art of Georgia O'Keeffe*. New York: Crown, 1985.

Claire, Jean. *Bonnard/Matisse: Letters Between Friends*. New York: Harry N. Abrams, 1992.

Collins, Bradley. *Van Gogh and Gauguin: Electric Arguments and Utopian Dreams*. Boulder, CO: Westview Press, 2004.

Cowling, Elizabeth, Anne Baldassari, John Elderfield, John Golding, Isabelle Monod-Fontaine, and Kirk Varnedoe. *Matisse Picasso*. New York: The Museum of Modern Art, 2003.

Drohojowska-Philp, Hunter. *Full Bloom: The Art and Life of Georgia O'Keeffe*. New York: W.W. Norton, 2004.

Duchting, Hajo. *Paul Cézanne, 1839-1906: Nature into Art*. New York: Taschen, 1999.

Elderfield, John. *Henri Matisse: A Retrospective*. New York: The Museum of Modern Art, 1992.

Essers, Vokmar. *Matisse*. Köln, West Germany: Taschen, 1987.

Fry, Roger. *Cézanne: A Study of His Development*. Chicago: University of Chicago Press, 1989.

Fuentes, Carlos. Introduction to *The Diary of Frida Kahlo: An Intimate Self-Portrait*. New York: Harry N. Abrams, and Mexico City: La Vaca Independiente, 1995.

Garrard, Mary. *Artemisia Gentileschi*. Princeton, NJ: Princeton University Press, 1989.

Gassier, Pierre. *Goya: A Witness of His Time*. London: Alpine Fine Arts Collection, Ltd., 1983.

Herrera, Hayden. *Frida Kahlo: The Paintings*. New York: HarperCollins, 1991.

Herrera, Hayden. *Frida: A Biography of Frida Kahlo*. New York: Harper & Row, 1963.

Higonnet, Anne. *Berthe Morisot*. New York: Rizzoli International, 1993.

Hoog, Michel. *Cézanne: Father of 20th Century Art*. New York: Harry N. Abrams, 1994.

Kemp, Marilyn, ed. *Leonardo on Painting*. New Haven: Yale University Press, 2001.

Klein, Mina C., and H. Arthur Klein. *Käthe Kollwitz: Life in Art*. New York: Holt, Rinehart and Winston, 1972.

Lamarche-Vadel, Bernard. *Giacometti*. New York: Konecky and Konecky, 1984.

Linscott, Robert N., ed. *Complete Poems and Selected Letters of Michelangelo*. New York: The Modern Library, 1965.

Loran, Erle. *Cézanne's Composition*. Los Angeles: University of California Press, 1943.

Matthews, Nancy Mowll. *Mary Cassatt: A Life*. New Haven: Yale University Press, 1994.

Nagel, Otto. *Käthe Kollwitz*. Greenwich, CT: New York Graphic Society, 1963.

Neret, Gilles. *Henri Matisse*. Köln, Germany: Taschen, 1999.

Perruchot, Henri. *Cézanne*. New York: World Publishing, 1961.

Peters, Sarah Whitaker. *Becoming O'Keeffe: The Early Years*. New York: Abbeville Press, 1991.

Prelinger, Elizabeth. *Käthe Kollwitz*. New Haven, CT: Yale University Press, 1992.

Rewald, John, ed. *Paul Cézanne Letters*. New York: Da Capo Press, 1995.

Richardson, John. *A Life of Picasso: 1907-1917: The Painter of Modern Life*. New York: Random House, 1996.

Roe, Sue. *The Private Lives of the Impressionists*. New York: Harper Perennial, 2006.

Sagner-Duchting, Karin. *Claude Monet*. New York: Taschen, 1998.

Schama, Simon. *Rembrandt's Eyes*. New York: Alfred A. Knopf, 1999.

Spurling, Hilary. *Matisse the Master*. New York: Alfred A. Knopf, 2005.

Spurling, Hilary. *The Unknown Matisse*. New York: Alfred A. Knopf, 1998.

Stevens, Mark, and Annalyn Swan. *De Kooning: An American Master*. New York: Alfred A. Knopf, 2004.

Stuckey, Charles F., and William P. Scott. *Berthe Morisot: Impressionist*. New York: Hudson Hills Press, 1987.

Sylvester, David. *Interviews with Francis Bacon*. New York: Thames & Hudson, 1975.

Taylor, Michael. *Rembrandt's Nose*. New York: Distributed Art Publishers, 2007.

Tibol, Raquel. *Frida Kahlo: An Open Life*. Albuquerque: University of New Mexico Press, 1993.

Wheelock, Arthur K., Jr. *Vermeer*. New York: Harry N. Abrams, 1981.

White, Christopher, and Quentin Buvelot, eds. *Rembrandt by Himself*. London: Thames & Hudson, 1999.

Wilson-Bareau, Juliet. *Manet by Himself*. New York: Little, Brown, 1991.

Wolf, Bryan Jay. *Vermeer and the Invention of Seeing*. Chicago: University of Chicago Press, 2001.

Zamora, Martha. *The Letters of Frida Kahlo: Cartas Apasionadas*. San Francisco: Chronicle Books, 1995.

Zigrosser, Carl, ed. *Prints and Drawings of Käthe Kollwitz*. New York: George Braziller, 1951.

About Life Change

Alboher, Marci. *One Person/Multiple Careers*. New York: Warner Business Books, 2007.

Andreasen, Nancy C., M.D., Ph.D., *The Creating Brain: The Neuroscience of Genius*. New York: Dana Press, 2005.

Bayles, David, and Ted Orland. *Art & Fear*. Santa Cruz: The Image Continuum, 1993.

Bennis, Warren, and Patricia Ward Biederman. *Organizing Genius: The Secrets of Creative Collaboration*. Reading, MA: Addison-Wesley, 1997.

Bratter, Bernice, and Helen Dennis. *Project Renewment: The First Retirement Model for Career Women*. New York: Scribner, 2008.

Braun Levine, Suzanne. *Inventing the Rest of Our Lives: Women in Second Adulthood*. New York: Plume, 2005.

Bridges, William., *Transitions: Making Sense of Life's Changes*. Cambridge, MA: Perseus Books, 1980.

Cameron, Julia., *The Artist's Way*. New York: Jeremy P. Tarcher, 2002.

Campbell, Joseph, ed. *The Portable Jung*. New York: Penguin Books, 1972.

Cohen, Gene. *The Creative Age: Awakening Human Potential in the Second Half of Life*. New York: William Morrow, 2000.

———. *The Mature Mind: The Positive Power of the Aging Mind*. New York: Basic Books, 2006.

Farrell, Michael P. *Collaborative Circles: Friendship Dynamics & Creative Work*. Chicago: University of Chicago Press, 2001.

Feynman, Richard. *"Surely You're Joking, Mr. Feynman!"* New York: W. W. Norton, 1985.

Freedman, Marc. *Encore: Finding Work That Matters in the Second Half of Life*. New York: PublicAffairs, 2007.

———. *PrimeTime: How Baby Boomers Will Revolutionize Retirement and Transform America*. New York: Public Affairs, 1999.

Gardner, Howard. *Creating Minds: An Anatomy of Creativity*. New York: Basic Books, 1993.

———. *Intelligence Reframed*. New York: Basic Books, 1999.

Ghiselin, Brewster. *The Creative Process: Reflections on Invention in the Arts and Sciences*. Los Angeles: University of California Press, 1952.

Goleman, Daniel. *Emotional Intelligence: Why It Matters More than IQ*. New York: Bantam Books, 1995.

Kimmelman, Michael. *Portraits: Talking with Artists at the Met, the Modern, the Louvre and Elsewhere*. New York: The Modern Library, 1999.

———. *The Accidental Masterpiece: On the Art of Life and Vice Versa*. New York: The Penguin Press, 2005.

Langer, Ellen J. *On Becoming an Artist*. New York: Ballantine Books, 2005.

Lawrence-Lightfoot, Sara. *The Third Chapter: Passion, Risk and Adventure in the 25 Years after 50*. New York: Sarah Crichton Books, Farrar, Straus & Giroux, 2009.

Leider, Richard J. *Repacking Your Bags: Lighten Your Load for the Rest of Your Life*. San Francisco: Berrett-Koehler, 1996.

Leider, Richard J., and David A. Shapiro. *Something to Live For: Finding Your Way in the Second Half of Life*. San Francisco: Berrett-Koehler, 2008.

Lesser, Elizabeth. *Broken Open: How Difficult Times Can Help Us Grow*. New York: Villard Books, 2005.

MacKenzie, Gordon. *Orbiting the Giant Hairball: A Corporate Fool's Guide to Surviving with Grace*. New York: Viking, 1996.

Maisel, Eric, Ph.D. *The Creativity Book*. New York: Jeremy P. Tarcher, 2000.

May, Rollo. *The Courage to Create*. New York: W. W. Norton, 1975.

McNiff, Shaun. *Creating with Others: The Practice of Imagination in Life, Art & the Workplace*. Boston: Shambhala, 2003.

Nachmanovitch, Stephen. *Free Play: Improvisation in Life and Art*. Los Angeles: Jeremy P. Tarcher, 1990.

Pascal, Eugene, Ph.D. *Jung to Live By*. New York: Warner Books, 1992.

Pink, Daniel H. *A Whole New Mind: Moving from the Information Age to the Conceptual Age*. New York: Riverhead Books, 2005.

Rowe, Alan J. *Creative Intelligence: Discovering the Innovative Potential in Ourselves and Others*. New York: Pearson Prentice Hall, 2004.

Sadler, William A., Ph.D. *The Third Age: 6 Principles for Growth and Renewal after Forty*. Cambridge, MA: Perseus, 2000.

Sadler, William A., Ph.D., and James H. Krefft, Ph.D. *Changing Course: Navigating Life After 50*. Centennial, CO: The Center for Third Age Leadership Press, 2007.

Sawyer, Keith. *Group Genius: The Creative Power of Collaboration.* New York: Basic Books, 2007.

Schlein, Stephen, Ph.D, ed. *Erik H. Erikson: A Way of Looking at Things.* New York: W. W. Norton, 1995.

Schwartz, Tony. *What Really Matters: Searching for Wisdom in America.* New York: Bantam Books, 1995.

Selhub, Eva. *The Love Response: Your Prescription to Turn Off Fear, Anger, and Anxiety to Achieve Vibrant Health and Transform Your Life.* New York: Random House, 2009.

Senge, Peter. *The Fifth Discipline: The Art and Practice of the Learning Organization.* New York: Doubleday, 1990.

Senge, Peter, and C. Otto Scharmer, Joseph Jaworski, Betty Sue Flowers. *Presence: An Exploration of Profound Change in People, Organizations, and Society.* New York: Doubleday, 2004.

Sheehy, Gail. *Passages: Predictable Crises of Adult Life.* New York: Ballantine Books, 1974.

Susanka, Sarah. *The Not So Big Life: Making Room for What Really Matters.* New York: Random House, 2007.

Tharp, Twyla. *The Creative Habit: Learn It and Use It for Life.* New York: Simon & Schuster, 2003.

Trafford, Abigail. *My Time: Making the Most of the Bonus Decades after Fifty.* New York: Basic Books, 2004.

ILLUSTRATION CREDITS